REFUGEES OR MIGRANTS

Refugees or Migrants

Pre-Modern Jewish Population Movement

ROBERT CHAZAN

Yale
UNIVERSITY PRESS
NEW HAVEN AND LONDON

Published with assistance from the foundation established in memory of Philip Hamilton McMillan of the Class of 1894, Yale College.

Yale University Press books may be purchased in quantity for educational, business, or promotional use. For information, please e-mail sales.press@yale.edu (U.S. office) or sales@yaleup.co.uk (U.K. office).

Set in Electra type by IDS Infotech, Ltd.
Printed in the United States of America.

ISBN 978-0-300-21857-2 (hardcover : alk. paper)
Library of Congress Control Number: 2018941453
A catalogue record for this book is available from the British Library.

This paper meets the requirements of ANSI/NISO Z39.48-1992 (Permanence of Paper).

10 9 8 7 6 5 4 3 2 1

CONTENTS

REFUGEES OR MIGRANTS

Prologue

Refugee or migrant? The conclusion of this evaluation can mean life or death for millions uprooted throughout the contemporary Middle East, South Asia, and Africa. These hordes have left their home territories for a variety of reasons: Some have been formally expelled from their homelands; others suffered under legislation that made their lives impossible or nearly impossible; yet others feared rampant violence that threatened life and limb; some sought simply to distance themselves from turmoil and achieve a measure of stability. These dislocated adults, children, and aged have set out on perilous journeys in order to find sanctuary in new, safe, and supportive settings. The photos and videos of these sojourners are horrific. Many of them perish during their dangerous journeys.

The need to manage the massive population movement unleashed by change, instability, and violence in the contemporary Middle East, South Asia, and Africa has moved Europeans and others to distinguish between two categories of dislocated humans: refugees, who have been forcibly displaced and cannot return to their places of origin or at least cannot return without fear for life and limb; and migrants, who are on the move essentially in pursuit of betterment for themselves and their families.

It is widely agreed that refugees have a moral claim to acceptance. To turn back fellow humans who cannot return to their places of origin or would risk their lives in so doing seems unconscionable. Although there is nothing inherently objectionable about migrating out of the desire for betterment, turning away such migrants under the current conditions does not seem immoral. Under normal circumstances, most societies accommodate immigrants; indeed, there is often a sense that immigrants serve useful purposes in their new host societies economically, socially, and culturally. The current circumstances of population flux, however, are by no means normal. The magnitude of the human tidal wave seeking to relocate requires the imposition of limits, and restricting acceptance to those requiring refuge seems to many a reasonable way of responding to the current human tragedy unfolding in major sectors of the world.

The distinction between refugees and migrants involves two dimensions—the host majority and the targeted minority. Host majorities can formally reject minority elements in society in a number of ways. Over the ages, governing authorities have enacted edicts of expulsion against many different minority groupings on ethnic, religious, racial, and economic grounds. Such edicts are definitive; they make the ongoing presence or the return of these minorities impossible. There are less definitive forms of majority rejection as well. In some cases, governments introduce legislation that is so limiting for minority groups as to make life nearly impossible. Much more commonly, popular animosity and the fear of violence are so overwhelming as to make life untenable for these minorities. This last form of majority rejection is very much the dominant concern for many of those presently seeking entrée to Europe and other areas of the West.

Another dimension of the refugee/migrant distinction involves those in motion and the level of judgment and volition they can exercise. When governing authorities decree expulsion, those expelled can exercise no judgment or volition whatsoever; they must leave and they cannot return. On the other hand, those faced with governmental limitations can exercise a measure of judgment and volition. They can assess the tenability of their circumstances under the new laws. They might decide that productive living, although difficult, remains possible; alternatively they might decide that productive living is in fact impossible. Exercise of judgment and volition can take place. The same is true for reactions to the threat of violence. In the face of danger, assessments can be made. Some might conclude that life under these dangerous circumstances is risky but possible; others might conclude that it is unthinkable.

Establishing status as a refugee involves both of these two dimensions. Those formally expelled from their home countries can readily establish their status as refugees. There is no possibility of return to their place of origin.

However, in the cases of harmful legislation and the more widespread instances of potential violence, the level of limitation and danger must be assessed. Does the legislation or the violence make life untenable, or can life be maintained despite these impediments? If the former, then the evaluation results in assignment to the category of refugee; if the latter, the individual involved is adjudged a migrant, despite considerable discomfort.

There is a widespread perception that the present humanitarian crisis of dislocation is unprecedented, and this perception seems warranted. In the first place, human population is now larger than ever before, which means that there are more potential human targets of dislocation. Moreover, while persecution is well documented throughout history, the capacity for persecution on a massive scale is now greater than ever before, and the same is true of the potential for effective relocation. The new modes of mass persecution and the new modes of mass relocation are both unprecedented. Finally, the current media bring the reality of contemporary dislocation to a level of public attention that it had never previously achieved. Almost every household in the modern West is pervaded day after day by frightful images—masses trekking across barren terrain; flimsy boats overloaded with passengers on the Mediterranean Sea; bodies being retrieved from the waters; masses straining tearfully before barbed wire fencing.

Even though forcible population dislocation has reached new levels and contemporary uprootedness has a hold on the popular imagination it never had before, the phenomenon is by no means new. Governments over the ages have expelled portions of their populations or introduced legislation that made the lives and livelihoods of segments of the population untenable. More commonly, internal animosities and the violence they engender are a commonplace of human history. From time immemorial, majorities have harbored hostility against minorities in their midst and have mistreated these minorities in ways that occasioned flight. Dislocation grounded in governmental edict or in popular hatred and violence is a well-established feature of human history, copiously documented for all times and places.

The Jewish people has elicited a considerable level of governmental attention and popular animosity. As a result, the history of this people shows instances of governmental expulsion, governmental limitation, and popular animosity and violence. There is a widespread consensus, both traditional and modern, that Jews have suffered an extraordinary level of majority maltreatment, which has occasioned constant population movement resultant from governmental expulsion, hostile legislation, and popular animosity and violence. In this widely shared view, Jews have been an unusually mobile human group, overwhelmingly composed of refugees.

The goal of this book is to challenge this consensus. The challenge leveled herein does not deny the reality of governmental expulsions of Jews, of majority limitations on Jewish life that forced Jews to relocate, or of violence that necessitated flight. All these are indisputable realities and must be fully acknowledged. The challenge to be leveled involves, first of all, recognition that in many instances Jews moved themselves and their families for betterment. Not all Jews in motion over the ages have been refugees; Jews have often been migrants and not refugees. Moreover, we shall see that there has been insufficient attention paid to the ubiquity of Jews as migrants. I shall argue that careful consideration of broad patterns of Jewish population movement shows that the majority of Jews relocating over the ages have done so in search of betterment, that Jews were overall more often migrants rather than refugees.

The earliest period of Israelite history, which is portrayed in rather mythic fashion in the first five books of the Hebrew Bible, shows considerable demographic relocation. Interestingly, this recurrent movement is not attributed to external persecution, either governmental or popular. Abraham and his immediate descendants move regularly in response to divine command, internal familial strife, or natural calamity, for example the famine in Canaan that forced the family of Jacob into Egypt. The massive Israelite movement out of Egypt was stimulated by Egyptian persecution, but it is not portrayed as involving human decision making and human initiative. It is God who is portrayed as leading the Israelites out of Egypt and into Canaan, often against the expressed desires of the Israelites themselves.

Beginning with the sixth book of the Hebrew Bible, the narrative style shifts from mythic to historical, and the portrayal of Israelite population dislocation changes as well. Population movement remains a prominent theme, but is portrayed quite differently. In the six historical books that begin with Judges and end with II Kings, the Israelites are portrayed as seeking to settle comfortably in Canaan, the land promised to them by the one and only God in the universe. Skirmishes with Canaanite neighbors abound. More menacingly, another group of newcomers to Canaan—the Mediterranean-based Philistines—invaded from the west and engaged the Israelites in a protracted struggle for dominance in Canaan.

These six books conclude with two major episodes of forced expulsion from Canaan. The first took place at the hands of the Assyrian Empire, which during the eighth pre-Christian century assumed control of Canaan. The Assyrians created an empire that was militarily powerful and sophisticated in its governance. The Assyrian emperors pioneered in techniques of governmental coercion designed to assure compliance on the part of the many disparate minority communities that made up the population of this realm. Especially noteworthy was the use of forced population movement to destroy sub-groups that resisted imperial authority. Such recalcitrant subgroups were expelled from their home terrain and scattered widely throughout the empire. As a result, the group disappeared, and the danger it represented was thus eliminated.

Part of the Israelite community in Canaan suffered this punishment. As the Assyrians sought during the eighth century to extend their empire westward from its Mesopotamian base all the way to the Mediterranean Sea, Canaan lay in its path. The diverse communities of Canaan were faced with the alternatives of accepting Assyrian hegemony or resisting. By this time, the Israelites had split into two separate kingdoms, and these two political confederations chose different responses to the Assyrian threat. The southern kingdom accepted Assyrian domination and became a subject community in the empire. In contrast, the northern kingdom resisted, was defeated, and suffered the consequences. The northern Israelites were exiled, scattered throughout the empire, and disappeared forever.

The danger to the northern kingdom and its eventual extinction created a serious theological challenge. Although the evolution of Israelite monotheism cannot be accurately traced, it seems clear that, by the eighth century and the eruption of the Assyrian crisis in Canaan, the notion of one

God that created and controls the universe in its entirety had taken root, at least in segments of the Israelite/Judean population. Thus, as the Assyrian danger became manifest, it evoked vexing theological questions. If the God of Israel is all-powerful and if this God has chosen Israel as his special community, how then could this community be severely threatened by the Assyrians? Does the danger of Assyrian victory and disastrous Israelite defeat reflect serious limitation of divine power, or alternatively does it raise doubts about the relationship between God and Israel? Both possibilities are theologically problematic.

The biblical books that follow the eleven historical books consist of the messages of the classical prophets of Israel and Judah, who preached from the eighth pre-Christian century and the Assyrian crisis down through the parallel crisis triggered by the Judean rebellion of the sixth century and its suppression at the hands of the Babylonians. These prophets addressed the issue of Israelite/Judean defeat and projected an innovative explanation. In the view of the prophets, Assyrian and Babylonian victory and Israelite and Judean defeat in no sense reflect negatively on God or on his love for Israel. The prophets shifted the focus of explanation from God to Israel. God had fashioned a covenant with the Israelite people. This covenant involved a set of obligations on the part of the human partners to the relationship, obligations that covered the entire spectrum of human activity. The divine partner to the covenant would reward or punish the human partner according to the level of fulfillment of these obligations. Reward revolved heavily around a safe, secure, and prosperous existence in the land promised by God to his covenantal partners. Punishment was to take multiple forms, dependent on the level of sinfulness—natural calamity in the Promised Land, invasion of the Promised Land by a foe serving as the rod of divine wrath, forcible exile from the Promised Land, and—most extremely—painful exilic displacements.

Toward the end of the seventh century, Assyrian rule over the vast Mesopotamian-based empire was challenged by the Babylonians. While the Babylonians were successful in displacing the Assyrians and in gaining control of the empire, the instability fostered by this transition encouraged the rulers of Judea to rebel against their ostensibly weakened imperial overlords. This rebellion was suppressed by the Babylonians, resulting once again in expulsion of the offending subjects. The fate of the Judean exiles, however, differed from the fate of their Israelite predecessors. Although the Judeans were by and large removed from Canaan, they were not scattered and thus destroyed as a cohesive group. A Mesopotamian Jewish diaspora was created, which was to enjoy creative existence for millennia.

This Mesopotamian Jewish diaspora forged a new stage in the development of Jewish religious thinking. The resulting evolution replaced the cult-centered Judaism of the pre-expulsion period with a text-centered Judaism. Although details of this shift are lacking, the books of Ezra and Nehemiah show the scribe Ezra instituting the reading and teaching of the sacred books as core religious ceremonies, with insistence on fulfillment of the demands adumbrated in these books as Israel's fundamental covenantal obligation. The biblical corpus that subsequently coalesced highlighted the prophetic notion that Israel's fulfillment or neglect of the covenant would determine its fate. Fulfillment would be rewarded, and neglect would be punished.

The most drastic of these punishments, to eventuate from the most serious sinfulness, was to include multiple elements—exile, exilic suffering, and regular and painful population dislocation. Profoundly influenced by the Assyrian and Babylonian forced expulsions, the biblical prophets established exile from the land of Israel and ongoing exilic dislocations as frightful. The prophets bundled forcible population movement into the complex of punishments that was to threaten the Israelites and their Jewish successors over the ages. Forcible dispersal of the Jews into a wide range of locales was to constitute the culminating and harshest element in divine punishment, the result of the most serious failures in fulfillment of the covenant.

Jews over the ages identified three separations and exiles from the land promised by God to his people. The first was reported in the Hebrew Bible as involving the forced descent of the sons of Jacob and their families into Egypt as a result of a devastating famine. This first exile reputedly lasted hundreds of years, during which time the families of the sons of Jacob evolved into a large and, from the Egyptian perspective, threatening nation; this first exile is portrayed as ending with the divinely orchestrated exodus from Egypt and subsequent reentry into Canaan.

The second separation and exile took place many centuries after resettlement in the Land of Israel and was forced upon the Judean kingdom in the early sixth pre-Christian century by its Babylonian overlords. This forcible expulsion was the result in terrestrial terms of a Judean rebellion against the imperial authorities; in theological terms, it was portrayed by the Judean prophets as reflecting the failure of their people to fulfill the demands of the covenant. Upon suppression of the rebellion, the Babylonians, in accordance with their general policy vis-à-vis disloyal subjects, expelled the Judeans from their homeland. The reign of the Babylonians did not last long thereafter, and their successors, the Persians, altered imperial policy for subjugated minorities, allowing some Judeans to return to the Promised Land. Thus, the second exile did not endure all that long and, according to the available biblical sources, was not all that arduous.

In traditional Jewish and likewise Christian thinking, a third exile began in the year 70, with the destruction of Jerusalem and its Second Temple in the aftermath of yet another failed Jewish rebellion against an imperial overlord. Viewing these events as parallel to the destruction of Jerusalem and its First Temple by the Babylonians, Jewish tradition created the imagery of yet another imperial expulsion, even though there was no such expulsion. Indeed, the suppression of the rebellion of 66–70 by the Romans resulted in no overall redistribution of worldwide Jewish population. Although the eastern and western diasporas probably grew to some extent, Palestine remained the dominant center of Jewish life for a number of centuries after the year 70. For traditional Jewish and Christian thinking, however, this supposed third exile, like the previous one, was the divinely imposed outcome of Jewish sinfulness. This alleged third, lengthiest, and most painful exile purportedly represented fulfillment of the horrific biblical predictions of exile, exilic suffering, and exilic wanderings, which had not been realized during the first and second exiles.

Over the ages, Jews have absorbed this biblical theology, its imagery, and its implications. They have viewed the biblical warnings of divine punishment as predictive of what they have identified as Jewish fate during the supposed third and lengthiest exile from the Promised Land. Traditional Jews over the ages believed that this third exile saw the fulfillment of the direst predictions of exilic Jewish suffering. Aware of their eventual dispersion far and wide, Jews interpreted Jewish displacements across the known world as realization of the biblical prophecies of the harshest aspect of exile. They perceived and projected their constant relocation as the profoundest pain of the divine punishment they were enduring.

In this traditional Jewish view, Jews were thus regularly refugees. The more benign imagery of Jews as migrants, seeking better circumstances for themselves and their families, did not fit this theological scheme. To be sure, traditional Jews viewed their purported punishment as temporary only. The same biblical legacy that projected punishment for Jewish sinfulness also insisted on eventual expiation of this sinfulness and an end to Jewish suffering. The God that inflicted harsh punishment upon his Jewish partners would ultimately redeem them and would return them to the Promised Land, where they would enjoy the bliss that a permanent home confers.

Christianity was born within the Jewish community of first-century Palestine and absorbed the sacred literature and underlying values and perspectives of that Jewish community. As Christianity slowly branched off from its Jewish matrix, it began to criticize that matrix as a misunderstanding and distortion of the Hebrew Bible, which the Church claimed to apprehend correctly. As a result of this broad projection of Judaism and the Jews and the dramatic imagery of Jewish rejection of Jesus and Jewish responsibility for his crucifixion, Christian thinkers maintained and indeed intensified the Jewish sense of serious Jewish sinfulness and harsh divine punishment. In the Church view, first-century Jews misread the divinely revealed biblical message and rejected Jesus as the promised Messiah; divine punishment was quick in coming, taking the form of exile and its attendant suffering following the year 70. The Church projected Jewish dispersion, already understood by the Jews themselves as the most painful form of exilic suffering, in similar fashion. For the Church, as for the Jews themselves, Jews wandering far and wide across the globe were obviously refugees, enduring punishment for their heavy sins.

Beginning in the seventeenth and eighteenth centuries, new patterns of Western thought began to replace the long dominant theological perspectives of Judaism and Christianity. Profoundly impressed with the achievements of the physical sciences, Enlightenment thinkers increasingly questioned and then rejected the intrusion of the divine into human affairs. Modern observers have dismissed supernatural intervention in human history, replacing it with natural causation. As a result of these changing views, many Jews and Christians began to question the notion of Jewish fate as reflective of divine punishment. The invocation of divine punishment gave way to a search for natural causes for what observers Jewish and Christian continued to project as the dolorous saga of historic Jewish suffering and forced population movement.

The search for the natural causes of exilic Jewish suffering took a number of directions, focusing on Jewish political identity, Jewish economic activity, Jewish societal placement, and historic Christian-Jewish tensions. What was common to all these naturalistic perspectives was the ongoing consensus that Jewish history was a continuous sequence of persecution and forced displacement. This biblically grounded conviction was shared by the Jewish minority and the Christian majority of the West. The views of the Christian majority and the Jewish minority thus regularly reinforced one another.

As the impact of the Reformation deepened, and as removing religious identity from its central role in political organization was first promoted by Enlightenment thinkers and then actualized in the course of the great eighteenth-century revolutions, other factors for creating and maintaining societal cohesion were introduced. The most prominent of these alternative factors was ethnic or national identity. States were to be organized as collectives of individuals with a shared ethnic or national identity. While the premodern focus on religion automatically moved Jews to the periphery of society, the implications of the new notion of social cohesion grounded in ethnic or national identity were less clear. For many, equal membership in the new societies was surely open to Jews as one of multiple European religious communities; for others, it was not, because Jews constituted more than simply a religious community; for yet others, there was uncertainty.

During the nineteenth century, the loose notion of ethnic or national identity gave way to the pseudo-scientific concept of racial identity, which was presumed to be more objective. Racial perspectives tended to produce yet more negative views of the Jews as outsiders to the new societies. The ongoing and contentious nineteenth-century debate over Jewish rights spurred an outburst of thinking and writing about Jewish ethnic/national and racial identity. Much of this writing was pejorative, in an effort to expose the inappropriateness and indeed the harmfulness of Jewish citizenship by identifying negative Jewish ethnic and racial characteristics. These purportedly negative Jewish characteristics served to explain for some modern observers historic Jewish suffering and forced dispersal. Not God, but the Jews themselves were responsible for their ongoing persecution and for the unceasing rejection that had turned them into historic refugees. Painful Jewish dislocation was self-inflicted, the result of negative characteristics that made others fearful of Jews.

At the same time that the modern West was grappling with the creation of alternative groundings for societal cohesion, it was simultaneously undergoing massive, exciting, and disorienting economic change. New economic forces, opportunities, and challenges became a reality, with resultant pain and disruption for many in Western societies. Accelerating awareness of the complex role of the economy in modern societies resulted in heightened sensitivities to Jewish economic strength, weakness, and impact. These new economic sensitivities as well were invoked to explain historic Jewish suffering. The purported Jewish propensity toward business and banking, broadly reviled in most societies, supposedly engendered intense anti-Jewish sentiment wherever Jews located themselves and resulted in the ubiquitous pattern of persecution and forced displacement purportedly so obvious in Jewish history.

Jewish observers understandably rejected these negative political and economic perspectives on Jewish suffering and forced dislocation and sought less condemnatory aspects of the Jewish past to explain the painful pattern. For one group of Jewish thinkers, the Jewish nationalists, the explanation for persecution and forced dislocation of Jews over the ages lay in sociological factors. Once again, these observers rejected the traditional view of divine causation for Jewish suffering and forced dislocation; however, they emphasized the deleterious impact of these traditional perspectives on the Jews themselves. Jewish dispersion, accepted by Jews as divinely ordained, was the critical factor, in this view, behind repeated maltreatment by the numerous majorities among whom Jews ensconced themselves. Minority status and the liabilities that flowed from it set the stage for the repeated expulsions that recurrently made Jews refugees. The cycle was truly vicious, as dispersion led to ongoing minority status and maltreatment, which then culminated in yet further forced displacement.

An alternative approach to the human causes of Jewish suffering focused on historical factors, specifically Christian views of Jewish sinfulness and resultant exile and suffering. Again rejecting the theological projection of Jewish sinfulness and divine punishment, modern observers both Jewish and Christian argued that this theological doctrine itself, espoused by leading thinkers and the Christian masses over the ages, bore central responsibility for the sad saga of Jewish suffering and ongoing forced dislocation. Christians of all kinds—Church leaders, governmental authorities, and the populace at large—were convinced of Jewish sinfulness and divine punishment, believed that the punishment was appropriate, and were thus emboldened to initiate diverse anti-Jewish actions. These Christians perceived their anti-Jewish behaviors as part and parcel of the divine plan for the Jews and therefore fully justified. In this view, Christian doctrine bore major responsibility for Jewish suffering in general and for forced Jewish displacement in particular.

Striking in all these modern efforts to explain in natural terms Jewish fate is the ongoing assumption of relentless exilic Jewish suffering and the related conviction that dispersion of the Jews far and wide was the most extreme manifestation of this suffering. While this diversified modern thinking rejected Jewish sinfulness and divine punishment as the mechanisms driving Jewish fate, it maintained the prior convictions of post-70 Jewish history as unendingly painful and—especially important for our purposes—of Jewish dispersion as unfailingly forced and hurtful. It is the latter of these ongoing assumptions that this book challenges.

Recent historians of the Jews have continued to reject the theologically grounded assumption of unending Jewish suffering during the supposed third exile and have raised important questions about the modern naturalistic continuations of this sense of interminable Jewish suffering. The innovator in a new and more positive perspective on the Jewish past was a young scholar named Salo Baron, who arrived in America from his native Europe in 1926. Over his long and remarkably productive career Baron introduced and maintained a protracted assault on what he dubbed "the lachrymose theory of Jewish history" in a multitude of publications, capped by the magisterial eighteen volumes of the second edition of his *Social and Religious History of the Jews.* Baron rejected both the theologically grounded and the modern naturalistic views of an endless cycle of Jewish suffering and forced dislocation.

Beyond the range and impact of Baron's writings, he also influenced an entire generation of American-trained historians of the Jews, who were his students and his students' students. By and large completing their doctoral studies in American universities rather than separate Jewish academic institutions, this generation of Jewish historians moved decisively beyond the theological perspectives on Jewish history and likewise beyond the modern naturalistic perspectives that maintained the traditional sense of interminable Jewish suffering.

Jewish history has been perceived and projected by these Jewish historians as composed of a wide range of geographic settings and chronological periods. In some of these settings and periods, Jews flourished; in others, Jews were badly mistreated and suffered. Understanding Jewish fate both positive and negative necessitates full comprehension of the majority societies in which Jews have found themselves. The quality of minority Jewish experience was a function not of Jewish sinfulness or even of purportedly negative Jewish characteristics. As a minority community, Jewish fate was bound up with the essential nature and directions of the non-Jewish ambience in which Jews were ensconced. As these new historiographic tendencies developed, the possibility emerged of envisioning Jews in motion as migrants rather than refugees.

This book focuses on one element only in the traditional and modern perspectives on exilic Jewish suffering—the assumption that demographic dislocation and resultant dispersion of Jewish population must be consistently treated as involuntary and painful, as divinely inflicted punishment of the Jews or as humanly instigated maltreatment of them because of their negative characteristics or problematic relations with others. The new insistence on understanding the majority milieu has now come to the fore. Students of Jewish population movement have begun to insist on consideration of the tendencies in majority societies toward persecution of minorities in their midst or, somewhat less commonly, toward expulsion of minorities from their midst. Noteworthy here is a new awareness that persecuting and banishing societies persecuted and banished multiple minority groups and not Jews only. Understanding the broad tendencies toward persecution and banishment represents a totally new perspective on Jewish population movement over the ages.

This study does not assume one and only one paradigm for Jewish population movement. Governmental expulsion of Jews and Jewish flight from intolerable circumstances were both realities. We shall examine with care instances of formal governmental banishment of Jews, which were real and painful, but were relatively limited in time and space. We shall likewise address instances in which Jews have confronted governmental repression or popular animosity. To be sure, in some instances this repression and animosity were not deemed by Jews sufficiently dangerous to warrant relocation. Even acknowledging the reality of harsh governmental legislation and dangerous situations that precipitated Jewish flight, I shall again argue that such situations, like formal edicts of expulsion, were relatively limited in time and space.

Ultimately, we shall follow major changes in Jewish demography—points in pre-modern Jewish history at which major redistribution of Jewish population took place—and assess the factors that led to these changes. We shall see that large-scale alterations of Jewish demography generally resulted from voluntary migrations, set in motion by the sense of better alternatives for prosperous and fulfilling living. Of course, voluntary relocation reflects some level of discomfort and dissatisfaction with the current setting; people fully contented with their present habitations do not move. However, a measure of dissatisfaction is by no means the same as being forced to leave. A measure of dissatisfaction and the perception that an alternative locale offers a better life involve a human decision about relocating and the exercise of volition and reason. Jews over the ages moved in this way far more frequently than as a result of governmental expulsions or overwhelming fear.

In this sense then, Jews were proto-globalists, ahead of their time in a willingness to contemplate demographic change, to undertake careful assessment of the pros and cons of relocating, and to accept the risks associated with uprooting. In the process, individual Jews regularly bettered their circumstances and enriched those areas in which they settled, although their contribution was by no means always acknowledged or appreciated. Jewish migrants regularly encountered the normal proclivity of indigenous populations to resent and distrust newcomers. In the world of globalization, there is recognition of this human tendency and likewise the sense that by and large the movement of people over the ages has produced better circumstances for both those in motion and those who accepted these migrants into their midst.[1]

PART ONE

Perspectives

ONE

Traditional Jewish and Christian Perspectives

The biblical Israelites and Judeans suffered the usual tribulations that are the lot of all humanity. In part, these tribulations involved the depredations of nature. Over their many centuries in the Land of Israel, the biblical Israelites and Judeans were subjected to insufferable heat and debilitating cold, to the ravages of drought and flood, to horrific pestilence and plague of all kinds. At the same time, the biblical Israelites and Judeans also endured the normally destructive buffetings of inter-ethnic rivalries and human cruelties—raids, pillage, and wars. Overall, Israelite and Judean circumstances were in all likelihood no better or no worse that the circumstances of many neighbors across the eastern shores of the Mediterranean Sea.

The biblical Israelites and Judeans differed from their neighbors, however, in the explanation they fashioned for this generic human suffering. For biblical Israelites and Judeans, eventually convinced of the power of the one God who created and controls the entire universe, their fate was by no means a reflection of blind forces operative in a mechanistic universe or of the interactions of competing divinities clashing with one another. Israelite and Judean fate came to be understood against the backdrop of the unchallenged dominance of the one true God and the dynamics of the unique relationship created by this God with the Israelite and Judean peoples. This unique relationship involved a fundamental quid pro quo: To the extent that the human partners—Israel and Judah—fulfilled the demands laid upon them, they would be blessed; to the extent they neglected or contravened these demands, they would be punished. Thus, when natural calamity or humanly induced catastrophe struck, either or both were projected as punishments imposed by God for failure to honor the divine-human covenant.

Early evidence for this conceptualization of Israelite and Judean suffering as divine retribution comes from the first wave of prophets whose utterances are preserved in the Hebrew Bible.[1] Beginning in the eighth pre-Christian century, the point when the westward expansion of the powerful Assyrian Empire threatened both the Israelite kingdom of the north and the Judean kingdom of the south, prophetic figures in both settings chastised their fellow Israelites and Judeans for contravening the covenant with God. Both communities were accused of abandoning the worship of the one true God, and both communities were likewise castigated for neglecting and even persecuting the unfortunate and needy in their midst. These serious breaches of the covenant between Israel and God would, according to Amos, Hosea, and the first of the Isaiahs, call down divine wrath in a multitude of forms.[2]

Although these early prophets occasionally forecast natural catastrophe, the unsettled political situation throughout the Near East at the time brought to the fore their concern with the destruction that would be inflicted by human enemies. Isaiah, for example, addressed a message of divinely ordained persecution at the hands of others to the kingdom of Judah.

> Why do you seek further beatings,
> That you continue to offend?
> Every head is ailing,
> And every heart is sick.
> From head to foot
> No spot is sound:
> All bruises and welts,
> And festering sores—
> Not pressed out, not bound up,
> Not softened with oil.
> Your land is laid waste,
> Your cities burnt down;
> Before your eyes, the yield of your soil
> Is consumed by strangers—
> A wasteland as overthrown by strangers!
> Fair Zion is left

Like a booth in a vineyard,
Like a hut in a cucumber field,
Like a city beleaguered.[3]

The violence and destruction envisioned by this early group of prophets was in fact visited upon the northern kingdom, which chose to challenge the Assyrian advance westward. The effort to resist the Assyrians failed dismally and resulted in the imposition on the northerners of the standard Assyrian punishment of banishment and dispersal, as a result of which the northern Israelites disappeared from history.[4] The Judeans of the south chose the path of acquiescence to Assyrian domination and thus survived as a vassal kingdom.

A little more than a century later, as rule over the vast Mesopotamian empire passed from the Assyrians to the Babylonians, the Judeans were emboldened to rebel, failed in their efforts, and likewise suffered exile. Once again, prophets, most prominently Jeremiah, interpreted the impending danger as the result of human shortcoming and divine anger. When defeat and exile had been suffered, the rebukes of Jeremiah, so painful and disagreeable to his Judean contemporaries, were transformed into a source of understanding and solace. His fulminations provided the Judeans with comprehension of the tragedy that had beset them and offered direction for regaining divine favor and thus improved circumstances. The Judeans, unlike their former northern co-religionists, were able to maintain their corporate identity in Mesopotamian exile. A Judean diaspora proved viable, became permanent, and eventually laid the foundation for renewal of Judean life in the Land of Israel.

Somewhat later, after Jewish life had revived in the Land of Israel, the author(s) of the book of Deuteronomy retrojected these earlier prophetic views of the covenant and the possibility of devastating divine punishment back into the period of the exodus from Egypt and the desert wanderings.[5] Deuteronomy, largely consisting of lengthy addresses by Moses, comes to a stirring climax as the divinely appointed leader prepares to take his leave of Israel. In the closing addresses, in which he delivers his final charge to the recalcitrant people he has led, Moses emphasizes one last time the covenant between God and Israel, the rewards for fulfillment of the demands of this covenant, and the punishments for its neglect. The finality and dramatic rhetoric of these closing addresses have made them critically important to traditional Jews and Christians.

About to take leave of the people he had led for so long and with so much difficulty, Moses highlighted the complex workings of the covenant. The positive aspects of the covenant should have been abundantly clear to the Israelites over the preceding decades, although they obviously did not absorb sufficiently the lessons from God's unstinting assistance to them. As a result of the covenant with the Patriarchs, God freed the Israelites from Egyptian bondage and supported them during decades of wandering through the wilderness. These Israelites were now poised on the verge of entry into the land promised to them as part of the covenant. Although the Israelites had yet to conquer Canaan and settle in it, the record of divine support during the wilderness wandering should have been reassuring. In the face of all these positives, Moses chose to emphasize the potential negatives. The Israelites whom he is addressing for the last time must understand their responsibilities and the price to be paid for failure. The covenant has its positive aspects, which the Israelites have experienced; it also has its dangers, which Moses explicated in great detail.

Portraying the punishments to be inflicted for neglect of the covenant between God and Israel, Moses highlighted prominently the Assyrian and Babylonian technique of expulsion (which emerged centuries after Israelite settlement in Canaan). This technique is introduced toward the end of the address and enjoys a kind of pride of horrific place. Given the setting, with Israel poised to enter the land promised to it, predictions of expulsion from that land are especially striking. Moses began his catalogue of the suffering to be inflicted in this new way with the following:

> The Lord will bring a nation against you from afar, from the end of the earth, which will swoop down like the eagle—a nation whose language you will not understand, a ruthless nation that will show the old no regard and the young no mercy.[6]

The depiction of this enemy from afar introduces into the climactic Mosaic address a radical and frightening warning.

> As the Lord once delighted in making you prosperous and many, so will the Lord now delight in causing you to perish and in wiping you out; you shall be torn from the land that you are about to enter and possess.[7]

The Israelites were poised to enter the land promised to their ancestors, in a joyous conclusion to the exodus from Egypt and the wilderness wandering. Moses wanted his listeners to comprehend the painful message that living in the Promised Land is not Israel's inalienable right. Prosperous existence in this land is dependent on fulfillment of the demands of the covenant. The gift of the land might well be lost, if the Israelites were to neglect the covenant. They could eventually be assaulted by an enemy that does more than invade, kill, rape, and pillage—an enemy that drives indigenous populations out of their homeland and scatters them mercilessly.

The description of the tribulations inflicted by this new kind of enemy exceeds all the earlier depictions of suffering at the hands of future enemies. This new suffering will be horrible, indeed worse than death.

> The Lord will scatter you among all the peoples from one end of the earth to the other, and there you shall serve other gods, wood and stone, whom neither you nor your ancestors have experienced. Yet even among those nations you shall find no peace, nor shall your foot find a place to rest. The Lord will give you there an anguished heart and eyes that pine and a despondent spirit. The life you face shall be precarious; you shall be in terror night and day, with no assurance of survival. In the morning, you shall say "If only it were evening!" and in the evening you shall say "If only it were morning!"—because of what your heart will dread and your eyes will see. The Lord will send you back to Egypt in galleys, by a route that I told you that you would not see again. There you shall offer yourselves for sale to your enemies as male and female slaves, but none will buy.[8]

This is the most frightening of the predictions in Moses's final address. The land into which the Israelites are about to enter will be lost, which was surely a drastic message for the people who had traveled for forty years through the wilderness in anticipation of reaching the land promised to their ancestors. Moreover, the loss of the Promised Land will lead to a scattering all across the known world. Life in this exile and dispersion among all peoples will be worse even than death, with profound pain, physical and psychological, at every moment. Eventually, the exiled Israelites will make their way ignominiously back to Egypt, where they will be unable even to resume their positions as slaves, since no one will be willing to purchase them. Abandonment of the covenant will precipitate loss of all the blessings promised in the covenantal bond with God.

This painful message is not, however, Moses's final word. The covenant will remain in effect, Israel's failures and the attendant punishment of exile from the land and scattering among the nations notwithstanding. Genuine repentance will evoke divine mercy and resumption of the blessings of the covenant.

> When all these things befall you—the blessing and the curse that I have set before you—and you take them to heart amidst the various nations to which the Lord your God has banished you, and you return to the Lord your God, and you and your children heed his command with all your heart and soul, just as I enjoin upon you this day, then the Lord your God will restore your fortunes and take you back in love. He will bring you together again from all the peoples where the Lord your God has scattered you. Even if your outcasts are at the ends of the world, from there the Lord your God will gather you. And the Lord your God will bring you to the land that your fathers possessed, and you shall possess it.[9]

This affirmation of the covenant highlights the punishment of banishment and scattering as the nadir of Israel's fortunes. However, Moses assured his listeners that God will at all times be prepared to accept Israel's repentance, to rescue his people once again from exile, and to bring them back to their rightful homeland.

According to the Mosaic warning, exile for neglect of the covenant and the God who fashioned it was to involve more than simply separation from the

Promised Land. God would punish disobedience by scattering his people far and wide, throughout the entire known world, and the fate of those thus scattered was to be worse than death. Jews were to become the most abject of refugees. This Mosaic emphasis on exile and recurrent forced displacement was to impact deeply subsequent Jewish thinking and Christian thinking as well. As Jews eventually became a people living largely outside its homeland, they came to view themselves and to be viewed by others, especially Christians, as suffering the consequences of their sinfulness, as mired in exile (lengthy from the Jewish perspective, and interminable from the Christian point of view), and as consigned to endless forced dislocation all across the face of the earth.

By the first Christian century, the Jewish community in Palestine had been revived and had reoccupied center stage on the world Jewish scene. To be sure, large numbers of Jews remained in the Mesopotamian diaspora, and smaller but not insubstantial Jewish settlements dotted the northern and southern shores of the Mediterranean Sea. The Jewish community of Palestine continued to live under imperial domination; it formed the easternmost outpost of the vast Roman Empire. As had been the case many centuries earlier under Babylonian rule, Palestinian Jews chafed under Roman control, and throughout the first century segments of Palestinian Jewry agitated for rebellion. Despite the threat of harsh Roman repression and the opposition of many within Judean society, war fever escalated in Judea.

Tensions exploded into violence in the year 66. Putting down the rebellion in Judea was no easy matter for the Roman authorities. Major deployment of troops and equipment and the appointment of experienced and effective generals reflected Roman recognition of the seriousness of the Judean threat. Despite difficulties, the Roman authorities were totally committed to suppressing the rebellion and thus maintaining control of the entire Mediterranean littoral. In the year 70, Roman troops finally achieved their objectives; they conquered Jerusalem, destroyed its temple, and killed or captured most of its population, creating yet another painful watershed in Jewish history.[10]

The Romans took harsh measures in the wake of their suppression of the Judean rebellion. Destruction of Jerusalem and its temple, perceived to be the epicenter out of which the rebellion emerged, was thorough. Like most victors in antiquity, the Romans took many captives to be sold as slaves back in the center of the empire. Such enslavement, while exceedingly painful, was nonetheless a far cry from the Assyrian and Babylonian policy of total depopulation and repopulation. In fact, the demography and cultural configuration of world Jewry remained stable, despite the costly losses of the war of 66–70. Palestine remained what it had become over the preceding centuries—the demographic and religious center of worldwide Jewish life, loss of the Jerusalem Temple and wide-ranging destruction notwithstanding. There were major differences between Babylonian suppression of the revolt of the sixth pre-Christian century and Roman suppression of the revolt of the first Christian century.

How did the survivors of the war of 66–70 assess this milestone? In the first place, the biblical conviction of divine control of the destiny of the Judeans in the name of the covenant remained in place, at least to a significant extent. Of course much had changed as a result of the Greek conquest of the Near East and the diffusion of Hellenistic ideas. Josephus, who composed a minutely detailed description of the war and its devastation, wrote a history that is radically different from the biblical historical narrative. Although he by no means denied the role of God in the Jewish catastrophe of 70, his focus on logistical, political, and social realities sounded a new note. Overall, however, despite the major cultural innovations that had taken place throughout Judea and the Near East, the sense of a catastrophe that reflected the hand of God remained.

A coincidence of timing reinforced the conviction of God's role in the new disaster. The destruction of Jerusalem and its temple by the Babylonians had taken place during the height of summer, and the same was true for the later destruction of Jerusalem and the Second Temple by the Romans. Although there were minor discrepancies between the two destruction dates, these discrepancies were readily resolved, and the ninth day of the summer month of Av became the commemoration date for both calamities. This ritual conflation of the two sets of destructions reinforced the conviction of parallel divine intervention, with the biblical emphasis on God, the covenant, and neglect of covenantal demands carrying over to the new disaster.

The second major legacy of the prior catastrophes involved the punishment of exile preached by the prophets and highlighted in Moses's dramatic closing address to his people. This central theme in the Mosaic speech was a direct outgrowth of the realities of Assyrian and Babylonian imperial rule, especially the harsh policy of mass deportations and scattering of those exiled. The Romans, however, did not adopt the Assyrian and Babylonian policy of depopulation and repopulation in general or in the wake of the 66–70 war in particular. The war and the destruction it entailed did not alter the overall demography of world Jewry. Nonetheless, parallels to the Babylonian catastrophe—destruction of Jerusalem, obliteration of its temple, and massive loss of life, coupled with the deportation of large numbers of prisoners to be sold into slavery—tended to efface this crucial difference.

Thus, subsequent Jews projected the year 70 as the onset of yet another divinely initiated banishment, which was destined to evolve into the longest and most painful of the Jewish exiles. The conviction emerged that on three occasions Jews were separated from the land promised to them: when the early Israelite tribes made their way into Egypt as a result of famine; when the Babylonians deported the Judeans into Babylonia; and when the Romans drove the Judeans from their homeland. The first exile was relatively lengthy, began on a positive note, and then evolved into slavery; the second was brief (at least the total separation from the Land of Israel was brief, although the diaspora community established in Mesopotamia was destined for an extremely long life) and did not seem to entail serious suffering; the third eventually proved itself the longest of the exiles by far and was projected as the harshest as well. The Mosaic warnings were understood to apply to the third and longest exile. Clearly, the horrific predictions of Moses could not apply to the first exile, which had already ended through Mosaic leadership of the exodus from Egypt; they could likewise not apply to the second exile, which showed none of the harshness predicted in the Mosaic address; the horrors predicted by Moses surely pointed to the third exile, the purported Roman exile.

There was yet a further biblical support for this sense of the exile that purportedly began in the year 70 as the longest and most painful of all. The biblical book of Daniel includes two visions that adumbrate the succession of world empires under which Jews would live. The first of these visions was seen by the Babylonian king Nebuchadnezzar and involved a great statue composed of a variety of elements, ranging from fine and superior to coarse and inferior. The focus of this vision lay in the quality of these succeeding empires, which makes sense given that the dreamer was a Babylonian king concerned with the status and standing of his dynasty. This vision reveals nothing of substance as to the fate of the peoples subjected to the rule of these successive empires.[11]

The second vision, found in the latter and later half of the book, depicts once again the succession of empires, but highlights the impact of these empires on their subjects, specifically on the Jews who would live under their domination. This second vision was conveyed to the Judean lad Daniel, concerned of course with the fate of his people. This second vision involved four ferocious beasts emerging from the sea, each beast more frightening than its predecessor. Interpretation of these beasts referred them again to four great world empires—Babylonia, Persia, Greece, and Rome in the Jewish reading of the vision and its interpretation.[12] The fourth of the beasts, the one interpreted by Jews as representing Rome, was depicted as the most ferocious of all. "After that, as I looked on in the night vision, there was a fourth beast—fearsome, dreadful, and very powerful, with great iron teeth—that devoured and crushed and stamped the remains with its feet."[13] This imagery, which Jews associated with the Romans in both their pagan phase and their Christian phase, clearly suggests horrible persecution by this beast/empire of its competitors and its subjects. Daniel 7 powerfully reinforced for Jews the conviction that the Mosaic warnings foretold Jewish suffering, indeed unique Jewish suffering, under Roman rule.

The biblically grounded Jewish conviction that post-70 Jewry was mired in a lengthy exile the pain of which had been fully portrayed by Moses was powerfully reinforced by Jewish ritual.[14] Public reading of the Hebrew Bible constituted a core element in post-biblical Jewish ritual. Public reading of portions of the Pentateuch took place sequentially on every Sabbath and twice each week during weekday services. Either in the course of each year or over a period of three years, Jews thus encountered the entirety of the all-important first five books of the Hebrew Bible. In this way, the centrality of the Land of Israel, foregrounded in these five books, was firmly reinforced in Jewish thinking, as was the concomitant sense of Israel's potential for shortcoming and resultant divine punishment in the form of exile and wandering. These regular Torah readings were supplemented by additional readings from the prophetic literature, which reinforced many of the core Mosaic themes of covenantal obligations, the punishments that would ensue from a failure to fulfill these obligations, and the path of repentance that would reestablish the divine-human nexus and bring Israel back to its Promised Land.

The cycle of the Jewish ritual calendar further reinforced the sense of exile for Jews. The three key agricultural/historical holidays of the Jewish calendar—Pesach (Passover), Shavuot (Pentecost), and Sukkot (Booths)—were pilgrimage festivals, the major occasions on which Israelites and Judeans would make their way to Jerusalem for the special temple rituals prescribed for each of these days. The very act of celebrating these pilgrimage festivals outside the Land of Israel highlighted the reality of exilic circumstances and the elements missing in full observance of these occasions. These three festivals involved a combination of historical and agricultural rationales that once again pointed to the gap between the ideal life in the Promised Land and the contemporary exilic realities.

The two most solemn holidays of the Jewish calendar, Rosh ha-Shanah (New Year) and Yom Kippur (Day of Atonement) with their more existential and less historical focus, reinforced the ubiquitous sense of exile. At the climax of the ten-day period of atonement, the solemn rituals of Yom Kippur highlight anguished recollection of the salvific temple rites. For Jews, these temple rites constituted the most effective means ever available to propitiate God and to assure a peaceful and prosperous new year. Jews immersed in the rituals of Yom Kippur thus confronted at every turn the realities of their exilic circumstances and the loss of the primary vehicle for attaining divine favor. Avenues to propitiate God remained, of course, but the loss of Jerusalem and its sanctuary pervades the day.

The Jewish calendar also includes a number of fast days in memory of historic tragedies. The major such fast days revolve at their core around the destructions of Jerusalem and its temples. In the sequence presented in the Babylonian Talmud, these fasts are: (1) the seventeenth of Tammuz, which commemorates the onset of Roman destruction of Jerusalem; (2) the ninth of the Av, which commemorates simultaneously the destruction of the First Temple by the Babylonians and of the Second Temple by the Romans; (3) the third of Tishrei, which recalls the slaying of the leader appointed by the Babylonians to head the Judean community in the wake of the destruction of the First Temple; (4) the tenth of Tevet, which recalls the onset of the Babylonian siege of Jerusalem.[15] These four fast days recollect simultaneously the tragedies of Babylonian and Roman destruction of Jerusalem, thus reinforcing the sense of identity between the two, despite the considerable differences we have noted. At the same time, they drive home for Jews observing them the reality of persecution, the punishment of exile, and the yearnings for return to the Land of Israel and the idealized state of Jewish life that this return would inaugurate.

Jewish immersion in the Hebrew Bible and the rich panoply of Jewish rituals confronted Jews at every turn with the basic contours of their existence as a people in exile, enduring the subjugation and degradation of exilic circumstances. In one particular locale of this exile—the areas of Christian control—Jews were confronted not only with their own traditional emphasis on the rigors of exilic existence; in these areas, they lived under the rule of a competitor monotheism that buttressed many of the arguments for its legitimacy in claims of Jewish shortcoming, divine punishment, and indeed divine rejection.

Important to the evolution of Jewish attitudes toward the Roman exile were major changes in Rome itself. Pagan Rome gave way under Constantine to Christian Rome, which reinforced and indeed intensified the preexistent Jewish sense of the Roman exile as the longest and harshest of all. To be subjugated to a competitor monotheistic faith raised painful new issues. Christian thinking, which began within first-century Palestinian Jewry, embraced as a matter of course the biblical views of history. Christians accepted fully the notions of divine control of history and of the covenantal relationship as key to the history of the Jews. These views lay at the core of the Christian conception of Jewish sinfulness that moved God to do more than simply expel the Jews from the Land of Israel. In the Christian view, Jewish sinfulness was so egregious as to necessitate God's dismissing the Jews as bearers of the covenant and replacing them with human partners new and more loyal.

Whereas Jewish thinkers often wondered about the sins that brought about the third, the longest, and the harshest exile, Christian thinkers had no difficulty whatsoever in identifying this decisive sin. For Christians, Jewish rejection of Jesus, culminating in the call for his death, constituted a religious failure of such magnitude that God had as it were no choice but to replace his original covenant partner with a new one. A lengthy, indeed interminable, exile was the result of the sin of rejecting and killing Jesus. This exile was no longer perceived simply as punishment for Jewish sinfulness. Rather, it was a new level of exile, involving rejection of the Jews and their replacement in the divine-human covenantal relationship. Christian political domination of the Jews was projected as decisive evidence of God's acceptance of the former and rejection of the latter. This stance of the Church, which highlighted Jewish exile and suffering, constituted a direct assault on the status and mission of the Jews as the unique divinely chosen covenantal community.

Church thinkers, led by the influential Augustine, reinforced the Jewish sense of ongoing forced demographic displacement as the most painful element in divine punishment by adding to the broad Jewish and Christian conviction of Jewish sinfulness and exilic wandering a further biblical image—the potent figure of the fratricide Cain.[16] According to the biblical tale, in the wake of the murder of Abel, God punished his murderous brother Cain with condemnation to perpetual wandering. Cain was to become a wanderer across the face of the globe. This constituted, according to Augustine and subsequent Christian thinkers, a perfect prefiguration of the Jews, Jesus, and Jewish dispersion. In this view, the Jews slew their brother Jesus in a parallel to Cain's slaying of Abel, and God punished them with condemnation parallel to that inflicted on Cain—ceaseless wandering. Wandering Jewish refugees, spread far and wide across the known world, were living out this punishment, so precisely akin to that of Cain.

The Church made the Hebrew Bible part of its sacred Scriptures, absorbed fully many of the doctrines and images therein, and interpreted these doctrines and images in new ways. The prophetic and Mosaic conception of the covenant became a core element in Christian thinking; the Mosaic addresses and the Cain saga became central to Christian self-perception and imagery of Jews; the conviction that the Jews had been rejected and that the Church had taken their place as the human partners to the covenant became a core conviction in Christianity.

This direct and powerful Christian assault required a thoughtful and convincing Jewish response. Jewish leaders had to provide their followers with a counter-perspective on Jewish exile, and Jewish leaders responded regularly to the Christian theological assault. The Jewish counter-perspective could not and did not deny the reality of Jewish exile and inferior Jewish circumstances. These were realities too tangible to be denied. Rather, the Jewish position had to insist on the totality of the biblical paradigm. Earlier Jews had sinned, and God had imposed the requisite punishment, which brought Jews into exile and scattered them throughout the nations. However, for Jews the biblical paradigm made a further assumption, which was that the bond between Israel and its God would never be broken. At some point, Jews would repent of their sinfulness; God would accept their repentance and redeem them from exile and its debilitating conditions. The Christian attack thus served to intensify Jewish absorption of and commitment to the biblical paradigm. Jewish sinfulness, divine imposition of exile and wandering, and eventual Jewish repentance and reacceptance by God had to be constantly uppermost in Jewish consciousness.

TWO

Modern Perspectives

Over recent centuries, the conviction that God controls the cosmos and human affairs began to dissipate. The major stimulus to this momentous change came from the increasingly impressive advances in the physical sciences. As scientific investigation accelerated and scientific knowledge expanded, the conviction deepened that ultimately everything in the physical universe could and would be understandable in completely natural terms. In the process, traditional religious teachings that posited divine intervention in the cosmos in general, especially in the form of miraculous disruption of the natural order, came to be viewed as problematic or even indefensible.[1]

Eventually, this sense of natural causation made its way into human affairs as well. The deist sense of God as setting the cosmos in order and then stepping aside removed the divinity from an active role in human affairs. The more radical agnostic or atheistic perspectives challenged notions of divine intervention in human history yet more forcefully. Thus, the biblical, Jewish, and Christian conviction that God had imposed exile, exilic suffering, and interminable forced dislocation on the Jews as the result of their ancestors' failure to fulfill the demands of the divine-human covenant slowly eroded in many quarters—Jewish, Christian, and otherwise.[2]

Interestingly, and importantly for our purposes, even though the removal of God from human history radically altered understanding of the mechanism that propelled Jewish history, assessments of Jewish historical fate as unfailingly painful—grounded in the prior religious thinking—survived intact. Observers of all kinds continued to project the Jews as an endlessly afflicted people and to highlight forced Jewish displacement as the most extreme element in the relentless tragedy of the Jewish people. The ongoing emphasis on Jewish suffering and hurtful demographic dislocation combined with the removal of God and divine causation from the historical arena sparked a search for new causative explanations for the long-established and widely shared views of the tribulations of the previous two millennia of Jewish history. These new explanations revised but at the same time reinforced the still regnant conviction that Jews have suffered incessantly since the onset of their purported third exile and that the most striking manifestation of this Jewish suffering has been forced Jewish population displacement.

The search for the natural causes of assumed Jewish suffering moved in multiple directions. One major direction involved the essential nature of Jews as a distinct community within larger societies. During the Middle Ages, religion was the core component in individual identity and societal cohesion. Jews as an identifiable religious community constituted a separate and secondary element in Western societies dominated by Islam, Eastern Christianity, or Western Christianity. Notions of equality for Jews in such societies were unthinkable. To be sure, both Islam and Christianity venerated the Jewish religion and established meaningful protections for its adherents.

The onset of the Reformation shattered the religious homogeneity of western Christendom, engendering seemingly endless violence among the competing Christian religious factions on the European scene. Eventually, this costly violence moved Enlightenment thinkers to seek alternative foundations for societal cohesion. The most prominent basis for societal cohesion advanced during the Enlightenment and indeed thereafter involved ethnic or national identity. Precisely how ethnic/national identity might be defined and achieved was not altogether clear. For some observers, Jews might be comfortably encompassed in the new ethnically and nationally defined societies; for others, they remained outsiders.

Subsequently, post-Darwinian thinking about human nature created a new possibility for categorizing humans. Humanity—it was increasingly urged—consists of a number of alternative racial groupings, whose physical and spiritual characteristics are shaped by their biological heritage. These racial groupings, like all other groupings in the animal world, are in constant tension with one another, as they compete for the limited resources that nature offers. Interracial tension and struggle constitute an entirely natural and thoroughly justifiable phenomenon. Individuals and communities must be alert to this unending battle and fight vigorously for their rightful place in the natural order. Both the ethnic or national identity and the racial identity of individuals and groups, Jews included prominently, became core issues in the fashioning of nineteenth- and twentieth-century Western societies.

The status of Jews in pre-modern Europe was based essentially on religious identity, and Jews were thus secondary members of society. Under the new circumstances of societal cohesion based on ethnic/national or racial identity, the status of the Jews became a murky and contentious issue. Many in nineteenth- and twentieth-century Western polities took the position that Jews were essentially a religious community and that elimination of religion as a factor in societal cohesion created an equal place for Jews in the new Western polities. Others argued that Jews constituted more than simply a religious community; for these observers Jews clearly constituted a recognizable ethnic or national group and could thus not be absorbed into the new Western polities. As racist thinking emerged and proliferated, it provided yet another consideration for evaluating the place of Jews in the new Western societies. Political parties grounded in the conviction of Jewish racial difference and resultant inappropriateness, indeed harmfulness, to Western societies proliferated and became a powerful force in nineteenth- and twentieth-century Europe.

As the debate over Jewish ethnic/national and racial identity expanded, those espousing negative perspectives came to portray Jewish shortcomings in increasingly broad strokes. They argued that Jewish ethnic and national separateness and Jewish racial uniqueness had long been recognized by host societies as threatening. Widespread historical recognition of Jewish separateness and harmfulness has thus constituted the natural basis for the ongoing suffering and forced displacement of Jews. Non-Jewish majorities over the ages long knew of the harm introduced by Jewish ethnic separatism and Jewish racial uniqueness and protected themselves from the dangers that Jews represented by regularly removing this problematic group from their midst. Not God, but the Jews themselves were the cause of the incessant forcible displacement of Jews.

A major voice in the nationalist and racist ranks of nineteenth-century European society was Houston Stewart Chamberlain.[3] Chamberlain, an Englishman by birth, became an important part of the retinue and eventually the family of the German composer Richard Wagner. Wagner himself was deeply committed to German nationalist and racial thinking and wrote harshly of the dangers that Jewish composers posed to the purity of German music.[4] An autodidact, Chamberlain was widely read and idiosyncratically learned. On the cusp of the twentieth century, he agreed to write a volume recapitulating the achievements, failures, and problems of the waning nineteenth century, as that century came to close. His voluminous *Foundations of the Nineteenth Century* became a classic statement of nationalist and racist thinking throughout the first half of the twentieth century.[5] While essentially arguing against a place of equality for Jews in the new Western societies, the scope of the Chamberlain argumentation meant that he ultimately advanced what he perceived and projected as the grounds for historic Jewish suffering and forced displacement.

For Chamberlain, the Jews have constituted over the ages a remarkably cohesive community, alien to Europe and all European peoples. The entry of the Jews into the history of the West signifies therefore beyond doubt the entrance of a definite element, quite different from and in a way opposed to all European races, an element that remained essentially the same while the nations of Europe went through the most various phases. In the course of a hard and often cruel history, the Jewish people never entertained proposals of fraternity, but, possessed as it was of its national idea, its national past, and its national future, felt and still feels all contact with others as pollution.[6]

Chamberlain adroitly combines in this passage Jewish national identity, Jewish racial identity, and Jewish religious ideas and ideals into a potent unity, which he projects as the foundation for the Jewish unbending resistance to toleration of others and change. Further on in his treatment of the Jews, he details the characteristics of the purported Semitic race and the unique nature of its Jewish branch; he likewise portrays the Jewish national identities, out of which the eventual historical Jewish nation derived; he identifies the fundamental religious ideas that infused and reinforced Jewish racial and national traits.[7] The end result of this potent combination is a

Jewish community that has been strengthened by every conceivable human bond—racial, national, and religious. This powerful mixture has resulted—in Chamberlain's eyes—in a unified, resolute, intolerant, and unassimilable element in European society. The liberal notion that Jews are simply a religious grouping and thus deserve an equal place in the new European states is, for Chamberlain, incredibly naive, ill-informed, and dangerous.

According to Chamberlain, insightful leaders of all times have recognized the dangers this unique group poses to Western societies.

> Now this political and social influence of the Jews has been very variously judged, but the greatest politicians of all times have regarded it as pernicious. Cicero, for example (no great politician but an experienced statesman), displays a genuine fear of the Jews. . . . Even before the destruction of Jerusalem the Emperor Tiberius, who was, according to many historians, the best ruler that the Roman Imperium ever possessed, recognized a national danger in the immigration of the Jews. Even Frederick the Second, the Hohenstauffen, certainly one of the most brilliant men that ever wore a crown or carried a sword, a more free-thinking man than any monarch of the nineteenth century, an enthusiastic admirer of the East and a genuine supporter of Hebrew scholars, nevertheless held it to be his duty, contrary to the custom of his contemporaries, to bar the Jews from all public offices, and pointed warningly to the fact that wherever the Jews are admitted to power, they abuse it.[8]

For Chamberlain, Jewish suffering over the ages was not the result of divine punishment; it resulted from the alien nature of the Jews and the resultant and widespread recognition of the danger that this unassimilable group posed to Western host societies.

As the reconfiguration of the political foundations of European states unfolded during the nineteenth century, the economic foundations of European life were being simultaneously altered in dramatic ways. Industrialization and the new forms of capitalism it fostered radically altered economic power and had a drastic impact on the circumstances of the European populace. Formerly secure elements in European society floundered; new groups emerged as successful and powerful. Here too the Jews came to the fore prominently. In the first and simplest way, the new and more open political structure combined with burgeoning economic opportunities to result in a growing number of Jews being attracted westward from the great reservoir of Jewish population in the more backward areas of eastern Europe. The Jewish population of the western European states grew rapidly, which was duly noted by the Christian majority. For many of those distressed by the economic changes taking place, the arrival of the Jews was very much associated with their accelerating economic discomfort.

In fact, there were identifiable links between the growing number and prominence of Jews on the European scene and the changing European economy. The Jews as a marginal group in European society were inevitably drawn to the new frontiers of economic activity. People from the margins always have great difficulty making their way into the established bastions of economic power. On the other hand, areas of new economic endeavor tend to be far more open. Thus, in a broad way, periods of rapid economic evolution tend to offer much greater latitude to members of marginal groupings like the Jews. Thus, the perception that there was a relationship between changing economic patterns and the growing numbers and prominence of Jews in European society had a foundation in reality.

Indeed, the relationship between the changing European economy and the Jews had a further constituent element as well. Although there is a longstanding perception of Jews as involved continuously over the ages in banking and finance, this in fact was not at all the case. The remarkable evidence of everyday Jewish life that survived in the storage room of a Cairo synagogue has enabled reconstruction of many aspects of quotidian Jewish life in the eastern Mediterranean toward the end of the first millennium. This extensive evidence was mined brilliantly by S. D. Goitein and his students, and the reconstruction of what Goitein called a Mediterranean society includes a full volume devoted to Jewish economic activity.[9] The results of Goitein's research are unequivocal: The Jews whose economic activities are richly detailed in the Cairo material show no evidence of any kind of specialization, including specialization in banking and finance. These Jews made their livings in every conceivable way, from the lowest rung of the economic ladder to the highest.

To be sure, the sense of Jews as deeply involved in banking and finance was not totally without foundation; the perception that undergirds Shakespeare's *Merchant of Venice* is not chimerical or fabricated. This depiction emerges not from the totality of Jewish history, or from purported Jewish national and racial proclivities. There was, however, a branch of the Jewish people whose unique historical development resulted in concentration in the money trade. Brief consideration of this branch of the Jewish people is required, since the reality and portrayal of Jewish specialization in banking and finance play such an important role in nineteenth-century Jewish economic success and economic representation.

At the end of the first millennium, Jewish population remained, as it had been from time immemorial, centered in a rectangular configuration that stretched from Mesopotamia in the east through the Mediterranean basin in the west. This area had for long harbored the overwhelming majority of the world's Jews. What occasioned the creation of a new branch of the Jewish people was the emergence of northern Europe from its historic backwardness. Long a hinterland to the productive and creative lands of southern Europe, northern Europe began to emerge from its torpor toward the end of the first millennium. Arable land increased; population grew; old towns expanded and new ones were formed; powerful states began to take shape; and the Roman Catholic Church matured in every way. By the end of the Middle Ages—five hundred years after the invigoration of northern Europe, Christian Europe, led by its northern component, dominated the West, and that domination continued down into modernity.

A curious byproduct of the rapid development of heretofore backward northern Europe was the attraction of Mediterranean Jews northward. Jews had already in antiquity fashioned voluntarily a significant western diaspora throughout the Mediterranean basin. During antiquity and the first half of the Middle Ages, the backwardness of northern Europe offered no incentive for Jewish migration from advanced Mediterranean regions to the retrograde territories of the north. As northern Europe began its remarkable invigoration, southern European Jews were for the first time attracted northward. This shift to the north became appealing to a slowly growing number of Jews.

Only a limited segment of southern European Jewry was in a position to take advantage of the new opportunities in the north. Within the economically diversified Jewry of the Mediterranean basin, many Jews were involved in occupations that allowed no option for mobility.[10] In effect, only the merchant class enjoyed the possibility of relocating to northern Europe, and the limited evidence of early Jewish settlement in northern Europe shows the immigrating Jews to be primarily merchants. Those Jewish merchants who made the decision to migrate northward faced daunting impediments. In southern Europe, Jews were a well-established element on the societal and economic scene; in the north they were newcomers in a monolithic population that was hardly happy to—was indeed reluctant to—accept and integrate them. The newness and otherness of Jews in northern Europe would plague this young and expanding Jewry over the ages, but these difficulties did not deter southern Jews from migrating northward and ultimately did not obstruct over time the transformation of this new set of Jewish communities into the dominant Jewry on the world scene.[11]

The need felt by many northern European rulers to introduce an urban and business population into their realms and to create new and more flexible sources of government revenue, and the desire of some southern European Jews to make their way northward, fostered a cooperative effort that benefited both sides. The support of the northern European ruling class for the Jewish immigrants and the successes of these immigrants in providing the business and urban stimulation and the governmental revenues required by the secular authorities worked to the advantage of both. The Jews contributed significantly but quietly to the transformation of northern Europe; the rulers provided the support that was essential to the founding of viable Jewish communities. Both sides contributed to a successful outcome, and both benefited from this successful outcome.

The twelfth-century assault on Christian moneylending mounted by the Church had far-reaching implications for Jewish life in northern Europe. We have already noted the resistance of the indigenous population of northern

Europe to the new Jewish immigrants. This resistance did not derail the Jewish immigration; it did, however, preclude economic diversification for the Jewish newcomers. The twelfth-century Church attack on Christian usury unintentionally provided the young and growing Jewish population of northern Europe with a useful, lucrative, and ultimately problematic new economic outlet.

During the twelfth century, the increasingly well organized and powerful Roman Church undertook vigorous campaigns against common breaches of Church law. One of these breaches involved Christians lending money at interest to fellow Christians. The injunction against this practice derives from the Hebrew Bible, specifically Deuteronomy 23:20: "You shall not deduct interest from loans to your countrymen, whether in money or food or anything else that can be deducted as interest." Although Pauline Christianity had freed gentile Christians from the obligations of Jewish ceremonial law, this prohibition was by no means ceremonial. Rather, this was an ethically grounded decree, intended to provide charitable (meaning interest-free) assistance to needy Israelites and subsequently to needy Jews and Christians.

The immediately following biblical permission for taking interest on loans to non-countrymen makes the charitable element in the ordinance obvious: "But you may deduct interest from loans to foreigners."[12] Providing interest-free loans to fellow Israelites, Jews, and Christians was not transformed into a universal moral obligation; it was an act of charity limited to the internal community only. Since Jews were permitted to take interest from non-Jews and since Jews were generally a minority in their diaspora settings, moneylending was thus a potential Jewish economic activity, although down through the end of the first millennium it was by no means a dominant Jewish economic activity. As the twelfth-century Church campaign against Christians taking interest from fellow Christians progressed, for the young and economically limited Jewry of northern Europe moneylending provided a new economic outlet and eventually became a Jewish economic specialization.[13]

As new patterns of European economic activity developed in nineteenth-century Europe, the familiarity of the Jewish population with the money trade served these Jews very well. They were in a comfortable position to take advantage of the new forms of banking that were developing. Once again, as members of a marginal group, Jews were attracted to the new, but in this case they were unusually well positioned to accommodate themselves to this new corner of the European economy. For those who suffered from the new economic environment, the visibility of Jews in the money trade—especially in the form of extraordinarily successful and prominent Jewish banking families and firms—aroused deep antipathy. Banking and finance are never very popular; in periods of change and discontent they tend to become utterly despised.

We can once again turn to Houston Stewart Chamberlain and *The Foundations of the Nineteenth Century*. Early in his chapter on the Jews, Chamberlain suggests that if he had been writing his volume at the end of the eighteenth century, he would certainly not have accorded them a separate chapter. Change had occurred in the place of the Jews in Western civilization during the nineteenth century, and that change was intimately related to the economic evolution, or revolution, that had transpired and the Jewish place in it.

> Herder in spite of his outspoken humanism had expressed the opinion that "the Jewish people is and remains in Europe an Asiatic people alien to our part of the world, bound to that old law which it received in a distant climate and which according to its own confession it cannot do away with." Quite correct. But this alien people, everlastingly alien, because—as Herder well remarks—it is indissolubly bound to an alien law that is hostile to all other peoples—this alien people has become precisely in the course of the nineteenth century a disproportionately important and in many spheres actually dominant constituent of our life. Even a hundred years ago, that same witness had sadly to confess that the "ruder nations of Europe" were "willing slaves of Jewish usury"; today he could say the same of by far the greatest part of the civilized world. The possession of money in itself is, however, of least account; our governments, our law, our science, our

> commerce, our literature, our art . . . practically all branches of our life have become more or less willing slaves of the Jews.[14]

Jewish financial prowess had enabled the Jews to take control of European life in its totality, according to his argument. The malaise fostered by the changing European economy gave rise to a sense of an alien community taking control of Europe.

Once again, the concerns of nineteenth-century European society gave rise to a focus on and negative views of the Jews, and these negative views of contemporary Jews were then projected onto the totality of the Jewish past. Jews over the ages, it was claimed, had used their financial expertise to enslave the larger societies in which they had found a place. Eventually, the enslaved majorities had slowly come to their senses, had realized their plight, and had persecuted and eventually expelled these harmful aliens from their midst. The spectacle of continuous persecution and banishment of Jews is a reality; however, this reality is not rooted in supernatural interventions. It is, rather, the harmful economic proclivities of the Jews themselves that suffice to explain the saga of Jewish suffering.

Negative views on nineteenth-century Jews as an alien, unassimilable, and harmful minority on the European scene expanded into broad perspectives on baneful aspects of the Jewish past that explained in naturalistic terms the unabated persecution of the Jews. Not God, but the Jews themselves, caused the unending sequence of disasters and forced dispersion they had suffered. Nineteenth-century Jews and their sympathizers battled ferociously to blunt the criticism of their detractors and to win equal status in the new European societies. What then were the lines of defense against the broader claims of historic Jewish shortcomings? How might the Jews and their sympathizers create naturalistic explanations for Jewish suffering that would not be grounded in negative Jewish characteristics and behaviors? How could persecution of Jews be explained in naturalistic terms without portraying Jews as harmful?

This important effort proceeded in two directions: The first laid blame for Jewish suffering on the Jews themselves, but without portraying Jews in harmful terms; the second laid blame on others, specifically Christians, their theological positions, and their resultant behaviors. In both cases, it was the impact of the traditional biblical paradigm of Jewish sin, divine punishment, and eventual divine redemption that set the Jewish problems in motion. In the first instance, it was Jewish espousal of this supernatural paradigm that triggered in natural ways the sequence of Jewish suffering; in the second case, it was Christian absorption of the biblical paradigm that occasioned the lengthy patterns of persecution, suffering, and forced dispersion.

The case for an equal place for Jews in the new European societies was grounded in categorization of Jews as a religious community. In societies that had abandoned religious identity as a requirement for citizenship, Jewishness should serve as no obstacle. As we have seen, opponents such as Chamberlain rejected these claims categorically. For such opponents, Jews had been and remained an ethnic/national community as well as a religious community. For most Jews in the western and central areas of Europe, where the new-style state was coming to dominate, renouncing Jewish national identity was reasonable and acceptable. As resistance to Jewish citizenship mounted, a small number of Jews lost faith in the new effort and concluded that Jews would never be accepted as equal citizens, should therefore accept the reality of their national identity, and should strive to realize it.

The situation of the Jews in eastern Europe was radically different. This area, where the largest number of Jews was concentrated by the nineteenth century, was organized quite differently. In eastern Europe, large multinational empires remained the norm, and the idea of equal Jewish citizenship in a cohesive western-style state was meaningless. Indeed, this area was rife with minorities organizing themselves to achieve national independence. Even as the majority of eastern European Jews remained highly traditional, those oriented toward new, different, and improved circumstances included many who sought to emulate their neighbors in seeking national independence.

As nationalist movements developed within nineteenth-century European Jewry, especially in eastern Europe, these Jews too accepted fully the traditional perception of unique Jewish travails and forced demographic instability. For these groups, the explanation for Jewish tribulations did not reside in divine punishment; for the Jewish nationalists, it was precisely Jewish acceptance of these traditional teachings that brought about a sociological deformation of the Jewish people. Committed to the notions of divine punishment and eventual divine redemption, Jews over the ages had submitted passively to living regularly as a minority within host majority societies. Jewish minority status was inherently unstable and dangerous; minority Jews—like minorities everywhere—bore the brunt of societal tension and disruption. Only when Jews would reject the traditional thinking and actively restructure themselves into a "normal" human majority society of their own would the cycle of Jewish suffering come to an end.

During the nineteenth century, traditional rabbis occasionally enunciated overtly the notion of human initiative to set the process of divine redemption in motion. In the middle of the century, for example, the distinguished Rabbi Yehudah Alkali voiced these sentiments in surprisingly modern form.

> We, as a people, are properly called Israel only in the Land of Israel. In the first conquest, under Joshua, the Almighty brought the children of Israel into a land that was prepared: Its houses were then full of useful things, its wells were giving water, and its vineyards and olive groves were laden with fruit. This new redemption will—alas, because of our sins—be different: Our land is waste and desolate, and we shall have to build houses, dig wells, and plant vines and olive trees. We are therefore commanded not to attempt to go at once and all together to the Holy Land. In the first place, it is necessary for many Jews to remain for a time in the lands of dispersion, so that they can help the first settlers in Palestine.[15]

Alkali introduces the traditional perspective with his "because of our sins" and with the notion of the majority of Jews staying in the diaspora, as was done in the days of what he viewed as the second settling of the land: the rebuilding of a Jewish community in the Land of Israel under Persian rule. At the same time, the focus on redeeming the land does not revolve for

Alkali around fulfillment of commandments and prayer. Rather, the new activism lies in quotidian activities of reviving a desolate area by building houses, digging wells, and planting vines and olive trees. Modernity intruded into even very traditional circles.

More robustly modern thinking appears in the writings of the earliest Zionist thinkers, such as Leon Pinsker, for whom locutions like "because of our sins" no longer resonated. Pinsker's somewhat loose position on the definition of Jewishness follows from his personal development. Pinsker represented a combination of traditional roots and thinking, on one hand, and a new-style life story on the other. Son of a distinguished and enlightened Jewish scholar, Leon Pinsker was educated in a way that was unusual for eastern European Jews. His education culminated in a medical degree from the University of Moscow, and he served with distinction as a physician in Odessa. Beyond his medical practice, Pinsker devoted himself to the campaign for educating eastern European Jews in ways that would prepare them for the egalitarian Russian society that he was for a time convinced would emerge.

The pogroms of 1881, sparked by the assassination of Czar Alexander II, shook Pinsker to the core, convinced him that the dream he had nurtured throughout his lifetime was untenable, and turned him toward recognition that the Jews constituted a national element that could not be assimilated into Russian society. The only realistic option for Jews was to acknowledge their national identity and seek to realize it. The pamphlet he wrote to express his new insight, titled *Auto-Emancipation*, represented a very effective combination of the traditional and the innovative.[16]

Pinsker opens his pamphlet strikingly in very traditional fashion by citing a well-known rabbinic dictum, attributed in the Mishnah to the early sage Hillel: "If I am not for myself, who will be for me? And if not now, when?"[17] Whatever Hillel intended by this injunction was certainly not what it meant to Leon Pinsker. For Pinsker, the Hillel statement was appropriate to the crisis of 1881, the need for Jews to take their fate into their own hands, and the necessity to do so immediately. Taking their fate into their own hands—auto-emancipation—was the key to Jewish survival in the face of the insuperable hostility of Western societies, of which the pogroms of 1881 had convinced Pinsker.

Pinsker begins his analysis of what he identifies as "the Jewish Question" with the brute fact that the Jews cannot be assimilated into the body of nations.

> The essence of the problem, as we see it, lies in the fact that, in the midst of the nations among whom the Jews reside, they form a distinctive element that cannot be assimilated. Hence the problem is to find means of so adjusting the relations of this exclusive element to the whole body of elements that there shall never be any further basis for the Jewish Question.[18]

In this opening statement of the problem and its solution, Pinsker opts immediately for identification of the Jews as a national element. Identification of the Jews as a national grouping directs from the outset Pinsker's analysis of the enduring nature of anti-Jewish hostility and thus of the seemingly interminable suffering and forced dislocation of the Jewish people. For Pinsker, the Jews constitute a national grouping, and their dolorous fate results from the uniquely problematic nature of their national identity.

To be sure, Pinsker had long labored for inclusion of the Jews in the new and hoped-for egalitarian state. The outbreak of anti-Jewish hatred and violence in western and especially eastern Europe had proven to Pinsker beyond a shadow of a doubt that this solution to the long-standing Jewish problem was doomed, that the peoples of the world viewed Jews as a foreign national element in their midst. Recognition of the indisputable reality that Jews would never achieve acceptance in non-Jewish societies convinced Pinsker of the ineluctable reality of Jewish nationhood and the very special circumstances of this Jewish nationhood—circumstances that had traditionally aroused and would continue to arouse the fear and hatred of non-Jews.

For Pinsker, Jews as a nation evoked the hostility of their neighbors for two reasons—one material and the other psychological, but both flowing from the unique nature of Jewish nationhood. The uniqueness of the Jews involved the special circumstance of nationhood without the reality of a nation-state. The material reason for anti-Jewish hostility is relatively straightforward. Human beings move about, which results in nationals leaving their own territory and sojourning in the territory of others. This movement inevitably arouses animosity. However, this animosity is tempered by the reality of reciprocity. As Frenchmen sojourn in Germany and arouse hostility, Germans are keenly aware of German presence in France. Thus, it makes sense for Germans to treat French visitors well, in order to elicit parallel positive treatment of Germans visiting France. In this respect, Jews are unique and find themselves in a special situation. Jewish sojourners can offer no potential for repaying kindness when others visit their territory. The circumstances of the Jews as a national entity without a national homeland allows for the fullest expression of anti-foreigner animosity, without the tempering influence of potential reciprocal treatment.

Pinsker advances a second explanation for ongoing Jewish hatred—a more convoluted explanation that for him clarifies the intensity and durability of anti-Jewish sentiment over the ages. Pinsker was a physician, and the medical world by the end of the nineteenth century was becoming increasingly cognizant of the power of the irrational. For Pinsker, much of Judeophobia falls into the realm of the psychological, specifically the fear of ghosts.

> The world saw in this people [the Jews] the uncanny form of one of the dead walking among the living. The ghostlike apparition of a people without unity or organization, without land or other bond of union, no longer alive, and yet moving about among the living—this eerie form scarcely paralleled in history, unlike anything that preceded or followed it, could not fail to make a strange, peculiar impression upon the imagination of the nations. . . . Judeophobia is a psychic aberration. As a psychic aberration it is hereditary, and as a disease transmitted for two thousand years it is incurable.[19]

This is a remarkable analysis of the phenomenon of hatred of and animosity toward the Jews. In Pinsker's view, the nations of the world are not culpable for their hatred and mistreatment of the Jews, grounded in the more realistic factors or the more psychological factors or both. Fear and hatred of Jews is lamentable, but thoroughly understandable. To the extent that anyone is responsible for this hatred and the persecution it has set in motion, only the Jews themselves bear this responsibility—only the Jews themselves allowed the emergence of this abject state. According to Pinsker, an unbiased observer would say to the Jews: "You are *foolish*, because you stand awkwardly by and expect of human nature what it has always lacked—humanity. You are contemptible, because you have no real self-love and no national *self-respect*."[20]

Pinsker singles out the traditional Jewish attitudes toward Jewish history and Jewish fate we have tracked as key elements in this historic Jewish failure.

> Moreover, the belief in a Messiah, the belief in the intervention of a higher power to bring about our political resurrection, and the religious assumption that we must bear patiently a punishment inflicted upon us by God caused us to abandon every care for our national liberty, for our unity and independence. Consequently, we really gave up every thought of a fatherland and did so the more willingly, the more we had to care for our material welfare. Thus we sank lower and lower.[21]

Unending Jewish suffering and dispersion are for Pinsker an indisputable reality. This painful reality has not evolved from harmful Jewish characteristics that aroused non-Jewish fear and hatred. Rather, Jews have suffered because of their fidelity to a traditional belief that robbed them of the initiative to pursue their own national state and instead to await divine intervention for eventual amelioration of their circumstances.

As the Enlightenment gained strength, it affected every domain of human activity and creativity.[22] One of these domains was the writing of human history. Slowly, history writing in Europe shifted toward more naturalistic examination of the past. This included full collection of relevant data, careful assessment of the reliability of these data, a more nuanced depiction of major historical developments, and investigation of the natural factors impinging on these developments. The hope was to bring the reliability of the physical sciences into the arena of history. At the same time, nineteenth-century Europe was undergoing massive political and cultural change. The new-style history writing offered the possibility of trenchant criticism of traditional political and cultural ideals and practices, with this criticism buttressed by the new prestige of purportedly scientific historical research.[23]

As Jews gained the opportunity—indeed were confronted with the obligation—to participate more fully in European life, enhanced Jewish involvement in contemporary intellectual trends became possible and eventually mandatory. Jewish integration into the intellectual life of nineteenth-century Europe became a major criterion in assessing the successes or failures of Europe's Jews in amalgamating into their majority ambience. Small groups of intellectually oriented Jews, usually young Jews, seized upon these new opportunities. Since one of the major developments on the academic scene was an innovative and more critical stance toward history, new-style Jewish history writing emerged. As was true in majority society, the new-style Jewish history writing offered the possibility of attacking and altering traditional perspectives on the Jewish past within both the Christian majority and the Jewish minority. For historians of the Jews, their histories became a major vehicle for critiquing and hopefully changing traditionally negative views of Judaism and Jews held by non-Jews and Jews alike.

Since previous European histories of Judaism and Jews were essentially Christian histories and thus decidedly negative, it was hoped that the new and ostensibly more objective histories might alter some of the widely disseminated negativity. To cite but one illustrative example, nineteenth-century Europeans assumed that Jews possessed no philosophical or aesthetic sensibilities. Christians and Jews agreed that philosophy and poetry were well beyond Jewish capacity. The exploration of Europe's libraries in search of fuller data for reconstructing the Jewish past resulted in the unearthing of a rich corpus of medieval Jewish philosophic literature and an equally impressive collection of medieval Hebrew poetry, thus contradicting sharply the regnant assumptions about Jewish intellectual and aesthetic limitations.

In the process of rebutting non-Jewish negativity toward the Jewish past and enhancing the image of Jews for a non-Jewish audience, the new-style Jewish historians were in fact simultaneously addressing Jewish readers as well. Indeed, the Jewish audience may have been even more important to these historians. As European Jews gained increasing access to majority society, they inevitably encountered the negative majority perspectives on Judaism and Jews. Absorption of these negative views by Jews themselves, no longer isolated from the majority and thus shielded from its attitudes, resulted in Jewish acceptance of many of the negative majority perspectives, fostering internal Jewish perceptions of shortcoming and inferiority, which in many cases led to abandonment of the Jewish community and Jewish life. Creating a Jewish sense of dignity and pride was thus a major objective of the new Jewish historical writing.

The uncovering of new data on the Jewish past during the first half of the nineteenth century proceeded at an impressive pace, and innovative treatments of important Jewish communities and central aspects of Jewish creativity, many previously neglected, proliferated. As this evidence and these histories accumulated, combining the new findings into overall syntheses of Jewish history constituted an obvious next step. Such syntheses offered the opportunity, indeed the obligation, to address the broadest aspects of the historic Jewish experience, to project new understandings of the dynamic of Jewish history, and to combat the Christian perception of Jewish history as reflecting Jewish shortcomings and divine rejection.[24]

During the second half of the nineteenth century, a number of overarching syntheses of Jewish history appeared. The most popular of these by far was written by the German-Jewish historian Heinrich Graetz.[25] Graetz brought to his task a number of important qualifications. He had a traditional Jewish education and was for some time very close to and influenced by Rabbi Samson Raphael Hirsch, the leader of Modern Orthodoxy in Germany. He was thus well versed in standard Jewish sources and fully cognizant of traditional Jewish attitudes and thinking. At the same time, Graetz was university trained, having completed doctoral studies at the University of Breslau, with a degree conferred by the University of Jena.[26] Thus, Graetz was in effect a blend of the old and the new, equipping him effectively for composing a synthesis of Jewish history that would simultaneously reflect traditional Jewish sources and thinking, the new historical methodology taught at Europe's universities, and the innovative intellectual and spiritual currents abroad in nineteenth-century Europe.

Graetz, in writing his highly influential eleven-volume *Geschichte der Juden*, utilized fully the newly discovered materials unearthed by early nineteenth-century scholars and the new historical techniques developed in nineteenth-century European universities. One of his major objectives was to dispel negative majority—that is, traditional Christian—perspectives on the Jews and their past. Graetz intended his magnum opus to advance the cause of Jewish emancipation by dismantling many of the negative views on the Jewish past current in European thinking, by convincing his fellow Germans and fellow Europeans of the positive contributions made by Jews to their host societies over the ages, and by imputing to the historic Christian majority—not the deity—major responsibility for Jewish suffering and wanderings.

Graetz argued that Jews suffered persecution at the hands of precisely those forces that important segments of nineteenth-century Europe were determined to combat, especially the Roman Catholic Church and its unpopular institutions, such as the Inquisition. Thus, Europe and its Jews were united—argued Graetz—by a common bond of victimization at the hands of malign forces and by shared opposition to these forces. More positively, he argued that the Jews of the past had pursued the kind of intellectual quest that animated much of nineteenth-century European liberal society. For Graetz, the bonds between the European majority and Europe's Jewish minority were extensive and meaningful.

Graetz's historical synthesis hardly represented disinterested historical inquiry. He was determined to portray the Jewish past in a way that would be appealing to both non-Jews and Jews. In the process, he absorbed much of the Enlightenment criticism of the European Middle Ages, utilized the new techniques of history writing, and altered traditional views of exilic Jewish suffering and forced displacement from supernatural causation to natural causation. Further, Graetz wrote in a vivid and colorful style that attracted readers and provided them with a sharp sense of history's (gentile, Christian) villains and (Jewish) heroes. This combination of the old, the new, and the vivid made Graetz's history extremely popular and influential, especially among Jewish readers seeking positive perspectives on the Jewish past that would include explanations of Jewish suffering that eliminated Jewish shortcomings and failures as key explanatory factors.

Graetz set for himself the difficult task of portraying the positive and creative aspects of the Jewish past while absorbing fully the traditional Jewish and Christian sense of historic Jewish suffering. This combination raised difficult questions. Since divine punishment no longer played a role in Graetz's understanding of history, what natural factors could have caused pre-modern societies to persecute and reject such exemplary inhabitants as the useful and creative Jews? Graetz had to identify some agent of persecution, and for him this was the Roman Church, which had so profoundly reinforced and disseminated the traditional Jewish sense of Jewish sinfulness and divine punishment and had built upon that traditional sense a panoply of regulations and images harmful to Jews. Graetz was in effect absorbing half of the traditional imagery, Jewish suffering, while rejecting the second half, Jewish shortcomings. Graetz was keenly aware of the contrastive perspectives he was attempting to balance—Jewish productivity and creativity on one hand and Jewish tribulations on the other; he created striking images to project both simultaneously.

Graetz began his eleven-volume history of the Jews with the fourth volume, which opens with what he perceived, in highly traditional terms, as the beginning of the third exile in the year 70. Because this was his very first volume, he made some initial remarks on the broad trajectory of Jewish history that this volume was introducing.

> The long era of the dispersion, lasting nearly seventeen centuries, is characterized by unprecedented sufferings, an uninterrupted martyrdom, and a constantly aggravated degradation and humiliation unparalleled in history—but also by mental activity, unremitting intellectual activity, and indefatigable research.[27]

This is a remarkable opening to Graetz's synthesis of Jewish history. It is obviously not intended as an overarching statement on the totality of Jewish history; it is expressly an introduction to the middle period of the Jewish past, which for Graetz stretched from the year 70 to something like the year 1770. The *terminus a quo* of 70 is clear. It reflects Graetz's absorption of traditional Jewish description of the year 70 as the onset of the third and lengthiest exile. The *terminus ad quem* of something like 1770 is less clear, but it suggests Graetz's sense that the restructuring of European states along Enlightenment lines ushered in a new and happier era in Jewish history.

Further notable in this remarkable opening statement is Graetz's highlighting of Jewish suffering, his argument that this suffering was "unparalleled in history" (surely a rather grandiose claim), his depiction of Jewish travails as "an uninterrupted martyrdom," and his insistence that Jewish suffering was counterpointed by remarkable spiritual and intellectual creativity. For non-Jewish readers, this was intended to suggest that Europe bore a debt to its long-suffering Jews and that Jewish intellectual commitments qualified Jews for the citizenship they were so earnestly attempting to achieve. For Jewish readers, this portrait was intended to evoke enormous pride, especially in the capacity to overcome unparalleled persecution through extraordinary intellectual creativity.

One of Graetz's strengths—at least in terms of his desire to attract and influence readers—was his capacity to create evocative imagery. Graetz encapsulated his sense of Jewish fate between 70 and circa 1770 in the following powerful lines:

> A graphic, adequate image of this era could only be portrayed by representing it in two pictures: the one represents the subjugated Judah with the pilgrim staff in hand, the pilgrim pack upon the back, with a mournful eye addressed toward heaven, surrounded by prison walls, implements of torture, and red-hot branding irons; the other exhibits the same figure with the earnestness of the thinker upon his placid brow, with the air of a scholar in his bright features, seated in a hall of learning, which is filled with a colossal library in all the languages spoken by man and on all the branches of divine and human lore.[28]

It is an extraordinarily vivid description. The first of the two metaphors reflects the core themes of traditional Jewish thinking about the purported third exile, evoking prison walls, implements of torture, and branding irons, which seem to conjure up echoes of the despised Inquisition. Graetz conveys Jewish demographic movement, which lies at the center of our interest, through the staff and pack of the pilgrim. Clearly, Graetz meant to project the Jewish peregrinations as forced and extremely painful. Where he diverges from the traditional Jewish and Christian view we have tracked is his attribution of this fate to gentile and especially Christian hatred and persecution of innocent Jews, rather than to divine punishment for Jewish sinfulness.

For Graetz, within the broad constellation of oppressive gentile forces that brought suffering and forced displacement upon the Jews throughout the lengthy third exile, the dominant element was the Roman Catholic Church. Graetz has very harsh words for the papacy, the Church councils, the crusades, and the Inquisition. To an extent, this was a safe target for his ire, since much of European liberal society despised these aspects of the Middle Ages as well, and Enlightenment authors harshly criticized the medieval Church for them. Laying the onus for Jewish suffering on religious intolerance, and more specifically on the medieval Church, was unlikely to arouse majority defensiveness, although on occasion it did. Graetz effectively absorbed and disseminated the well-established Jewish and Christian sense of exilic suffering and forced dislocation; however, in accounting for this suffering and compelled wandering he replaced the traditional insistence on divine causation with destructive human agents and sinful Jews with innocent and productive Jews.

Precisely because of the capacity to integrate the old and the new, the Graetz synthesis had enormous impact during the latter decades of the nineteenth century and the early decades of the twentieth century. The overall outline of Jewish history that he advanced was by and large grounded in traditional Jewish and Christian thinking and was thus readily and widely accepted. This outline emphasized what was commonly projected as the extremely painful middle period of Jewish history, extending from the year 70 into the late eighteenth century. Graetz's sense of endless Jewish suffering during this middle period of Jewish history resonated positively in many circles. Here again, he integrated the old and the new effectively, reinforcing the traditional Jewish sense of exilic tribulations but supplying a new culprit for them, essentially medieval Christendom and the Roman Church.

Graetz's highlighting pre-modern Jewish virtues and achievements and identifying the Catholic Church, its institutions, and its teachings as the culprit in undeserved Jewish suffering made his historical synthesis congenial and valuable to Jewish readers, and to some but by no means all Christian readers as well. His suggestion that the proposals for restructuring Western societies that emerged in the seventeenth century and began to be realized toward the end of the eighteenth century constituted the beginning of a far better period in the history of the Jews enabled Graetz to bring the trajectory of Jewish history to an innovative and optimistic close.

The traditional Jewish and Christian views of Jewish history grounded Jewish suffering and dispersion in divine causation. Jewish failure to observe the divine-human covenant properly had aroused God's anger and fostered the punishment the prophets and Moses had predicted. Jewish population displacement was understandable according to this scheme and could be rectified by a return to the covenant. As the sense of divine control of history diminished in Western societies, thinkers of many stripes proposed new mechanisms for explaining Jewish suffering and Jewish peregrinations. Strikingly, however, the conviction that Jewish dislocations were forced and inevitably painful was so deeply entrenched that it remained a firm foundation for all of the innovative efforts to understand historical Jewish circumstances and thus an unquestioned truth for both traditional and post-traditional Jews and Christians.

The ultimate objective of this book is to challenge this widely accepted axiom—to show that not all Jewish wanderings were compulsory, that in many and indeed most instances Jews freely chose to uproot themselves in search of improved circumstances, and that quite often these Jews realized their objective. These claims by no means deny the reality of forced banishment of Jews and attendant suffering. Such banishments are fully documented and beyond doubt. The argument, rather, is proportional: How much of Jewish population movement was forced and painful, and how much voluntary and productive? It will eventually become clear that, in the majority of their peregrinations over the ages, Jews uprooted themselves of their own volition, did so in hopes of achieving better conditions for themselves and their families, and regularly achieved their aspirations.

THREE

Innovative Recent Perspectives

Recent historians of the Jews have continued to reject the supernaturally grounded assumption of unending Jewish suffering during the supposed third exile; many of them have also distanced themselves from the modern and naturalistic continuations of this sense of interminable Jewish suffering. The first major challenge to the received wisdom came in 1928 from the young Salo Baron (only thirty-three years old at the time), newly arrived in the United States from his native Europe. In an essay titled "Ghetto and Emancipation: Shall We Revisit the Traditional View?" Baron undertook a fairly limited assault on traditional Jewish thinking about exilic pain.[1] Focusing on the French Revolution and the beginnings of the process of emancipation of Western Jewry, Baron examined the centuries immediately preceding the revolution—generally viewed as the darkest centuries in the history of pre-modern Jewry—and the immediate post-Emancipation period. He argued that the former was nowhere near so horrific as usually projected and that the latter was nowhere near so idyllic.

Baron closed his brief essay with the following striking sentence: "Surely it is time to break with the lachrymose theory of pre-Revolutionary woe, and adopt a view more in accord with historical truth."[2] Precisely what Baron meant by "the lachrymose theory of pre-Revolutionary woe" is not clear—perhaps it was not even clear to Baron himself. One possibility is restricted intention—that it was time to break with the lachrymose view of Jewish life in the sixteenth through eighteenth centuries, which is the pre-revolutionary period upon which Baron focused in his brief essay. On the other hand, the words "the lachrymose theory of pre-Revolutionary woe" taken simply at face value would seem to refer to the view of Jewish life altogether prior to the eighteenth-century revolutions.[3] Even if Baron intended his call to be read in a limited way as a concluding observation to his study of European Jewry immediately before and after the French Revolution, he eventually expanded his 1928 argument into an all-out assault on the regnant view of Jewish history as a saga of suffering and forced dislocation.

Nothing in Salo Baron's background presaged this break with the traditional and modern views of Jewish history as a tale of unending persecution and pain. He was brought up in Poland in a moderately observant home, which surely included inculcation of traditional perspectives on the Jewish past. In his late teenage years, Baron made his way to Vienna, where he fairly quickly completed three doctorates and a rabbinical degree. During his studies, he was fully exposed to the newer views of Jewish history, which reinterpreted the mechanisms of Jewish history, but remained committed to the sense of unending Jewish tragedy, at least until the era of emancipation if not later.[4]

Given the enormous impact of Baron's call to reject the lachrymose perspective on Jewish history, a renewed look at what Baron did and did not say in his 1928 essay is useful. While the features of the Jewish past reconstructed by Baron are noteworthy, even more important are the methodological considerations that led him to his revolutionary conclusions. Baron espoused innovative methodological principles in this very early essay and maintained fidelity to these principles throughout his lengthy career. These principles became the foundations of his subsequent research in Jewish history and that of most recent historians of the Jews as well.

For all of the attention Baron's "Ghetto and Emancipation" has attracted—predominantly its closing sentence—the essay is rather slight. It was not intended as a major statement on Jewish history or history writing, but rather as a polemical reflection on Jewish political circumstances and policies, grounded in an appeal to the realities of the Jewish past. This rather brief essay shows none of the characteristics of the later Baron oeuvre, renowned for lengthy, somewhat ponderous, and carefully balanced writing and rich in extremely long and detailed footnotes. Nonetheless, the essay became immensely influential among later historians of the Jews, whose enterprise owed much to the leadership and stature of Salo Baron. Especially important was the memorable closing sentence, its critique of perspectives on pre-revolutionary Jewish life as steeped in lachrymosity, and parallel criticism of Jewish thinking about emancipation as far too optimistic. Baron himself extended his 1928 call for abandoning lachrymosity well beyond its originally limited parameters, and many subsequent historians of the Jews dedicated themselves to pursuing and expanding his effort.

In his introductory remarks to the 1928 essay, Baron established his focus as comparative. For the sharp contrast between pre- and post-emancipation Jewish life, he cited at some length the views of the then dominant authority on Jewish history, Heinrich Graetz, and added a critique of other predecessors:

> Emancipation, in the judgment of Graetz, Philippson, Dubnow and other historians, was the dawn of a new day after a nightmare of the deepest horror, and this view has been accepted as completely true by Jews, rabbis, scholars, and laymen, throughout the Western world. It is in terms of this complete contrast between the black of the Jewish Middle Ages and the white of the post-Emancipation period that most generalizations about the progress of the Jews in modern times are made.[5]

Identification of the prevailing consensus led immediately to the brash challenge issued by the young Baron.

> Unfortunately, in the light of present historical knowledge, the contrast on which these hopes [Jewish hopes for expanding Jewish rights and eventually achieving full equality] are built is open to great qualification. A more critical examination of the supposed gains after the Revolution and fuller information concerning the Jewish Middle Ages both indicate that we may have to revaluate radically our notions of Jewish progress under Western liberty. A wider, less prejudiced knowledge of the actual conditions of the Jews in the period of deepest decline—during the sixteenth, seventeenth, and eighteenth centuries—seems to necessitate such a revision. If the status of the Jew (his privileges, opportunities, and actual life) in those centuries was in fact not as

> low as we are in the habit of thinking, then the miracle of the Emancipation was not so great as we suppose.[6]

While this introductory statement articulates sharply the polemical objectives of the piece, describing the need for a rethinking of pre- and post-revolutionary Jewish life, it also contains a curious ambiguity. On one hand, these rich sentences seem to augur a dual focus—revising the prevailing negative portrait of the Jewish Middle Ages that preceded emancipation and at the same time reconsidering the rosy projection of the post-emancipation Jewish experience. However, the final sentence in this citation highlights a changing grasp of the medieval Jewish experience as crucial. If that experience was not as dire as widely assumed, then the gains attendant upon its replacement could not be as great as normally projected. Baron seems to point to a genuinely comparative study on one hand, but to a focus on the pre-modern Jewish experience on the other.

The contents of Baron's famous essay are in fact heavily oriented toward revision of the prevailing understanding of pre-revolutionary Jewish history. Baron divided his essay, short as it was, into three unequal segments: the widely accepted and intensely negative imagery of Jewish legal and theoretical circumstances during the Middle Ages and its shortcomings;[7] the equally widely accepted and equally intensely negative perceptions of the realities of Jewish life during this period and their inaccuracies;[8] and limited but significant reflections on some of the threatening aspects of post-emancipation Jewish life.[9] The actual content of the essay thus focuses heavily on the medieval Jewish experience and what Baron saw as modern misrepresentation of this experience. The dramatic final sentence, already noted, exhorts historians "to break with the lachrymose theory of pre-Revolutionary woe," without an explicit call for similar reevaluation of the modern Jewish experience.

In his essay, Baron in effect focused on what he called the Jewish Middle Ages. In the only footnote in the popularly oriented essay, he clarifies the meaning assigned to the notion of the Jewish Middle Ages.[10] Using the terms "Middle Ages" and "Dark Ages" interchangeably, Baron begins by noting, in accord with an observation by Leopold Zunz, that the Jewish Middle Ages were not at all identical with the general European Middle

Ages.[11] While he does not define the parameters of the European Middle/Dark Ages, he does make important observations on the Jewish Middle/Dark Ages, noting that, "until the Crusades a majority of Jews lived under Islamic rule under relatively good circumstances." Thus, the Jewish Middle/Dark Ages as a period of intense disabilities and suffering did not, according to Baron, begin before the twelfth century.

Baron further suggests that during this period of Islamic domination of Jewish life, which can be dated from the seventh through the twelfth centuries, "even Western Jewry [which seems to mean the Jews in Christian Europe] was far superior to its Christian neighbors in culture and status." This leads to the following somewhat unclear statement: "Only in the last centuries of the European Middle Ages did the Jewish Middle Ages set in." This suggests that during the closing centuries of the European Middle Ages, which are not specified but obviously postdate the twelfth century, Jewish life declined, with the decline reaching its nadir in the sixteenth through eighteenth centuries, which are generally viewed in terms of European history as post-medieval.[12] Thus, Baron proposes that European Jewish life began to decline sometime in the twelfth through fifteenth centuries and reached its lowest point in the sixteenth through eighteenth centuries. Baron's utilization of these latter centuries in his discussion of pre- and post-emancipation Jewish life is thus largely a polemical device, through which he intended to show that medieval Jewish life at its very worst was not as harsh as commonly assumed.

Notable immediately in this lengthy footnote are two important methodological innovations. The first is insistence upon introducing into discussion of the Jewish past the entirety of that past. Since modern study of Jewish history was essentially a European project, there was inevitably a danger that the focus would be the European Jewish experience. Baron in his lengthy footnote on the Jewish Middle Ages warns his readers that Jewish life was to be found elsewhere in the pre-modern world. Indeed, he notes that for many centuries the center of Jewish existence was in the Islamic rather than the Christian world.

The second methodological innovation was the need for comparative sensitivity, grounded in full knowledge of the broad environment in which Jews found themselves. Thus, he insists that, during the seventh through twelfth centuries, "even Western Jewry was far superior to its Christian neighbors in culture and status." The historical situation of the Jews cannot be judged against some abstract standard (which usually means simply a modern standard, as we shall see); rather, the circumstances of the Jews of the past must be weighed against the broader backdrop of the period under discussion. The Jewry of the Christian West from the seventh through the twelfth centuries, when viewed in its context, was not persecuted and downtrodden; it was in fact "superior to its neighbors in culture and status." The difference between this view and the Graetz perspectives cited in the previous chapter is obvious and immense.

Baron proceeds in the first segment of his analysis to apply this latter methodological principle. He identifies the key elements in negative projections of Jewish legal and theoretical circumstances during this purportedly most dismal period of the sixteenth through eighteenth centuries and tempers these negative projections by placing them in historical context. The initial item in the prevailing negative depiction of medieval Jewish life that Baron challenges is the claim that during this period "Jews did not have 'equal rights.' "[13] Baron's rejoinder to this claim reveals immediately the need for a thorough grasp of the majority culture of all periods of the Jewish past. To the claim that Jews lacked equal rights, Baron responds brusquely and dismissively: "The simple fact is that there was no such thing then as 'equal rights.' "[14] Thus, Jewish lack of equal rights can hardly be advanced as an index of desperate Jewish circumstances.

To be sure, more was called for than the simple observation that there was no such thing as equal rights, and Baron proceeds further. He addresses the basic structure of the medieval and early modern European state and notes its essentially corporate organizational pattern. The state was composed not of discrete individuals, but of clearly defined corporations, including prominently the nobility, the clergy, the urban populace, and the peasant masses. Thus, for Baron the crucial question in identifying and evaluating Jewish legal and theoretical circumstances is not the equal standing of Jews in society as individuals, but rather the comparative standing of the Jewish corporation within the corporately organized state. Baron argues that this comparative standing—even in the most dismal period of the sixteenth through eighteenth centuries—was hardly as desperate as generally depicted.

With respect to the nobility and clergy, Baron notes that, while Jews had fewer rights than nobles and clergymen, they also bore fewer responsibilities. Medieval Jews were, Baron asserts vigorously, incomparably better off than the peasant masses. The element in the majority population that was closest to the Jews in status was the urban populace. Although Jewish rights relative to this group declined during the second half of the Middle Ages and into the early modern centuries, Jews were by no means devoid of rights. Therefore, the notion of lack of equality must, according to Baron, be radically reformulated. As a group, Jews were hardly unique with respect to their rights. In fact, as a group they enjoyed far greater rights than the vast majority of the inhabitants of medieval and early modern Europe.[15]

Baron's discussion of the legal and theoretical circumstances of medieval European Jewry constituted a sharp revision of prevailing views of Jewish life in pre-revolutionary Europe. Baron introduced and examined emotional symbols like inequality, serfdom, ghetto, and inquisition dispassionately and stripped them of much of their significance. Noteworthy in the light of his subsequent writings, Baron insisted on moving from the theoretical to the practical. "Legally and in theory, we have seen, the status of the Jew was by no means an inferior one. But did actual events—persecutions, riots, pogroms, monetary extortions—reduce their theoretical legal privileges to fictions in practice? Even here the traditional answers of Jewish historians do not square with the facts."[16] This insistence on the practical and the quantifiable became one of the hallmarks of Baron's subsequent historical writings.

The point at which Baron chose to begin his examination of the practicalities and realities of Jewish life is characteristic. He commences with demographic statistics. The question he poses involves the rate of growth or decline of Europe's Jewish population during the purportedly bleak sixteenth through eighteenth centuries. Not only does Baron claim rapid growth of the Jewish population throughout this allegedly dismal period, he notes that Jewish population growth far outstripped the population growth of the non-Jewish majority during these centuries. Indeed, Jewish population, Baron contends, grew at four times the rate of general population growth from the sixteenth through the eighteenth centuries. While anti-Jewish violence is documented for this period and is usually highlighted by historians of the Jews, the impact of this violence could hardly have been devastating, given the overall Jewish population explosion. For Baron, this is a decisive indication that the lachrymose view of this period is misguided and must be tempered.

The second major index of the realities of Jewish circumstances lay in the area of economics. The picture that Baron paints is one of Jewish economic achievement, indeed achievement far beyond the median level of Christian economic success. In fact, claims Baron, Jewish economic activity, often judged harshly, set the stage for much modern Jewish success. "Paradoxical as it may seem, the very restrictive legislation [endured by Jews] proved in the long run beneficial to Jewish economic development. It forced them into the money trade, and throughout the Middle Ages trained them in individual enterprise without guild backing, compelled them to set up international contacts . . . , and equipped them with vast sums of ready cash. With the dawn of early capitalism, and the need for ready money for the new manufactures and international trading ventures, the Jew fitted readily into the new economic structure."[17] Rather than projecting Jewish involvement in the money trade as unqualifiedly negative (the normal perspective), Baron suggests that this specialization had some very useful aspects to it.

Little wonder that Baron's brief and polemical 1928 essay made such a striking impression. It leveled a potent challenge to the findings of the reigning authorities on pre- and post-revolutionary Jewish life in Europe, to the thinking of the bulk of the contemporary Jewish community about both these periods, and to political positions that flowed from these findings and this thinking. In the process, the essay also established a number of methodological guidelines for the developing field of Jewish history. These included: the need for comprehension of the broad contours and organizational patterns of the majority societies in which Jews found themselves; constant comparison of the Jewish minority to diverse elements in the non-Jewish majority; consideration of the full range of Jewish experience; attention to the quantitative realities of population and economics; and resolute resistance to the emotional impact of compelling slogans and dramatic events.

Finally, the 1928 essay reflects a certain cast of mind in the young Salo Baron—a recoiling from simplistic absolutes and an embrace of complexity and nuance. For Baron, comparisons were acceptable, indeed useful. The situation of Jews in medieval Christian Europe was better than that of the serfs and inferior to that of the nobility; these Jews lived in circumstances inferior to those of their brethren in the earlier Islamic world. What was not useful or acceptable was what Baron identified as the "complete contrast between the black of the Jewish Middle Ages and the white of the post-Emancipation period." Human life—in his mind—does not admit of such stark contrasts; human life is too complex for such oversimplifications. Viewed retrospectively, this essay signaled the onset of a new view of the Jewish past, although this was hardly its raison d'être or its central thrust.

In 1926, Baron had accepted a temporary invitation to teach at the Jewish Institute of Religion in New York. He rapidly established himself as a productive scholar and an effective teacher, and he decided to remain in New York. Not too long after, Baron was invited to fill the newly created Miller Chair in Jewish History, Literature, and Institutions at Columbia University.[18] This position afforded him a unique opportunity—indeed a unique responsibility—to investigate the Jewish past from a dispassionate and comparative perspective. The move to Columbia certainly had a decisive impact on the crystallization of his innovative perspectives on the history of the Jews. For Baron, who was already well on his way to new perspectives on the Jewish past even before his move to Columbia, the experience of teaching in a general history department at a major American university strengthened the tendency toward engaging the history of the Jews in new ways. Moving to the new and broader environment of a general university reinforced the tendencies already evident in the 1928 essay—the tendencies to see Jews in the context they found themselves in, and to view Jewish history from a comparative perspective. Baron's transition from the Jewish Institute of Religion to the department of history at Columbia radically altered the course of his academic career and arguably the future of Jewish studies on American university campuses.

As the newly appointed Miller Professor at Columbia, Baron gave ten Schermerhorn Lectures in 1931 under the title "Jewish Society and Religion in Their Historical Interrelation." The title of these lectures reflects nicely the shift from the parochial setting of the Jewish Institute of Religion to the broader Columbia setting. In these lectures, Baron addressed the important methodological issue of the relationship between societies and their patterns of religious expression through a case study of the Jews. In this way, he sought to establish the academic and non-parochial character of the Jewish history that he would teach in the Columbia setting. Baron subsequently used these lectures as the foundation for his three-volume *Social and Religious History of the Jews*, published by Columbia University Press in 1937. The published volumes absorbed the Schermerhorn Lectures' methodological focus on the combination of the social and the religious. However, these volumes were presented unabashedly as moving beyond the methodological to a substantive history of the Jews.

In 1937, ensconced in the Columbia University department of history, Baron was still a rather young forty-two, and the range, erudition, and innovativeness of his three-volume history are truly remarkable. The three volumes of the *Social and Religious History* actually consist of two volumes of text and a third volume of extensive notes, bibliography, and index.[19] The two volumes of text, divided into twelve chapters, take the reader through the entirety of Jewish history, from the origins of the Israelites through the twentieth century. The notes are voluminous—vintage Baron. As a result of the relative compactness of the two-volume treatment of the lengthy trajectory of Jewish history, Baron was able to present clearly his narrative sense of the Jewish past, thus allowing a wide range of readers to follow his structuring of the history of the Jews, its major developments, and its central themes. In the process, Baron launched a full-scale assault on the dominant lachrymose perspective on Jewish history, challenged the reigning periodization of Jewish history, and established a neutral and descriptive rather than a programmatic framework for treating the Jewish past.

In his essay from 1928, Baron focused on the period immediately before emancipation and on the geographic area in which emancipation eventually took place, that is to say late medieval and early modern Christian Europe. We have noted his brief effort at specifying the temporal limits of the Jewish Middle Ages, which were roughly the thirteenth through eighteenth centuries. However, the prevailing lachrymose view of Jewish history was hardly limited to the Jewish Middle Ages as defined by Baron. The time frame for most lachrymose presentations of Jewish history, both traditional and modern, was far more inclusive. For traditional and modern Jewish thinkers, most of Jewish history was a sequence of suffering that began with Roman suppression of the Jewish rebellion in the year 70 and would end with one or another form of redemption.[20] Although in the essay Baron's polemical purposes led him to limit his assault on lachrymosity to what he called the Jewish Middle Ages, in the *Social and Religious History* he altered his definition of the lachrymose to cover a far broader span of Jewish history.

Baron explicitly addressed lachrymosity in chapter 9 of his 1937 history (the placement is significant). He discussed it in a brief but important section titled "Lachrymose Conception of Jewish History."[21] This terminology constitutes a departure from that of 1928, and the changes are significant. "Theory" of the 1928 essay was replaced with "conception," which projects a stronger sense of the views that Baron found problematic and was determined to combat. "Pre-Revolutionary woes" was replaced with "Jewish history," reflecting Baron's sense that his predecessors—both traditional and modern—created a view of Jewish history that encompassed far more extensive portions of the Jewish past than merely the immediate pre-emancipation period. As Baron's stature rose and as his call for abandonment of lachrymosity exerted more authority, the revised 1937 formulation came to dominate.

In his comments on what he now labeled the lachrymose conception of Jewish history, Baron makes a number of telling points beyond his brief exhortation in the 1928 essay. He immediately defines this conception more fully. He identifies the lachrymose conception of Jewish history as "viewing the destinies of the Jews in the Diaspora as a sheer succession of miseries and persecutions," stating explicitly his awareness of the broad temporal extent of the lachrymose conception.[22] If for the polemical purposes of the 1928 essay Baron focused only on the lachrymose approach to pre-revolutionary Jewish experience in Europe, in the broader context of the *Social and Religious History* of 1937, he identified the comprehensive lachrymose approach that portrayed all of post-70 Jewish life as steeped in suffering.

Equally important, in this work Baron overtly associated lachrymosity with the exilic experience of the Jews. He defined the lachrymose conception as "viewing the destinies of the Jews *in the Diaspora* as a sheer succession of miseries and persecutions" [emphasis added]. Baron challenged this conception, suggesting that both pre-70 and post-70 Jewry in the Land of Israel experienced severe persecutions, including for example the bloody suppression of the second revolt against Rome and decrees against key Jewish practices in the wake of the second uprising and its suppression. Moreover, Baron notes that exilic experience did not begin in the year 70 and did not always involve Jewish suffering. In the wake of Babylonian suppression of an earlier Jewish uprising, for example, an exilic community was created in Mesopotamia that exhibited for millennia a low level of persecution and a high level of religious creativity. The focus on exilic suffering among lachrymose historians of the Jewish past was not the result of immersion in the available data; like much else in the lachrymose conception, it was deeply rooted in a theological construct, even among thinkers and historians who had abandoned traditional religious beliefs in divine control of history.

Baron's 1937 clarifications concerning the lachrymose conception are highly significant and identify aspects of Jewish historiography that he insisted required revision. But how did Baron himself carry out this mandate in the *Social and Religious History*? In his preface, Baron described how his twelve chapters fell into four broad periods: "After an introductory chapter, Chapters II–IV deal with the history of ancient Israel down to the Restoration; Chapters V–VII treat the period between Alexander and Mohammed; Chapters VIII–X discuss the medieval period from the rise of Islam to the seventeenth century; while Chapters XI, XII, and the Epilogue are devoted to modern Jewish history."[23]

This four-part periodization is noteworthy from a number of perspectives. First of all, it reflects Baron's insistence on linking Jewish history to broader developments. Periodization of the Jewish past in the *Social and Religious History* is organized largely around developments from without rather than from within—the restoration under the Persians; Alexander; Muhammad; the rise of Islam; and the seventeenth century, meaning the changes in European society during the seventeenth century. As already stated in his 1928 essay, Baron was adamant about projecting the history of the Jews against the broader canvas of majority history. This was in and of itself a major advance in the conceptualization of Jewish history.

This highly innovative 1937 periodization also represents significant implementation of the call to abandon the focus on the lachrymose in Jewish history and reveals Baron's awareness of the lachrymose views of traditional Jewish historical thinking and of his modern predecessors like Heinrich Graetz and the nationalist and Zionist historians. For both of these perspectives, the disaster of the year 70 marked the beginning of a new, lengthy, and painful period of Jewish history; the disaster of 70 played no such role in the periodization Baron established. The defeat at the hands of the Romans in the year 70, which dominated previous Jewish historical thinking, both traditional and modern, was simply absorbed by Baron within the lengthy time frame that stretched from Alexander to the rise of Islam. The war of 66–70, identified by Baron as the Great War, is accorded less than four pages in chapter 6 of the *Social and Religious History*. In contrast, the same chapter has five pages on "The Rise of Christianity" and six pages on the "Pauline Schism."[24] Baron's attack on lachrymosity now extended well back in time, and he was determined in his own history to overcome this tendency, to a significant extent by diminishing the importance of the defeat of the year 70 at the hands of the Romans, the razing of the Second Temple, and the destruction of the city of Jerusalem.

The negation of lachrymosity also characterizes the medieval section of the 1937 *Social and Religious History*, which begins with a chapter on Jewish life in the Islamic world titled "The Infidel." While this might be considered an evocation of negative features of Jewish life under Islam, in fact both Jews and Christians were identified as infidels. Moreover, these two sets of infidels enjoyed considerable protections in the Islamic world. The positive perspectives of this chapter are established at the outset. Baron depicts the closing centuries of late antiquity in both the Roman Empire and the Mesopotamian world as a period of decline, which entailed diminution of Jewish fortunes as well (once again Baron insists on the impact of the larger environment on the Jewish minority). He portrays the rise of Islam, the Islamic conquests, and the reconstruction of life throughout the vast Islamic empire as rejuvenation, and it is no surprise that he depicts the Jews of the Islamic realm as participating in and enjoying the benefits of this remarkable rejuvenation. Thus, the first half of the Middle Ages, as generally defined in European history, is portrayed in positive terms.[25]

The period between the seventh and twelfth centuries in the vast Islamic world is covered in the *Social and Religious History* in one chapter; the period between the thirteenth and seventeenth centuries in European Christendom is accorded two full chapters. This arrangement is partially a reflection of the growing corpus of sources available for the later period; at the same time, it also reflects the greater interest of Baron and his readers in European Jewry. Indeed, four of the twelve chapters in the *Social and Religious History*, which constitute one-third of this overall survey of three thousand years of Jewish history, are concentrated on the most recent seven centuries and the European Jewish experience.

The chapters on medieval and early modern European Jewry, "The Wanderer" and "Within the Ghetto Walls," reflect central themes discussed already in the 1928 essay, in which Baron showed great sensitivity to the distinction between external forces and their impact on medieval and early modern Jewish life and the internal structures of Jewish life. In Baron's view in 1928, the opportunities afforded by the corporate nature of medieval and early modern society and by the topography of Jewish life, with its separate neighborhoods, created the backdrop for a high level of Jewish independence and creativity, which the Jews exploited fully. Chapter 9 of the *Social and Religious History*, devoted to the external forces, balances a range of positives and negatives; chapter 10, focused on the internal aspects of Jewish life, is much more consistently positive.

The title of chapter 9—"The Wanderer"—is noteworthy, for it breaks the pattern of chapter titles. The previous eight chapter titles were essentially neutral, bearing no overtones of Jewish suffering or degradation; "The Wanderer" points unmistakably to negative developments in Jewish circumstances.[26] Always in search of balance, Baron begins the chapter by connecting Jewish fortunes in Europe to the positive Jewish circumstances in the medieval Islamic world, showing how Jewish achievements in the East under medieval Islam were carried over into the West as well, especially on the Iberian peninsula. In Spain, where Muslims controlled most of the peninsula from the early eighth century on, Jews prospered, and Jewish creativity flourished.[27]

After this brief exposition of the positive aspects of Jewish experience, the tone of the chapter changes markedly. The section headings that follow this brief opening are: "Economic Decline"; "Elimination from Agriculture"; "Money Trade"; "Few Periods of Affluence"; "New Legal Status"; "Jewish 'Serfdom' "; "The Wandering Jew"; "Lachrymose Conception of Jewish History"; "Religious and Economic Intolerance"; and "Latent Nationalism." The negativity of these section headings is patent. Something clearly took place in Christian Europe that diminished the circumstances of the Jews considerably. To be sure, Baron had labored to ameliorate this sense in his polemical essay in 1928. Once again, the broader thrust of the *Social and Religious History* dispelled the polemical argumentation and allowed Baron fuller latitude in depicting the historical realities. He opened his portrayal of Jewish life in medieval and early modern Europe by pointing in a positive direction to Jewish circumstances in Spain; he closed it in similarly positive fashion with sections titled "Close Judeo-Christian Relations" and "The Church and the Jews." Despite the opening and closing positives, the decline of Jewish circumstances in medieval Europe was not disguised in Baron's 1937 history.

Between 1928 and 1937, the elements in declining Jewish fortunes in western Christendom identified by Baron shifted somewhat. In 1928, Baron had highlighted purportedly negative developments in medieval European Jewish life as inequality, serfdom, ghettoization, and Inquisition, and had moderated or denied each. In addition, when proceeding from theoretical and legal circumstances to the realities of Jewish life, he had pointed to violence and monetary extortion. While acknowledging these negatives, Baron had argued that the growth in Jewish population meant that these harmful developments were hardly overwhelming.

In his 1937 treatment of medieval and early modern European Jewish life, Baron continued to identify serfdom as a modest disability and continued to insist on the benefits of ghettoization, devoting an entire chapter to the rich internal life of the medieval European Jews in their ghettos. Interestingly, anti-Jewish violence is not highlighted, but two new negative developments make an appearance—economic decline and expulsions. In the *Social and Religious History*, Baron began his depiction of Jewish life in medieval Europe with what he portrayed as the economic decline suffered by these Jews. In fact, he made economic decline the basis for the emergence of new and increasingly negative Jewish status. "Economic developments helped to shape the political destinies of the people. The more limited their function in society, the more restricted were their numbers and their rights."[28]

The second new theme in 1937 is Jewish demographic dislocation, the importance of which is reflected in the title of chapter 9, "The Wanderer." The opening sentences of the section titled "The 'Wandering Jew' " show the weight Baron placed on this development.

> In these words [The Wandering Jew] is well epitomized the greatest transformation in the life of medieval Jewry. It was in medieval Europe that the Jew became the "Wandering Jew." Anti-Semitism had existed in one guise or another, wherever Jews lived in dispersion. In the Graeco-Roman, as well as in the Persian worlds, under the domination of the eastern as well as the western caliphs, there had frequently occurred bloody persecutions of Jews; and even legal attempts to eliminate or reduce this alien minority had not been wanting. But nowhere else than in medieval Europe did persecutions follow in such quick succession, assume such universal character, or have such lasting effects. Moreover, nowhere else did the practice of *expulsion* [Baron's emphasis] become such a prominent factor in the relations between Jew and Gentile.[29]

Given the focus of this book, this is a critically important statement, which we shall examine in great detail in the next chapter.

The lachrymose conception of Jewish history, according to Baron's newer definition, involved the projection of post-70 diaspora life as an undifferentiated sequence of disasters. Baron's approach in 1937 represented a clear rejection of this approach. The previous citation reflects full awareness and presentation of the disabilities of Jewish life in antiquity and the early Middle Ages. These disabilities, as portrayed by Baron, are viewed comparatively, balanced by sensitivity to the disabilities suffered by others in society and by portrayal of the positive and creative aspects of Jewish life. Explaining that the negative aspects of Jewish life intensified in medieval Europe by no means signals reembrace of the lachrymose conception.

Baron's awareness and presentation of the difficulties of Jewish life in medieval western Christendom led him to a striking conclusion. He argued that these difficulties were in fact responsible for the creation of the lachrymose conception of Jewish history. "The lachrymose conception of Jewish history, viewing the destinies of the Jews in the Diaspora as a sheer succession of miseries and persecutions, a conception from which Jewish historiography has not been able to free itself to this day, took hold of the imagination of the people."[30] Baron thus asserts that the lachrymose conception was not a legacy of the classical periods of the Jewish past, during which the guiding principles of Jewish life were adumbrated. Rather, it was formulated during the Jewish Middle Ages, ostensibly as a result of some of the debilitating characteristics of that period.

Baron points to two important sixteenth-century Jewish authors—Samuel Usque and Joseph ha-Kohen—as examples of Jewish thinkers who embraced the lachrymose perspective.[31] This clarification of the genesis of lachrymosity has important implications. On one hand, the lachrymose conception by no means constitutes essential Jewish doctrine, which means that abandoning it does no damage to core Jewish views.[32] At the same time, the modern historians, whose emphasis on the lachrymose Baron challenged, did not create the paradigm themselves. They simply absorbed and extended a medieval Jewish perception. Thus, abandoning this medieval Jewish perception offers no real offense. The medieval lachrymose conception, like so much else bequeathed from the Middle Ages, could and should be left behind.

In this brief but important section on the lachrymose conception, Baron made one more telling point: He claimed that the lachrymose conception of Jewish history was absorbed by medieval Christians as well. Baron's formulation is striking: "The more frequently Jews were seen abandoning their homes, bundles on their backs, for unknown destinations, the more deeply was the conception stamped on the mind of the masses that these 'aliens' by race and religion were merely temporary sojourners."[33] This Christian absorption of the lachrymose conception of Jewish history reinforces the significance of "the wandering Jew" as a central feature of Jewish life in medieval and early modern Christian Europe, and hence Baron's focus on the subject for an entire chapter in the *Social and Religious History*.[34]

The assault on the "lachrymose conception of Jewish history" constituted a major thrust of this work, but it challenged other and equally important staples of traditional and earlier modern Jewish history writing. Baron sought to leave behind the prevailing teleological and programmatic judgments on Jewish experience. The teleological judgments were grounded in the traditional tripartite division of Jewish history. Jews, like so many other peoples, divided their history into three qualitatively distinct segments—a distinguished early period, a diminished middle period, and a resplendent final period.

For traditional Jews, this meant a period of greatness in the Land of Israel in antiquity, the painful exile initiated in the year 70, and the divine redemption that had been promised and would certainly eventuate. With the onset of the Enlightenment and one or another form of Jewish acceptance of modern perspectives on historical process, the same tripartite scheme was nonetheless maintained. In many ways, the Zionist thinkers and historians remained closest to the traditional lines. For them, there was a period of dignified independent Jewish living and flourishing Jewish creativity in the Land of Israel prior to the year 70, the deformities of exile from 70 onward, and the future reconstruction of independence and creativity in the Land of Israel. For Enlightenment thinkers and historians and for Diaspora nationalists, the same two initial periods remained firmly in place. The third and eventually brilliant phase of Jewish history would take place outside the Land of Israel and would involve for the former group full acceptance of Jews into the emergent European states, and for the latter group the establishment of Jewish political and cultural independence somewhere in the Diaspora. In all four cases, there was simplistic presentation of three diverse phases of Jewish history, two highly positive and one unrelievedly negative.

Baron led the way in replacing these simplistic presentations of the assumed phases of the Jewish past with a more rigorously and consistently descriptive portrayal of the varied experiences of the Jews. To an extent, this was an offshoot of his assault on lachrymosity. At the same time, however, it was a separate innovation, one that reflected his independence of mind and the influence of the Columbia environment and its non-parochial character. For Baron in 1937 and subsequently, the diverse periods of the Jewish past were to be portrayed in nuanced fashion, without attributing overall well-being or suffering to them. Discerning movement from well-being to suffering and then eventually from suffering back to well-being is not—in Baron's view—an element of the historian's craft. It is appropriate for the historian to discern improvement or deterioration in Jewish life, as Baron himself did on occasion, associating for example the onset of Islamic rule with improvement of Jewish circumstances and identifying Jewish life in medieval western Christendom as a period of decline. These do not, however, constitute the simplistic assessments of well-being and suffering imposed by traditional Jewish thinking, emancipationist Jewish thinking, and nationalist/Zionist Jewish thinking.

In the process of dissociating himself from these simplistic and teleological assessments of phases of the Jewish past in traditional and modern Jewish historical thinking, Baron also eschewed the programmatic stances associated with such broad assessments of Jewish fortunes. For the traditionalists, their analysis of the post-70 suffering of Jews leads to a prescriptive stance for the improvement of Jewish circumstances, which is acceptance and fulfillment of the obligations of the covenant. For the emancipationists, the trajectory of Jewish suffering and well-being requires fullest possible immersion in the life of Western societies in order to bring historic Jewish suffering to an end. For the nationalists/Zionists, Jewish well-being will derive from realization of the dream of Jewish political independence. Baron's nuanced descriptive approach to the complexities of the Jewish past precludes such prescriptive stances for improving Jewish life.

Perhaps at very best, readers of the early Baron oeuvre might have come away with a sense of the extreme complexity of the Jewish experience, the need to see the experience of Jewish communities against the backdrop of the specific environment in which these Jews found themselves, and the necessity of grasping as fully as possible the challenges and opportunities of these specific environments. Baron himself, in his 1928 essay, had advanced a number of suggestions for the improvement of modern Jewish circumstances. These suggestions were grounded in specific aspects of modern Jewish life; they were not overarching programmatic suggestions based on a global and all-encompassing theory of the trajectory of Jewish history.

Baron's writing Jewish history continued into the ninth decade of his life; his teaching career at Columbia lasted almost four decades. Throughout the rest of his voluminous writing, Baron addressed a wide range of sites of Jewish habitation, periods of the Jewish past, and aspects of Jewish experience, all while maintaining the core principles he had first adumbrated back in 1928 and refined in the *Social and Religious History of the Jews* in 1937. In 1952, he began publication of what would eventually become the eighteen-volume second edition of the *Social and Religious History of the Jews.* Although the second edition served a somewhat different purpose from its predecessor, it fully maintained the methodological commitments of the first edition.

The expansion of the original two volumes almost tenfold resulted in the creation of a rather different work. The second edition is a dense and richly documented history of the Jews that can no longer be read by a broad audience in order to grasp the overall trajectory of the Jewish past. It has come to serve largely as a resource for scholarly investigators—both those focused on Jewish history and others in alternative fields but needing the most up-to-date insight into the history of the Jews in their areas of expertise. The lengthy footnotes have increasingly become a research tool of major significance, mined regularly by scholars in a wide range of fields.

Although the second edition of the *Social and Religious History of the Jews* has had little influence on broad popular perceptions of the history of the Jews, the impact of Baron's teaching at Columbia has been enormous. As America emerged in the wake of World War II to a position of dominance on the world scene, American universities recognized their responsibility to introduce their students to the widest possible range of cultures.

Additionally, internal changes in American society, triggered by the civil rights movement and accelerating immigration, reinforced the drive for communicating fuller knowledge of a broad range of cultures. One of the results of these new university commitments was the remarkable efflorescence of Jewish studies across the length and breadth of North America, in a diverse cross-section of American universities and colleges.

As the proliferation of American universities and colleges offering Jewish studies and especially Jewish history intensified, Baron's teaching at Columbia had at least two major impacts. The first was simply providing the sense of Jewish studies as a rigorously academic field. The fact that a major American university had for decades seen fit to teach Jewish history and that the professor of Jewish history was a widely acclaimed scholar provided significant justification for the introduction of Jewish history and Jewish studies elsewhere. The second edition of the *Social and Religious History of the Jews*, even though it was not all that widely read, provided a conviction in universities and departments considering the addition of Jewish studies that this new field had already achieved high academic standards.

More important was Baron's leadership in providing a new generation of university-trained young academicians, fully prepared to take their place on university campuses. During his early years at Columbia, Baron had attracted a number of gifted students who were eventually unable to find a place in American academia; in his later years, his students found ready employment and began training their own students for academic careers.

For all those completing doctoral studies in Jewish history or other fields of Jewish studies and proceeding to research and teaching careers, the new assumptions of a universalist research and teaching environment, full attention to the broad contexts in which Jewish minorities have existed, and consideration of the comparative dimensions of Jewish experience have become the standard, replacing the earlier focus on the Jews only. The present study will reflect this new-style attention to context and the comparative dimensions of Jewish population movement.

PART TWO

Jews as Refugees

FOUR

Governmental Expulsions

For traditional Jewish and Christian thinking, God created the universe and controls history, especially the fate of his chosen human partners. To the extent that these human partners do his will, they flourish; to the extent they fall short, they suffer. This has meant to traditional Jews and Christians that Jewish behaviors have brought about historic Jewish suffering: according to Jews, temporary; according to Christians, permanent. When this theocentric view of history eroded, modern observers Jewish and non-Jewish abandoned the sense of Jewish sinfulness and divine punishment, but clung to the imagery of incessant Jewish suffering. These modern observers provided a variety of naturalist explanations for this purported persecution of Jews and Jewish suffering, explanations largely rooted in claimed Jewish shortcomings.

Methodologically, those studying the past from a naturalist perspective should have understood that analysis of the fate of Jews as a minority community should properly begin with a focus on the majority societies in which Jews have been embedded. It is the nature and tensions of majority society that play the dominant role in Jewish fate, with Jewish characteristics significant but secondary. Nowhere is the need to focus on majority cultures more important than with respect to the phenomenon of expulsion, purportedly unceasing throughout the course of Jewish history. In fact, however, the use of expulsion as a tool of governance has been sporadic, playing no role in governmental policies for very long spans of Jewish history. The overall history of expulsion must serve as the backdrop to understanding the formal banishments of Jews that have taken place.

Expulsion of rebellious ethnic-national minorities was carried out regularly by the Assyrian and Babylonian imperial authorities. Clearly, the expulsions of the eighth and sixth centuries were traumatic for the Judeans who survived as a cohesive community in exile and for their descendants who were eventually able to rebuild Jewish life in the Land of Israel. Ceaseless expulsions and scattering constituted the direst warning in the closing Mosaic speeches recorded at the end of Deuteronomy. In this way, the Assyrian and Babylonian expulsions dominated subsequent Jewish thinking, even though these expulsions of rebellious ethnic-national minorities were not emulated by rulers of Jews over the subsequent ages.[1]

Two decades ago, a prominent medievalist, Benjamin Z. Kedar, lamented the lack of serious attention to the broad phenomenon of expulsion, urged fuller study of this neglected aspect of world history, and offered some guidelines to the investigation he deemed necessary. Kedar set out three foundations for the required investigation:

> First, corporate expulsion—unlike the kindred but distinct phenomena of deportation, eviction in the wake of defeat in an armed conflict, ousting of criminals, refusal to admit unwanted aliens, and imposition of exile for political reasons—constitutes a characteristic of Western European civilization. Second, this characteristic took shape during the Middle Ages. Third, an examination of this characteristic, its evolution, and its recurrent manifestations may serve as an additional point of departure for understanding that late-comer among world civilizations, Western Europe.[2]

In addressing the general phenomenon of expulsion, Kedar sets forth the requisite foundations for the proper comprehension of expulsions of Jews over the ages. He argues that expulsion has not been a commonly invoked governmental technique throughout history. He suggests that in fact expulsion as a governmental technique in the West can only be traced back as far as the European Middle Ages. The implications of these simple assertions for understanding properly expulsions of Jews are momentous. Kedar is certainly aware of the Assyrian and Babylonian expulsions of Jews and others in early antiquity. He is thus suggesting that for almost two millennia expulsion did not surface as a governmental technique for dealing with recalcitrant subcommunities. Expulsions were hardly a ubiquitous feature of Western history. Kedar's general observations mean that between the Babylonian banishment of the early sixth pre-Christian century and the European banishments of Jews that began in the late twelfth century, Jews—along with the rest of Western humanity—did not suffer governmental expulsions. This represents a major reorientation of traditional Jewish and Christian thinking about the historical fate of the Jewish people, especially the allegedly endless cycle of forced population movement as a result of governmental edicts.

The first important observation on formal banishments of Jews involves what did not happen, rather than what did happen.[3] The Jewish rebellion that broke out in the year 66—once again an ethnic-national uprising against an imperial overlord—was profoundly threatening to the Roman authorities. A breach of Roman control of the Mediterranean shoreline had to be resisted at all costs, and it was. Roman suppression of the revolt was harsh and thorough, with major losses for the Palestinian Jewish community in lives, property, and institutions. Josephus provides enormous—indeed implausible—numbers for the casualties of the war, in order to convey to his Jewish readers Roman strength, determination, and cruelty and thus to discourage any repetition of what he saw as the insanity of the rebels and the rebellion.

Jewish casualties were surely high, even if not as high as Josephus claims. Beyond the loss of life, Jerusalem was destroyed and its temple demolished—devastating losses for Palestinian and world Jewry. Jewish religious life was decisively impacted by the Roman suppression of the rebellion of 66, as destruction of the Jerusalem Temple necessitated new forms of Jewish religiosity and new institutions of Jewish religious leadership. However, subsequent traditional Jewish thinking went much further, projecting the catastrophe of the year 70 as impacting much more than Jewish religious life; for traditional Jewish and Christian thinking, the year 70 and purported Roman expulsion of the Jews from the Land of Israel mark the beginning of the third, longest, and harshest of the Jewish exiles—a cataclysmic watershed in the history of the Jewish people.

Traditional Jewish thinking posits three exiles from the Promised Land: the first in very early antiquity as the result of a devastating famine; the second as the result of Babylonian imperial suppression of the failed Judean revolt; and the third as the result of parallel Roman imperial reaction to the failed Jewish revolt of 66. In fact, however, there was no such Roman edict of expulsion parallel to the earlier Assyrian and Babylonian decrees of banishment. The grounds for this assertion lie in two realities, the reality of Roman imperial policy and the reality of Jewish life in Palestine subsequent to the year 70. Imperial Roman responses to disloyalty on the part of subject people were intense and generally cruel; they did not, however, include the forced relocation of rebellious ethnic-national minorities decreed by the Assyrian and Babylonian emperors. The victorious Romans in the year 70 certainly brought back to Rome large numbers of captives, who were eventually sold on the Roman slave markets.[4] As painful as these deportations were, they were far less thorough than the wholesale depopulation enacted by the Assyrians and Babylonians. Loss of life and deportations notwithstanding, the bulk of the Jewish population of Palestine remained in place following the year 70.

A sober look at the demography of the Jewish people post-70 suggests that, despite all the destruction and pain, the demographic, political, and religious configuration of world Jewry in the wake of Roman suppression of the rebellion of 66–70 remained unchanged. Palestinian Jewry continued to be what it had been prior to the year 66—the largest, the politically most influential, and the religiously dominant Jewish community on the world scene. Despite Roman destructiveness in Palestine, the diaspora communities remained what they had been before the year 66—secondary in numbers, political significance, and religious strength to the Palestinian center. While this may seem strange given the evidence of the harm inflicted by the Romans, it is nonetheless the reality.

The ongoing demographic vigor of Palestinian Jewry is reflected, inter alia, in its continued agitation against Roman domination. Little more than half a century after suppression of the first revolt against Rome, the Jewish community of Palestine was strong enough and determined enough to mount a second uprising against Rome, which began in 132 and ended in 135. Like the first rebellion, this second one seriously threatened Roman control of the Mediterranean littoral and required the investment of significant

Roman resources to put it down. Although we know far less of this second uprising than we know of the first—thanks to the extensive reportage of Josephus on 66–70, there is enough evidence to suggest the strength of the Jewish insurrection. Most simply, the second uprising took almost as much time to suppress as the first. Rome was determined to quash the uprising at all costs, and it did so. Once again, this involved a multiyear effort that was costly to the Romans and costlier yet to the Jews.[5]

There is one difference in Jewish demography that emerged in the wake of the suppression of the second uprising. After 135, the center of Jewish life in Palestine passed out of Judea and northward into the Galilee. Nonetheless, despite this shift within the Land of Israel, Palestinian Jewry remained the demographic center of worldwide Jewish life for yet a number of centuries, despite the terrible casualties inflicted during two unsuccessful insurrections against Rome. It continued to function as the political center of Jewish life in the Roman Empire and the religious center for worldwide Jewish life.

The Jewish community in Palestine had to reconstruct a religious and political structure in the wake of the suppression of the revolts and the losses suffered, and it eventually did so. The destruction of the Second Temple and with it the religious and political base of the priesthood created a vacuum that had to be filled. Out of the diverse factions of early first-century Palestinian Jewry, the Pharisaic party emerged over time into a position of religious and political primacy. Precisely how quickly and how smoothly this process took place is difficult to ascertain. Later rabbinic sources suggest immediate replacement of the temple and the priesthood by the synagogue and the Pharisees/rabbis. Modern scholars are more cautious in their reconstruction of the process through which new and effective religious and political structures and leadership emerged in Palestine. These modern scholars emphasize the chaotic circumstances in the wake of 70 and 135 and the slow reconstruction that such chaos necessarily entails.[6] Eventually, however, the rabbis and their religious authority came to the fore, which formed the basis for Roman recognition of their usefulness and Roman support for them.

By the second half of the second century, the rabbinic academies of the Galilee and the leadership they vested in the Patriarch had begun to create effective patterns of political and religious authority. The Romans needed a center of internal Jewish authority with which to engage, and they found it in the rabbis and their leader, the Patriarch. Like the earlier political power of the priesthood, the political power of the rabbis and the Patriarch was ultimately rooted in their internal religious authority. The temple was gone, and the religious focus of the post-70 Jews eventually lay in fulfillment of the covenant struck between God and the Jewish people. Key to fulfillment of the demands of the covenant was the exegetical expertise and judgment that could and would clarify the details of these demands. The rabbis claimed for themselves this expertise, grounded in their meticulous deciphering of the biblical texts and their sophisticated grasp of the needs of the community they were leading, and the Romans built their relationship to Palestinian Jewry on this foundation.

By the early third century, the combination of rabbinic midrash—that is, authoritative deciphering of the biblical legacy—and rabbinic law was emerging to prominence. Under the political and religious leadership of the powerful Patriarch Judah, a corpus of rabbinically formulated Jewish law was promulgated in the form of the Mishnah. The religious authority of the Mishnah, like the earlier religious authority of the temple, extended beyond Palestinian Jewry into both the eastern and western diasporas. Its authority was global for Jews and long-lasting as well, forming the cornerstone of rabbinic Judaism from then until now.[7]

Thus in demographic, political, and religious terms, the traumatic events of 66–70 and 132–135 by no means destroyed the strength and vitality of Palestinian Jewry, which remained firmly ensconced at the center of worldwide Jewish life. Indeed, out of post-70 Palestinian Jewry emerged also the seeds of Christianity. Initially one of the many Jewish sects of early first-century Palestine, the followers of Jesus were able to survive his crucifixion, maintain his movement and legacy, and eventually take his movement and legacy in radically new directions. For our purposes, this is yet one more index of the vitality of post-70 Palestinian Jewry. Indeed, the subsequent development of Christianity suggests yet another facet of Palestinian Jewish religious creativity. Both Rabbinic Judaism and Christianity, especially its gentile branch, proved exportable, eventually capable of striking root in alternative settings across the ancient, medieval, and modern worlds.

Recognizing that there was no Roman expulsion of Palestinian Jewry in the year 70 constitutes an important clarification of the history of expulsions of Jews. This recognition alerts us to the fact that, from the early sixth pre-Christian century down into the second Christian millennium, formal banishments did not play a role in the population movement of the Jewish people. For most of this period, Jews lived under the rule of polytheistic governments and then subsequently under the rule of monotheistic governments; both chose to control recalcitrant subjects by means other than formal banishments. Also for most of this period (more than a millennium and a half) Jewish population was by and large confined to the traditional spaces that Jews had occupied from time immemorial—Mesopotamia, westward across the eastern shores of the Mediterranean Sea, and then farther westward through the Mediterranean basin. In these areas, Jews were an established fixture in the population and occasioned little or no governmental attention. The onset of a new series of expulsions of Jews—indeed of an entirely new form of expulsion of Jews, now projected as a dissident religious community—took place against the backdrop of the rise of a new force in the West, of innovative patterns of governance introduced by this new force, and of the emergence of an entirely new branch of the Jewish people.

During the early fourth century, Rome, which had been troubled by the appeal and rapid spread of Pauline Christianity and had tried to slow this spread through persecution, reversed its prior policy under Emperor Constantine, who embraced the Christian faith. For the first time, a monotheistic religious faith achieved power in a vast empire, and for the first time Jews were subjected to rule by monotheistic overlords. The implications of this shift were enormous. Jews were now projected as religious dissidents spread throughout the empire. To be sure, the struggle to assert Christian control of the Roman Empire was protracted, and thus the implications of Christian control for Jewish life took considerable time to manifest themselves. By the early sixth century and the time of Augustine, the outlines of the new status of Jews, now treated as a dissident religious community rather than an ethnic-national entity, were becoming clear.

What has often been identified as the "Augustinian synthesis" involved three major elements: the right of Jews to live securely as Jews within Christian society; the obligation of Jews to conduct themselves in such a way as to pose no danger to or inflict no insult on the ruling Christian faith; ongoing responsibility to preach Christian truth peacefully and sympathetically to Jews.[8] Nowhere in this "synthesis" is there reference to expulsion of Jews; indeed, nowhere in this "synthesis" is there identification of the penalties to be imposed if Jews in some way pose a danger to or inflict an insult on the ruling Christian faith. Through the initial centuries of the Christianization of the Roman Empire, Jews continued to live within the traditional confines of Jewish settlement, and there is no evidence of serious disruption of Jewish life and certainly no evidence of expulsions.

During the early years of the seventh century, a third Western monotheism emerged on the Arabian peninsula. In many ways, the stance of this new monotheism, Islam, to its two predecessors was far simpler than the stance of Christianity to Judaism. Its founder, Muhammad, proclaimed a revelation that vouchsafed to him a new and fuller truth delivered by the one universal God to a new human partner community. He asserted that the previous two revelations were genuinely divine and therefore demanded respect. The only shortcoming of these two revelations was incompleteness. Thus, even more clearly than in Christian policy toward Judaism and Jews there was respect for these non-Muslims as religious minorities and insistence on their right to safe and secure existence within the realm of Islam.

Demographic realities reinforced the safe and secure existence of Jews in the realm of Islam. In one of the most stunning conquests in world history, the forces of Islam, initially raiding parties and then armies, conquered completely the areas long dominated by the old Mesopotamian empires, which became the center of Islamic authority; vast swaths of the Byzantine Empire in Asia Minor and down the eastern shore of the Mediterranean Sea; all of the holdings of the western Roman Empire along the southern shores of the Mediterranean Sea; and even segments of the European mainland. When this remarkable conquest was completed by the early eighth century, the Islamic empire had emerged as the most powerful religio-political force in the Western world. In the process, it had become home to the overwhelming majority of the world's Jews, perhaps as large a share as eighty to ninety percent of worldwide Jewry. These Jews enjoyed unusually tranquil circumstances. They were protected by formal Islamic doctrine; they constituted only a small grouping within a richly diversified population; and they were long-time and well-established residents in their home areas. There was little anti-Jewish agitation, little anti-Jewish violence, and no evidence whatsoever of governmental expulsion.

At the beginning of the second Christian millennium, circumstances in the West were relatively stable. The vast realm of Islam constituted the most potent force in the West; the Byzantine Empire remained strong; and western Christendom was weak and constantly threatened by its two more powerful rivals. The augurs for the future of western Christendom were hardly encouraging. Yet unexpectedly, this weak sector of the West was vitalized and strengthened in every way. Politically, militarily, economically, and culturally, western Christendom emerged by the year 1500 as the dominant force in the West and maintained that position well into modernity. The process by which western Christendom achieved its reversal of fortune is not at all well understood, but the dimensions of this reversal have been widely recognized and fully described.

For our purposes, it is important to note that this reversal held enormous meaning for the history of the Jews. The Jewish population of western Christendom went from minuscule in the year 1000 to considerable by the year 1500 to dominant on the world scene by the year 1900. In the process, Jews encountered a new set of governing authorities and new governmental stances. Equally important, the geographic contours of Jewish life were altered radically. Most importantly, a large and ever expanding segment of world Jewish population relocated itself in the entirely new setting of northern Europe, an area in which Jews had never previously been settled in significant numbers and in which they were perceived from the outset as newcomers and treated with the hostility that is regularly the lot of newcomers. In addition, the foundations of Jewish economic life in northern Europe were radically revised, as was the relationship of the northern European Jews to their governmental overlords. Out of all this emerged a complicated set of opportunities, challenges, and difficulties for this new Jewry.

There also emerged a new set of expulsions of Jews—the first in more than a millennium and a half—and indeed a new set of expulsions for the West altogether.[9] The formal banishments that began during the twelfth century bore no resemblance whatsoever to those of early antiquity, and their complex and innovative contours must be investigated and understood. The expulsions of antiquity were simple. The northern Israelites and later the southern Judeans rebelled; these rebellions of ethnic-national minorities were suppressed; the rebellious communities were expelled and scattered in order to destroy them as cohesive ethnic-national entities and threatening political forces. The expulsions from northern Europe were grounded in an altogether different perception of the nature of Jews as a minority community and show none of this simplicity. These banishments are extraordinarily complex in their background and in their motivations, and we must carefully chart this complexity.

Understanding the innovative and complex contours of the European expulsions of Jews that were first enacted in northern Europe toward the end of the twelfth century must begin with attention to the governing authorities. The young and dynamic governments of northern Europe that first emerged during the twelfth century primarily in northwestern Europe were less rooted in hoary antiquity and its purported legacy, were more focused on the ethnic and religious core of a more homogeneous constituency, and were much more aggressive in pursuing the welfare of their society and their own ruling interests than had been the case during late antiquity and the first half of the Middle Ages. As northern Europe evolved stunningly and unexpectedly into great strength, its ruling class was very much influenced by the sense of innovation that pervaded northern European society and exhibited willingness to undertake new ventures, support new modes of societal growth, and create new techniques of governance.[10]

The new and more aggressive governmental attitudes meshed nicely with Jewish interests to foster the growth of Jewish population in northern Europe, an area previously uninhabited by Jews in any significant numbers. As rulers in northern Europe, especially northwestern and north-central Europe, sought to reinforce the rapid development of their domains, they recognized the importance of healthy urban centers and the value of urban settlers in creating or expanding such centers. Efforts to attract useful urban settlers included extension of invitations to Jewish settlers. Some southern European Jews were much interested in accepting these invitations. Jewish economic activity in the traditional areas of Jewish settlement was highly diversified, and many Jews were in no position to make the radical move to the north.[11] Jewish merchants, however, enjoyed the option of relocation in search of opportunity and responded to the governmental overtures. In this modest way, the foundation was laid for the development of northern European Jewry, fated eventually to dominate world Jewish population and life.

Economic opportunity and governmental support provided the grounding for the emergence in northern Europe of a new center of Jewish settlement. However, the lot of the new Jewish settlers was by no means easy. They faced a number of significant impediments. The first was simply the reality of newcomer status. Newcomers are never readily accepted in their new environments, and the Jewish settlers in northern Europe proved no exception. Moreover, these Jews were moving into areas that were unusually homogeneous in composition. Most strikingly, the population was almost entirely Christian, and the intrusion of non-Christians—who were the descendants of those regularly portrayed as the enemies of Jesus to boot—was resented by many in the population. This resentment expressed itself in multiple ways. Occasionally, it led to anti-Jewish violence, although the governmental authorities that had invited and supported the Jewish settlers generally provided effective protection. More insidiously, there was social and economic resistance. The latter precluded the possibility of normal economic diversification for the new Jewish settlers.

Precisely how this economic limitation might have played itself out cannot be determined, because a major ecclesiastically initiated innovation intruded and reshaped Jewish economic activity in northern Europe. One of the features of newly invigorated western Christendom was a better organized and more assertive Roman Church. Late in the eleventh century, this more assertive Church created an entirely new and precedent-shattering initiative, the crusades. In the twelfth century, the Church maintained its support for crusading while at the same time undertaking more traditional campaigns to eradicate sinfulness from Christian society. One of the sins thus attacked was Christian usury, that is, the taking or giving of interest on loans made between Christians. This practice was prohibited in Scripture for Israelites, was outlawed in later Jewish law, and was introduced into ecclesiastical law for Christians as well. Although Pauline Christianity had freed Christians from the obligations of Jewish ritual law, the prohibition of usury was not projected as a ritual concern; it was seen rather as a moral issue, the extension of assistance to fellow Christians fallen upon hard time. Church efforts to combat the sin of Christian usury were intense throughout the twelfth and thirteenth centuries, with a considerable measure of success.

The combination of Church assault on Christian usury and the economic needs of a rapidly growing society and expanding economy could have been disastrous. However, a way out of the dilemma was readily available. There was a small element on the northern European scene that could answer the need for the smooth flow of capital. Understanding of the Deuteronomic prohibition of the taking and giving of usury was explicitly limited to intracommunal lending transactions—Israelite, Jewish, and Christian.[12] Thus, Jews in northern Europe were perfectly free to take interest from their Christian contemporaries. To be sure, the Jews constituted but a tiny percentage of the population of northern Europe, however only a modest number of moneylenders could fill the societal need for flow of capital. Eventually, another group of lenders made an appearance as well, and these were the Italian moneylenders, who made the same kind of contribution to the economy, aroused similar opposition, and suffered eventually many of the same problems as the Jewish lenders, including expulsion by the ruling authorities.[13] As a result of the growing domination of this northern European Jewry on the world Jewish scene, moneylending has been projected as the historic Jewish economic specialization, which it certainly was not. The unique combination of factors in northern Europe—the need for flow of capital, the Church campaign against Christian usury, the Jewish right to lend at interest, and governmental support for this Jewish economic activity—served to create this new Jewish specialty.[14]

Like Jewish immigration into northern Europe, so too the new Jewish economic specialty in moneylending required and received governmental support. The rulers of northern Europe were aware of the danger to the burgeoning economy posed by the Church campaign against Christian usury. Just as they had earlier been supportive of Jewish immigration out of their concern for the general economic development of their domains, the same thinking affected their support for Jewish moneylending also. There was a second parallel factor in governmental support for Jewish immigration and Jewish moneylending. Both forms of support offered the possibility of significant governmental revenue. During this period of rapid economic and political development, northern European governments became far more ambitious in their undertakings. However, the financial resources at their disposal were very limited. New taxes on the Christian majority were difficult to impossible. Thus, an outsider group like the Jews—newcomers unprotected by tradition and deeply dependent on their protectors and supporters—offered themselves as valuable financial resources. They could be taxed almost at will and were. The most advanced rulers in northern Europe led the way in supporting their Jewish clients and at the same time enjoying the financial benefit accruing from this support.

With respect to Jewish moneylending, there was a further complication worthy of note. The major concern of lenders has always been ensuring the return of the funds extended to the borrower. The simplest way of securing this return was to take as security an object equal to or greater than the value of the principal extended and the anticipated interest. Should the borrower eventually default, the lender held in his possession an object of sufficient value to offset this failure. There has always been yet a further alternative for securing loans. In those instances of strong governmental power, governments could assume responsibility for insuring loans. Written records of loans guaranteed by governmental authority afforded lenders a very high level of certainty while at the same time enabling them to lend money against land, a prominent form of security that could not be transferred directly into the possession of the lender. Written records of Jewish loans appeared as a major feature of Jewish lending early in twelfth-century England, which was arguably the most advanced of the aggressive new states of northern Europe. These written records constituted for the Jewish lenders a double-edged sword. On the one hand, Jews were assured of return of the sums they disbursed. On the other hand, the same written records that offered security to the lenders also provided detailed and reliable information on Jewish wealth that made exactions from these Jewish lenders easier for the rulers of England and resulted in extensive taxation of England's Jews.

Jewish moneylending thus provided the Jewish immigrants to northwestern and north-central Europe a new and useful economic outlet—useful in terms of the general economy and also in terms of governmental revenues. At the same time, this burgeoning Jewish economic specialty aroused widespread opposition and animosity, both in Church circles and among the populace. In Church circles, there was awareness that the ecclesiastical campaign against Christian usury had spawned the unintended consequence of Jewish moneylending. Ecclesiastical concern first manifested itself over perceptions that Christian borrowers, especially the neediest among them, were suffering grievously under the harsh terms imposed by their Jewish creditors. The Church, which had long assumed a role as protector of the unfortunate in Christian society, began to lobby for limits on Jewish lending, and this lobbying regularly proved successful. Under Church pressure, many limitations on Jewish lending were introduced.[15]

Eventually, some churchmen came to question the right of Jewish lenders to take interest from Christian borrowers. The arguments adduced were generally casuistic, for example the suggestion that Jews and Christians, despite the distance and opposition between them, were actually from a broader perspective brethren, united by their shared biblical legacy. Since the key verses in Deuteronomy prohibited the taking of interest from brethren, Jews were thus precluded from taking interest from Christians. While this argument feels forced, it was occasionally advanced by Church leaders.[16] More important, this argumentation provides a useful gauge of the growing Church discomfort with Jewish moneylending. Increasingly, preachers railed against Jewish lenders, either because of the harm they were allegedly inflicting on Christian borrowers or even because the activity was deemed inherently sinful.

More pervasive than ecclesiastical condemnation of Jewish moneylending was popular anger against it. Like animosity toward newcomers, so too anger toward bankers and moneylenders has been ubiquitous in most societies. To be sure, careful reflection suggests that societies cannot exist without the flow of capital that is carried on by those who profit from this flow of capital. Moneylending is, as it were, a necessary evil. However, the necessity of moneylending and banking has never shielded moneylenders and bankers from the hatred of the masses. On occasion, this hatred could break out into anti-Jewish violence. Notable, for example, is the outbreak of anti-Jewish violence purportedly sparked by crusading in York in 1190. After attacking and killing most of the Jews of York, the rampaging mob quickly turned to the repository of Jewish loans documents kept for safety in the local cathedral. The cathedral was invaded; the documents were seized; and they were publicly destroyed. It is therefore reasonable to wonder whether this violence was rooted in crusader hostility toward Jews or alternatively in antipathy toward Jewish lending. In any case, the English authorities took energetic steps to quell the violence and ensure against repetition.

We have identified thus far energetic and innovative northern European rulers, supportive of Jewish presence and economic activities and benefiting handsomely from these economic activities. As Jewish economic activities evolved into the unpopular enterprise of moneylending, the authorities by and large supported these unpopular activities that were arguably useful to general economic well-being and development and were—at the same time—highly lucrative to the rulers themselves. To be sure, support of the Jews evoked opposition in Church and popular circles. Clearly, the advantages to the ruling class in supporting Jews outweighed the disadvantages. However, with the passage of time a new constellation of options presented themselves to the innovative and aggressive rulers of northern Europe. One highly innovative and aggressive young ruler—profoundly vulnerable at the outset of his reign—recognized the possibility of maximal profit on multiple levels by altering his predecessors' policy of protection of Jews and Jewish interests.

This young ruler was King Philip Augustus of France, weak and vulnerable in multiple ways upon his accession to the throne in the wake of the premature death of his father. What this young ruler, who eventually proved to be one of the most resourceful and powerful monarchs in French history, recognized was that exploitation of the Jews and their lending might be turned in a radically new direction. By expelling his Jewish clients, King Philip might achieve the following: considerable revenue through confiscation of Jewish land and debts; the approbation of churchmen deeply displeased with Jewish lending; and the support of a populace profoundly resentful of Jewish lending. This was a stunningly innovative and daring move, characteristic of the monarch who would eventually lay the foundations of expanded French power on the broad European scene.[17]

The resulting expulsion of 1182 from the small French royal domain was totally different from the simple expulsions of Jews in antiquity—in its impact on the Jewish victims, in its understanding of the nature of the problem the Jews purportedly represented, in the formal legitimization of expulsion, and in the motivation of the ruler enacting the decrees. The expulsions of early antiquity were occasioned by rebellion on the part of semi-autonomous and relatively powerful ethnic-national groups that dominated their home territories; they were aimed at destroying the cohesion and thus the existence of these groups—Israelites and many others. The Assyrian effort in this direction was thoroughly successful in eliminating for all times the northern Israelite tribes of Canaan; for reasons that are not entirely clear, the parallel effort of the Babylonians to obliterate the identity of the Judean community of southern Canaan was not similarly successful, with enormous implications for subsequent Western history. In contrast, the expulsion of 1182 was enacted against a small and weak religious group in French society and involved no effort to destroy this community; indeed there was no interest in the fate and fortune of this community. The Jews of France were banished from the royal domain, with no concern whatsoever with where they might relocate and how they might fare. There was no intention of destroying the Jews as a community, perhaps the result of the Augustinian doctrine with respect to the place of Jews in Christian society.

What then was the motivation of the expulsion of 1182, if not a genuine concern with the Jews expelled or even with their purportedly harmful activities? The motivation clearly lay with the enhancement of governmental power, through enrichment of the royal treasury, through eliciting ecclesiastical approval, and through garnering widespread popular support. This was a innovative, brazen, and callous effort at augmentation of royal power.

William Chester Jordan, who has examined in meticulous detail Capetian actions vis-à-vis the Jews of France, has argued the central role of royal policy toward the Jews in emerging French statecraft and by extension in governmental policies in medieval and early modern Europe altogether. "To study policy toward the Jews, its formulation, application, and effect, is to explore at once the essence of French state-building and, to some degree, the essence of state-building in the West as a whole where the majority of countries that have been successful have followed the French model."[18]

Jordan urges convincingly that Capetian policy vis-à-vis Jews, including prominently the innovative expulsion decreed in 1182 by King Philip Augustus, was central to the emergent and highly influential French state-building model. In the process, this policy, including the emergent new component of expulsion, became a core element in the subsequent stances and behaviors of numerous medieval European governments toward their Jews. The Jordan view dovetails perfectly with the suggestion already noted by Benjamin Kedar of the onset of expulsion as a governmental tactic in western Christendom during the early centuries of the second millennium. It was precisely in the vibrant northern sectors of western Christendom that this innovative tactic for the enhancement of governmental resources and power was first introduced. The new and small Jewish minority, by virtue of the unique circumstances we have traced, played a central role in the creation of this new governmental tactic, although its utilization would by no means be limited to Jews only.[19]

The innovative expulsion of 1182 affected only a small number of Jews and in all likelihood affected them only minimally. That is to say, the Jews expelled by King Philip Augustus could easily make their way short distances and find for themselves new homes. What was truly significant in the minor event of 1182 was the precedent it created. By the end of the 1190s, with accelerating ecclesiastical preaching against Jewish usury, a number of northern French barons emulated the action of their sovereign and expelled their Jews. Although we are not at all well informed as to the specifics and motivations of these baronial banishments, it certainly seems reasonable enough to suggest parallel considerations—seizure of Jewish assets, ecclesiastical approval, and popular approbation.

Strikingly, the French monarch himself exploited these new expulsions to reintroduce Jews into the royal domain in 1198, to the consternation of the clerical biographers who applauded so heartily the expulsion of 1182. Both Rigord of St. Denis and Robert of Auxerre lamented what they perceived to be a reversal in royal policy from warranted opposition toward Jews and their moneylending to support of Jews and their moneylending. Reflected in the disappointment of the clerical biographers is their failure to appreciate the underlying motivation of King Philip Augustus in both the expulsion and the recall. In both moves, the monarch was concerned above all with royal profit and royal power. This is reflected clearly in the post-1198 Jewish policies of the king. Subsequent to the return of Jews to his domain, Philip Augustus was focused on securing his rights—especially his taxation rights—over Jews who belonged to him and thus maximizing revenues from them. King Philip Augustus and fellow northern French barons were careful to introduce limitations on Jewish lending that reflected Church demands regarding the plight of Christian debtors. In this way, they could ensure maximal profit from Jewish moneylending while maintaining the requisite posture of adherence to ecclesiastical concerns.

Subsequently, in France two stances toward Jews and their moneylending emerged—support for the Jews and their lending business and exploitation of it, on one hand, and total opposition to this Jewish enterprise on the other. The former perspective dominated, with the latter represented most prominently by the unusually pious King Louis IX, who probably espoused the ecclesiastical view that Jewish lending was inherently sinful. Saint Louis, as he came to be known, hated Jews viscerally, eventually prohibited the Jews themselves from lending at interest, refused to benefit in any way from Jewish moneylending, and ordered those Jews unwilling to live by his prohibition of Jewish usury to leave France. This unusual move—expelling Jews unwilling to abide by the royal prohibition of Jewish usury—reflects the normalization of the new technique of banishment, utilized in an alternative way by the pious grandson of the far less pious King Philip Augustus.

More usual was the exploitative policy initiated by King Philip Augustus. As increasingly more powerful rulers emerged in northwestern Europe, the notion of utilizing the small, marginal, and weak Jewish communities for multiple benefits gained increasing traction among these rulers. As suggested by Jordan, the Jews, because of their economic resources, their visibility, and their weakness and marginality, served as a remarkably effective vehicle for augmentation of government power. Governmental expulsions could simultaneously provide valuable financial resources, win ecclesiastical approbation, and gain popular support. All of this constituted a windfall for aggressive political authorities. By the end of the thirteenth century, expulsions of Jews became increasingly commonplace, dominated by the 1290 expulsion from England, which remained in force for many centuries, and the 1306 expulsion from royal France, which was rescinded for a time and then fully and permanently decreed in 1394. These expulsions all reflected the Philip Augustus model, rather than the Louis IX model.

Two interesting special cases are notable. In one fascinating departure from the norm, Count Charles of Anjou and Maine, a member of the French royal family, introduced in 1289 a new way of benefiting financially from expulsion of his Jews. His decree of expulsion opens with a striking catalogue of the crimes that his Jews were allegedly committing, which served as legitimization of his banishment. As we recall, the Augustinian doctrine stipulated safe and secure existence for Jews in Christian society and therefore required justification for anti-Jewish actions like expulsion. The count notes explicitly the Jewish revenues that his expulsion would cost him. Rather than confiscating Jewish holdings, Count Charles imposed a tax on the inhabitants of his domain to compensate for his loss of revenue as a result of banishing his Jews. He further proclaimed that the expulsion was intended to be permanent and that, should any of his heirs revoke his edict, they would be obligated to return the taxes paid by the inhabitants of Anjou and Maine for the privilege of having the Jews banished.[20]

A second notable wrinkle to the normal pattern of expulsion is discernible in the wake of the expulsion of 1306 from royal France. King Philip IV followed in the footsteps of his great-great grandfather Philip Augustus, intending to profit from confiscation of Jewish goods of all kinds. Elaborate bureaucratic arrangements were instituted for maximizing the proceeds from the expulsion of the Jews. However the royal profit was clearly disappointing. The difficulties in realizing the anticipated material gains of the expulsion resulted in a recall of at least some Jews to royal France in 1315, so that they might assist in tracking down debts owed, with the proceeds split between the government and the helpful Jews.[21] Exploitation of the profits from expulsion of Jews could take a multitude of creative forms.

The areas of north-central Europe did not achieve the cohesive political organization that emerged further westward in England and France. The kind of centralized expulsions that emerged in England and France could not be replicated in the Germanic lands. Nonetheless, the innovative expulsion of Jews did become known and was imitated. In the Germanic lands, expulsions tended to be localized, to be less oriented toward governmental profit, and to reflect largely popular animosity. As a result, expulsions in the Germanic territories were often temporary only, with Jews returning before too long and often being expelled multiple times.[22] The scope and permanence of the expulsions further westward was not replicated.

The expulsions of Jews in early antiquity were simple, as were the explanations of subsequent real and alleged expulsions over the ages. For traditional Jewish and Christian theistic thinking, Jewish sinfulness had elicited divine punishment; subsequent naturalistic thinking maintained the sense of unremitting Jewish suffering—including expulsion as a standard feature of Jewish existence—and advanced simple causes for this suffering, including Jewish racial characteristics, Jewish usury (erroneously posited as a ubiquitous feature of Jewish economic life), the detrimental effects on Jews and Christians of the traditional theistic perspectives. Our analysis of the emergence of expulsions of Jews in the new sector of Jewish settlement in northern Europe has revealed them to be anything but simple. What has emerged is a complicated amalgam of new patterns of governance and new patterns of Jewish life.

Our analysis of the emergent phenomenon of expulsion of Jews has focused on northern Europe, an area in which societal life and governance took some decidedly new turns, in which Jews settled only at the end of the first millennium and the onset of the second, and in which Jewish life assumed new contours. At the conclusion of this analysis, it is worth noting that the new and painful phenomenon of expulsion in no way sapped the strength or slowed the growth of this new Jewry. As we have seen, the expelling authorities—unlike the Assyrians and Babylonians of antiquity—had no interest in destroying Jewish life and were in fact uninterested in how or where the Jews they expelled resettled. Perhaps curiously, the Jews expelled did not retreat to the older areas of Jewish settlement in southern Europe. Despite the obstacles they had encountered in northern Europe, the Jews forced into movement opted to remain within the exciting new civilization developing across the north.

In fact, these Jews in motion recapitulated core features of the earlier phases of Jewish settlement in the north. Despite their rejection in northwestern sectors of Europe and occasional rejection in the north-central sector as well, these Jews received invitations from northeastern European rulers to settle in their domains, with guarantees once again of physical protection and economic support, focused largely on the new Jewish specialization in moneylending. Jews made their way into these welcoming territories and maintained the momentum of Jewish growth across northern Europe. The progress of northern European Jewry toward dominance on the world Jewish scene was in no way impeded by the major expulsions from northwestern Europe or the lesser expulsions from north-central Europe. During the early centuries of the second millennium, expulsion emerged as a new phenomenon in Jewish life. Its impact on those Jews expelled was surely extensive and painful; its impact on overall Jewish life in northern Europe was not.

In analyzing the reemergence of expulsions into Jewish life after an extremely long hiatus, we have focused on the new Jewish communities in northern Europe, where the circumstances of general and Jewish life created the backdrop for innovative governmental edicts of banishment. With the passage of time, many of the new and negative features of northern European Jewish life made their way southward into the older areas of Jewish settlement. These included: the new Jewish specialization in moneylending; the damning and dangerous stereotypes of Jewish malevolence and murderousness that were generated in the north during the twelfth and thirteenth centuries; and the occasional outbursts of violence that erupted in the north beginning toward the end of the eleventh century. Yet another export from the north to the south was governmental banishment.

The Jewish populations of southern Europe were old and well established. As longtime residents of southern Europe, these Jews were, unlike their fellow Jews of northern Europe, relatively well integrated into their home environments. As the new tendencies generated in the north slowly manifested themselves across the south as well, the older pattern of comfortable Jewish living began to erode. Across areas of Latin Christendom in southern Europe, the Jewish communities of southern France had long been part of the French monarchy and thus had been included in the fourteenth-century expulsions, which culminated in 1394. Italy like the Germanic lands did not achieve unification, and Jewish population, scattered and not very large, suffered occasional expulsions along the same lines as the Jews of the Germanic lands. The largest Jewish communities of southern Europe were located in the various kingdoms of the Iberian peninsula, and these Jewish communities eventually suffered expulsion, indeed the most jarring of the medieval expulsions. Because of the long and stable history of Iberian Jewry, this expulsion, the last in the sequence of major medieval expulsions, was the largest and far and away the most traumatic.[23]

By the late fifteenth century, expulsion of Jews had become an accepted reality in western Christendom. Given the long-acknowledged Augustinian policy on Jews, banishments required legitimization, and the Iberian monarchs, like their northern predecessors, provided the requisite rationales. These rationales, however, constituted a striking departure from the focus on Jewish usury customary in the north. As a result of the wave of anti-Jewish violence that erupted across Spain in 1391, Spanish society was filled with "New Christians," converts from Judaism or descendants of such converts. These New Christians encountered considerable social resistance among the Old Christian population of Spain and aroused serious doubts as to the genuineness of their new religious identity. Many Old Christians suspected them of maintaining fidelity to their Jewish religious identity. By the closing decades of the fifteenth century, a small but powerful network of inquisitorial courts had been established. Whether these courts in fact revealed massive backsliding among the formerly Jewish New Christians was not clear to Christians and Jews during the late fifteenth century and has been debated ever since.[24]

Whatever the reality might have been, the Spanish monarchs who expelled their Jews in 1492 utilized the issue of backsliding by New Christians and alleged Jewish influence on such behavior as legitimization for their edict of banishment. In the words of the monarchs:

> Because we were informed that in our kingdoms there were evil Christians who Judaized and apostatized from our holy Catholic faith and that this was chiefly caused by communication of Jews with these Christians, in the Cortes that we held in the city of Toledo in the year 1480 we ordered that the said Jews be separated in all the cities, villages, and places of our kingdoms and seignories and that they be given Jewish quarters and separate places where they could live, hoping that this separation would remedy [the problem]. Moreover, we have sought and given the order that an inquisition be conducted in those kingdoms and seignories, which as you know has been done and is continuing. Through it, many guilty individuals have been discovered, which is well known. According to this, we are informed by the inquisitors and by many other religious persons, ecclesiastical and secular, that it is evident and apparent that great damage to Christians has resulted from and does result from the participation, conversation, and communication they have had with Jews, who try always by whatever means possible to subvert and to draw away our faithful Christians from our holy Catholic faith.[25]

Like their predecessors up north, the Spanish monarchs identify a major Jewish crime against Christianity and Christians, indicate serious efforts on their part to correct the situation, portray the failure of these efforts, and conclude by asserting that only removal of the Jews can solve the problem. Expulsion of the Jews is a necessity in order to protect Christian society from Jewish harm. The Jews have in effect transgressed the limits set for them by the Augustinian doctrine and have thus forfeited the protections promised in that doctrine. Expulsion of the Jews is legitimate—indeed failure to expel would constitute dereliction of duty on the part of proper Christian rulers.

In analyzing expulsions, we have regularly distinguished between justification and motivation. In the north, we have identified motivations for banishing Jews that were quite different from the formal justifications advanced. Students of the Iberian expulsions have done likewise. They have begun by questioning the extent of backsliding among the New Christians and have disputed even more stridently the role of Spanish Jews in subverting the Christian faith of the New Christians. At the same time, these students of the Spanish expulsion have not been attracted to the motivations for banishment we have discerned in northern Europe. Late medieval Spain was too far along in its governmental maturation to use the Jews as vehicle for augmentation of governmental profit and power.

Careful analysis of late-medieval expulsions—including expulsions of Jews—has been provided by Nicholas Terpstra. Terpstra notes the earlier introduction of expulsion into western Christendom as a tool of governance. He urges, however, that by the late fifteenth century the motivations for banishments had evolved. With the erosion of religious homogeneity in western Christendom, which would soon overtly erupt into the Reformation, rulers became in Terpstra's view concerned for the purity of their realms.

> As power began to flow towards monarchs and central government, French King Henry IV's goal of "one faith, one law, one King" took hold across the continent. Those who fell outside this unity were not just alien, but also impure and possibly contagious. Any society that took its responsibilities to God seriously might have to purge itself in order to purify the population and so maintain its own health. The sharp language of purification and purgation came out of medicine, but was adopted by religious reform movements. The drive to purge and purify reshaped Europe and the globe throughout the early modern period.[26]

To be sure, viewing Jews as aliens threatening to the Christian majority simply by virtue of their otherness ran counter to the Augustinian doctrine that promised Jews a safe and secure existence within Christian societies. Thus, the Spanish monarchs legitimized the expulsion of 1492 by pointing in traditional fashion to specific Jewish harm allegedly inflicted on Spanish Christians and Christianity. In Terpstra's view, however, the motivation for this expulsion lay with the new objective of a more cohesive Christian society, with alien elements removed. For Terpstra, the expulsion of Jews in 1492 was a harbinger of the new-style expulsions that would occur in early-modern Europe.

The impact of the expulsion of 1492 upon those expelled was devastating. In this instance, we have growing evidence of this personal suffering and pain.[27] On the broader level, the expulsion of 1492 had more grievous implications for southern European Jewry than the earlier expulsions had for northern European Jewry. Whereas the growing numbers and power of the latter were not adversely affected by the expulsions from northwestern and north-central Europe, the older Jewry of Iberia as a whole was adversely affected. Places of refuge within the southern sectors of western Christendom were minimal, and the Spanish Jews were in effect forced out of western Christendom and into areas of the globe whose period of great power was passing. Although the Spanish Jews were welcomed by the Ottoman authorities and flourished with their support for a time, the long-term fate of this area was disadvantageous. The descendants of the southern European Jews expelled in 1492 slowly fell behind the descendants of the northern European Jews in numbers, economic strength, and cultural creativity.

The Mosaic warning of interminable and painful banishments from place to place across the globe was by no means realized in the trajectory of post-biblical Jewish history. For very long stretches of that history, expulsions were not at all a feature of Jewish life. In realistic terms, the onset of expulsions reflects major changes in the structure and governance of majority Christian society, now with a growing Jewish minority. Jewish characteristics, likewise shaped by the broad realities of the non-Jewish ambience, played only a secondary role. The areas of northern Europe, newly settled by Jews from late in the first millennium, led the way in introducing governmental banishments into Jewish life. These expulsions were legitimized by appeal to the damage inflicted by Jewish usury and the failure of governmental efforts to wipe out this scourge. In fact, the real motivation lay elsewhere—in amassing substantial funds for the governmental treasuries, in winning ecclesiastical approbation, and in eliciting widespread popular commendation. Expulsion of Jews proved a very useful tool in the augmentation of royal power in northern Europe. Those Jews expelled of course suffered grievously. However, these banishments did not appreciably detract from the growing size and strength of this still young Jewry.

In the south, where Jewish life was well rooted, the innovation of governmental banishment was surely smoothed by the precedents that had taken place in the north. To be sure, the legitimation of expulsion took a different form—the claim that Jews had impeded the full Christianization of the formerly Jewish New Christians. Once again, the motivation lay elsewhere—in southern Europe in the desire for a more homogeneous Christian populace as Christian uniformity was in fact slipping away. Once again, the personal pain of those Jews expelled was intense. Additionally, southern European Jewry was more broadly affected over the succeeding centuries as a result of its uprooting from the European soil that had so long nourished it.

Southern European Jews wrestled with the tragedy that had afflicted their community in new ways, foreshadowing some of the modern approaches to human history that were beginning to surface. The combination of this wrestling with the biblical predictions we have highlighted resulted in the sense that expulsions had been a feature of Jewish existence over the ages. This popular sense, however, was in fact erroneous. From the Assyrian and Babylonian expulsions of the eighth and sixth pre-Christian centuries to the onset of the new and different expulsions from northern Europe first observable at the end of the twelfth century, almost two millennia had elapsed, and the world—both the non-Jewish majority and the Jewish minority—had evolved radically. The medieval European expulsions constituted a new phenomenon altogether.[28]

FIVE

Flight from Governmental Repression or Popular Violence

Beginning in the twelfth century, edicts of expulsion set in motion for the first time since early antiquity forced Jewish population movement. There have arguably been two further sources of pre-modern involuntary Jewish migration—repressive governmental edicts that made Jewish life spiritually or materially impossible and popular violence so threatening as to necessitate flight. Neither of these pressures is clear-cut in its impact, as were the edicts of expulsion from European states that began in the late twelfth century. The impact of both these pressures on Jewish population movement is often uncertain and must be carefully assessed.

Both Christianity and Islam disputed the Jewish claims to religious truth; at the same time, the formal doctrines of both faiths proclaimed unequivocally the right of Jews to remain Jews and to live safely and securely as such. Both Christianity and Islam prohibited the use of force in bringing Jews into their religious folds and—even further—prohibited any violence against Jews based on the simple fact that they were Jews. In both Christian and Muslim societies, Jews were to live safely and securely as Jews. This status was not unique to Jews. In Christian societies, Muslims were to enjoy the same fundamental rights, and in Muslim societies Christians likewise enjoyed the right to safe and secure existence. This safety and security did not at all imply equality. Jews and Muslims in Christian settings were second-class members of society, and the same is true for Jews and Christians in Muslim settings.

The traditional perspectives on Jewish history include the conviction that Jews living in either Christian or Muslim pre-modern settings regularly suffered discrimination and persecution and on occasion even had their right to live as Jews abrogated. There seem to be documented instances of abrogation of basic Jewish religious rights, expressed as governmental demands that Jews convert to the ruling faith. In fact, however, the evidence for such abrogation of the Jewish right to safe and secure existence in premodern Christian or Muslim societies is minuscule, and even this minuscule evidence is deemed questionable by contemporary researchers.

There are three well-known instances of governmental demands that Jews convert to the ruling faith—one in seventh-century Christian Spain; a second in early eleventh-century Christian northern France; and the third in twelfth-century Muslim Spain. The first evidence of a governmentally enacted decree that would seem to have made Jewish life untenable comes from seventh-century Visigothic Spain. Sources mention royal decrees ordering conversion of Jews or banishment, but data about the execution of these decrees are nonexistent. Moreover, there is no context that explains these decrees. Given the basic Church doctrine that assured Jews the right to live undisturbed as Jews, this departure in policy is difficult to understand. In any case, these governmental edicts do not constitute direct banishment of Jews, but rather the demand for change of religious identity that would result in nullifying Jewishness or—failing that—leaving Spain. Close recent analysis of these decrees has concluded that they were policy statements only and were not in fact carried out in any significant measure and thus did not result in involuntary Jewish migration.[1]

A second instance of abrogation of fundamental Jewish rights comes from eleventh-century northern France. A curious Hebrew narrative tells a striking tale of a royal decree offering Jews the stark choice between conversion or death (rather than banishment). The language of the narrative is heavily folkloric, absorbing imagery and phrases from major biblical sources. Following is the presentation of the royal demand:

> My desire is for one unified people. You will be powerful and respected. Turn to our teaching because it is more correct than yours. If you refuse, I shall put you to death by the sword. Now take counsel and answer on this matter.[2]

According to the narrative, the Jews did as ordered. They took counsel and opted for death, rather than baptism. The narrative claims that many Jews were killed and many others—especially women—took their own lives.

According to the narrative, one prominent Jewish leader from the town of Rouen in Normandy, where the same policy was ostensibly instituted, challenged the edict, arguing that only the pope could enact such a decree. The duke of Normandy rejected the Jew's claim and prepared to kill him. At that point, a miracle took place, as the palm of the duke's hand was pierced by the tassel on his sword. The duke saw this as a divine sign and allowed the Jew and his retinue to make their way to Rome, where meetings with the pope were successful. A papal bull was elicited, which proclaimed the formal Church doctrine of the Jewish right to safe and secure existence in Christian society, thereby nullifying the purported order that Jews convert. The entire tone of this Hebrew narrative is so folkloric as to warrant a high level of doubt.[3] In any case, even the narrative itself makes no suggestion of involuntary Jewish migration, since the Jews affected by the decree are portrayed as choosing death over flight.

The third case of governmental action that made Jewish life impossible comes from twelfth-century Muslim Spain. According to Abraham ibn Daud, the Almohade rulers of North Africa and parts of Muslim Spain instituted a policy of forced conversion, unique in the annals of medieval Islam. This purported policy of forced conversion resulted, according to ibn Daud, in the flight of many Jews from the affected areas, with the relocation focused on nearby Christian Spain and southern France. Ibn Daud's own family was seemingly part of this forced migration.[4]

Many modern scholars have come to question the reality of this decree, especially as they have delved into the Islamic sources for the incident. While it is clear that there were occasional forced conversions under the Almohades, some current scholars project these conversions as stemming from violent circumstances and Jewish fear of physical harm, rather than a governmental edict. Even when there were forcible conversions, many of the Jewish converts remained in place and loyal to their Jewish roots, a reality recognized by both Muslims and fellow Jews. The fullest collection of materials relative to this incident and the most careful assessment of the reliability of these sources, undertaken by David Corcos, conclude that there was no formal Almohade decree demanding conversion or death. Corcos acknowledges the reality of forced conversions, but attributes them to unsettled circumstances and fear.[5]

Most Jews forcibly converted seem to have been willing to make a formal and essentially meaningless statement of adherence to Islam and await what they fully anticipated as the inevitable return to more stable circumstances and normalcy. This is the advice offered by the great Maimonides, and there has been a recurring suggestion that his family might well have followed this path. Even accepting the reality of a formal Almohade decree and Jewish migration as a result, this incident and its population displacement would have constituted only the tiniest percentage of Jewish migration over the two millennia under consideration. Overall, it seems safe to conclude that governmental edicts that made Jewish life spiritually impossible, for example by demanding conversion to the ruling faith, generated little or no forced migration of pre-modern Jews.

Another form of repressive governmental legislation involved radical limitation of Jewish economic activity. In the older areas of Jewish settlement, Jewish economic activity was highly diversified, so there was no possibility of such legislation. However, in the newer areas of Jewish settlement in northern Europe there was—as we have seen—considerable popular resistance to the new Jewish settlers and resultant limitation of Jewish economic opportunities. What emerged out of the curious combination of restricted Jewish opportunities and the Church assault on Christian usury was a useful but problematic Jewish concentration in the money trade. This spurred considerable Church concern and even greater popular resentment. This combination resulted in occasional governmental efforts to limit Jewish moneylending and even on occasion to outlaw Jewish moneylending altogether. Were such efforts successful, Jews might well have faced the necessity of emigrating.

Moves to limit and occasionally to prohibit Jewish moneylending emerged in both thirteenth-century England and thirteenth-century France. In France, as we have seen, the genuinely pious King Louis ordered that Jews cease their moneylending or leave his realm. Here we see the combination of limitation of Jewish economic activity and forced displacement. However, there is no serious evidence of Jewish emigration from royal France and likewise no evidence of Jews abandoning their lending. With the death of Saint Louis, the stance of the French monarchy reverted to the more utilitarian approach of Philip Augustus, and evidence of Jewish lending abounds. This suggests that carrying out the prohibition of Jewish moneylending could well have proven virtually impossible.

Indeed, in his edict of 1290 expelling the Jews from England, King Edward I argued plaintively that he had made every effort to remove baneful Jewish lending from his realm, but that the Jews with their cunningness circumvented every such effort. In the face of Jewish circumvention of the effort to eliminate Jewish usury, King Edward suggested that he had no alternative other than to expel the Jews. This is curious confirmation of the sense that prohibiting Jewish lending would have been very difficult to enforce and limitations on Jewish lending or even its prohibition would have been unlikely to result in forced Jewish dislocation. The evidence suggests that significant governmental limitation of either Jewish spiritual or material rights had little impact on Jewish displacement.

Popular anti-Jewish violence is far better documented than repressive governmental edicts as a feature of pre-modern Jewish history, allowing for a greater possibility that such violence played a role in involuntary Jewish population movement. As modern conflict has increasingly moved beyond formal armies and well-defined battlefields, civilian populations have been increasingly imperiled. At this early point in the twenty-first century, the media bring to public attention on a daily basis the images of war- and violence-torn areas, with terrified civilians fleeing out of fear. These images are heart-rending, and those seeking refugee status in safe settings regularly argue that they must be accepted, since return to their original home environment would result in nothing other than death.

In earlier times when warfare was generally less threatening to civilian populations, certain minority groups could and did become special targets of popular animosity and violence. Perceived as harmful in one way or another, these groups were sometimes attacked and as a result fled out of fear, which is clearly a form of involuntary population movement. As a marginal minority within pre-modern majority Muslim and Christian societies, Jews were on occasion the objects of such violence. Indeed, Jews have often been projected as a marginal minority uniquely exposed to such popular violence, giving rise to the sense of involuntary Jewish population movement set in motion by both formal banishment and the threat of violence. Jews are often perceived as especially susceptible to dangerous levels of popular violence, which resulted in regular forced migration out of fear.

We have already seen that formal expulsion of Jews was by no means a recurrent feature of pre-modern Jewish life. While not denying the reality of such banishments, we have noted that they occurred far less frequently than predicted by Moses or than assumed by later Jewish and non-Jewish observers. Violence as the source of extensive involuntary Jewish population movement is yet more problematic. Again, the intention is not to deny the reality of instances of Jewish flight from violence or the threat of violence. Rather, the question involves once again the ubiquity of forced Jewish population movement as a result of the reality or fear of violence.

Fear of violence surely sparked involuntary Jewish relocation on occasion. Identifying specific instances of such flight is not easy, however, and in many instances cannot be achieved. There are two major problems in identifying with certainty fear of violence as the key factor in Jewish population movement. The first is simply the drama attending violence and the threat of violence. Violence is generally dramatic, much more dramatic than governmental expulsion. This raises the possibility or indeed the likelihood of exaggeration of effect. Moving accounts of a limited number of dramatic deaths can often result in loss of proportion. An attack with scores of Jewish victims dramatically portrayed takes on greater significance than less dramatic events involving thousands or tens of thousands of Jewish victims. Guarding against overemphasis resulting from the drama inherent in violence is critically important in analysis of involuntary Jewish relocation out of fear.

The second problem is that assertions of flight out of fear require reconstruction of psychological states. Present-day testimonies of refugees fleeing violence, captured richly and at the moment, are beyond reasonable doubt. Reconstructing the perceptions and feelings of earlier generations ranges between difficult and impossible. To what extent were earlier sufferers aware of the threat of violence? To what extent did they have confidence in the authorities of state and church to protect them from impending danger? To what extent did they perceive alternative locales as providing requisite security? These questions are generally difficult to answer. They are in fact increasingly difficult to answer the further back in time one proceeds, due to the diminishing sources for reconstructing early realities.

A few brief general observations on pre-modern anti-Jewish violence are in order. The first involves its frequency. As noted early on, the biblical view of the Jewish future projected harsh divine punishment for Jewish failure to observe the divine-human covenant. Included in this harsh punishment would be regular involuntary population movement, upon which we are focused; even more common in this harsh punishment would be incessant anti-Jewish violence. Traditional biblically grounded Jewish and Christian views of the arc of Jewish history projected the reality of regular forced migration and constant anti-Jewish violence. Modern views of Jewish history that broke with the theistic perspective on historical causation maintained nonetheless the same sense of Jewish suffering, albeit explaining this suffering as the result of Jewish shortcomings or the deleterious results of Jewish and non-Jewish embrace of the biblical perspectives.

As noted, these perspectives on the Jewish past, dubbed by Salo Baron as early as 1928 as "lachrymose," were challenged and battled by Baron throughout his lengthy career and by his students and his students' students. The present study of Jewish population movement is rooted in the Baron assault on lachrymosity. The Baron assault targeted the notion of incessant anti-Jewish violence. Baron, in his opening salvo in 1928, argued that during the sixteenth through eighteenth centuries—the period viewed by most observers as the worst in terms of anti-Jewish violence—Jewish population in Christian Europe grew at a remarkable rate, which very much contradicts the sense of widespread and damaging anti-Jewish violence. More recent studies have tended to question the level of anti-Jewish violence at major junctures in the medieval and early modern periods. Diminution of the sense of incessant anti-Jewish violence in and of itself reduces the likelihood of massive involuntary migration set in motion by such violence.

A second preliminary observation involves the nature of anti-Jewish violence. Much such violence was local and unpremeditated—violence that flared up suddenly, often as a result of a local incident, and then subsided equally quickly. Such unanticipated violence did not allow for the laying of carefully planned responses, especially plans for relocation. Local and unpremeditated anti-Jewish violence was unlikely to stimulate Jewish migration. In attempting to analyze involuntary migration in order to escape violence it is necessary to focus on instances of wide-ranging violence that stretched over a substantial time period and a broad spatial expanse. Only plentiful time and space would have set the circumstances for the careful consideration required for successful Jewish relocation.

The earliest of the broad instances of anti-Jewish violence often adduced is related to the innovative Church policy of crusading, initiated toward the close of the eleventh century. Up to that time, Church policy had legitimized only defensive resorts to arms by Christian warriors. As western Christendom began its vitalization at the turn of the millennium, it quickly exhibited incipient militancy in its efforts to reconquer areas of the Iberian peninsula that had earlier been under the domination of Christian rule. In 1095, Pope Urban II announced a new direction for this militancy, as he for the first time legitimized offensive military violence in the name of Christian ideals—the conquest of the sacred sites of the Holy Land—and valorized the Christian warriors who committed themselves to this effort.

The papal call to the new venture made no mention of Jews, and there is a consensus that the pope and his colleagues envisioned no implications of this campaign for Jews. Indeed, the well-organized crusading armies drew no anti-Jewish conclusions from their mission. Across areas of northern Europe, however, some of the poorly organized crusading militias did extract an anti-Jewish message from their crusading mission. Their unwarranted reasoning suggested that they were traveling enormous distances to destroy Muslim enemies, while Jewish enemies, projected as far worse than the Muslims because of their role in the crucifixion of Jesus, lived peacefully in their home territories. This faulty reasoning, which could draw no support from accepted Church doctrine, combined with the anti-Jewish immigrant sentiment we have already noted to foster outbreaks of anti-Jewish violence in a few urban centers across northern Europe. These outbreaks have often been interpreted as the onset of the decline of early northern European Jewry, which they clearly were not.[6]

These attacks have likewise been projected as the beginning of the persecutions of Europe's Jews that culminated in the Holocaust. This view as well is vastly inflated. Again, the dramatic portrayal of the killing of a few thousand Jews should not be conflated with the subsequent destruction of millions of Jewish lives. Resisting the impact of the dramatic has already been established as a critical element in responsible analysis of anti-Jewish violence over the ages. The anti-Jewish assaults associated with the First Crusade were limited, and the Church, taken by surprise by the outbreak of this unanticipated violence in 1096, initiated strong and effective measures to ensure that anti-Jewish violence not be repeated during subsequent crusades. Thus, the crusades, both the first and those that followed, do not represent a major disaster in European Jewish history.[7]

Nonetheless, the First Crusade provides a useful vehicle for examining the place of fear in forcing Jewish migration. The First Crusade, limited impact notwithstanding, constituted a broad effort that involved a vast span of territory over a protracted period of time; it provided potential Jewish victims with considerable forewarning of impending dangers; the rich records, especially Jewish but non-Jewish as well, composed in the wake of the assaults enable us to examine in some detail the steps that Jews took in the face of the dangers threatening them, of which they were keenly aware.

The crusading campaign that began during the late eleventh century has left rich narrative records on the crusading anti-Jewish violence of 1096 and the Jewish responses. According to the oldest of these narratives, the Jews of the Rhineland, who proved to be the major sufferers of crusade-related violence, were forewarned of the dangers associated with the new enterprise. It is reported that the Jews of France, which is the area in which the First Crusade was initially organized, were aware of the potential for anti-Jewish violence and warned their Rhineland brethren of the threat. Interestingly, the advice given did not include the suggestion of relocation, perhaps because the crusade and the threat it might represent were anticipated to be pan-European. The only concrete advice offered was to seek divine aid in the face of the threat.[8]

The initial appearance of the crusading forces in the Rhineland sparked a more terrestrial response on the part of the Rhineland Jews—providing material assistance to the crusading forces. These initial responses include no hint of flight.[9] This assistance seems to have been helpful, at least to an extent, with some of the disorganized crusading bands. Eventually, however, anti-Jewish violence broke out in Speyer, with eleven Jews killed by a combined force of popular crusaders and townsmen. The Jews thus endangered and attacked were, however, assiduously protected by the local bishop. The ploys utilized by the bishop included gathering the endangered Jews into his fortified palace and eventually moving them out of town into fortifications under his control.[10] This was by no means, however, forcible migration; this movement was clearly intended to be temporary only. In fact, before long the threat of violence subsided, and the endangered Jews returned to their homes in Speyer.

Knowledge of events in Speyer moved the Jews of Worms to seek safety, but not by fleeing Worms. Rather, they sought out the protection of either sympathetic burghers or the authorities. Ultimately, neither element in Worms was able to provide the requisite assistance, and the Jews of Worms became the first major victims of popular crusading violence. Much the same pattern is discernible in Mainz, where the largest number of Jews succumbed to the popular crusading violence. Again there is no suggestion of flight as a potential response to the impending danger.[11]

A slightly later source provides fuller information on the fate of the Jewish community of Cologne. There too the local authorities made strenuous efforts to protect their Jews. Once again, the major technique was to move Jews temporarily out of the town and into rural fortifications, on the theory that the crusading bands moving eastward would make their way through urban centers that might provide resources to the ill-provisioned bands. Rural fortifications, it was assumed, would be of little or no value or interest to these bands. This tactic proved relatively successful for the Jews of Cologne. Once again, when the crusading bands were gone and stability restored, the Jews of Cologne returned to their town.[12]

The onset of the crusading movement, with all the uncertainties and ambiguities attendant upon new movements, spawned as a by-product marginal bands that translated the call to battle against the forces of Islam in the Holy Land into rationalization for violence against the newly settling Jews of northern Europe. Jews across northern Europe became aware of the threat of violence, which in a few cases materialized. These Jews took protective steps, which focused on pleading for divine aid and soliciting the assistance of the authorities and their sympathetic neighbors. Jews were sometimes relocated by the authorities in an effort to protect their Jewish clients. These relocations were clearly intended to be temporary only and were fairly quickly undone. Although there is clear evidence of Jewish perceptions of danger, there is no indication of permanent population movement as a response to the perceived threat.

The same pattern is discernible upon the arousal of later wide-ranging dangers to Jewish life. When the Black Death broke out in 1348, there were clear signs of the potential for diversion of societal fear and animosity against the Jews of the plague-stricken areas. Once again, Jews were not oblivious to the threat of violence, and the violence in fact materialized. Nonetheless, there is no evidence of significant Jewish relocation. Here too the Jews sensed that the plague and the anti-Jewish reactions to it were pan-European, and thus safety through relocation could hardly be perceived as a solution to Jewish insecurity. When the turbulence of 1348–1349 was over, the Jewish population of Latin Christendom was surely reduced, as a result of the plague itself and of the plague-related anti-Jewish violence. There is, however, no evidence of Jews relocating in significant numbers out of fear of impending violence.

Much the same seems to be true of the wide-ranging violence that afflicted Iberian Jewry in 1391. These attacks seem to reflect serious socio-economic grievances combined with perceived weakness on the part of the Iberian governing authorities. Once again, the persecution encompassed broad areas and a lengthy period of time. Jewish losses were very heavy. In addition to the slaughter of numerous Jews, many others elected to save themselves from death through baptism. Many of these Jews were aware of the Church's prohibition of forcible conversion and believed that with the return of normalcy their conversions would be annulled. This conviction proved erroneous and was one among many factors in the emergence of the problem of backsliding Jews adduced as the rationale for the expulsion of 1492. In any case, there is once again no evidence of significant numbers of Jews emigrating, despite considerable knowledge of the dangers threatening them.[13]

A significant early modern persecution of Jews took place in the Ukraine, as an element in a powerful nationalist uprising against Polish domination during the middle of the seventeenth century. This uprising, led by a charismatic figure named Bogdan Khmelnitsky, resulted in virulent attacks on Ukrainian Jewish communities, accurately perceived as accomplices of the hated Polish overlords. The losses were considerable and were deeply mourned by contemporary eastern European Jews and their descendants.

The 1648–1649 attacks have recently been subjected to careful analysis by Shaul Stampfer, who set out to provide a reasonable estimate of the losses.[14] Previous estimates have varied very widely, from well over 100,000 to something on the order of tens of thousands. Stampfer introduces a variety of considerations in deciding in favor of the lower estimates, coming to an eventual conclusion that the Jewish losses were in the range of 18,000 to 20,000, which is certainly a terrible toll, but a far cry from the suggestions of more than 100,000.

One of the major arguments advanced by Stampfer to buttress his lower estimate is that Jews in threatened areas of the Ukraine were quickly aware of impending assaults and fled to temporary havens of safety, thereby reducing dramatically the mortality rate. To reinforce this suggestion, Stampfer notes the impressive Jewish population figures for the mid-eighteenth-century Ukraine derived from the census of 1764. In this census, the Jewish population of the Ukraine emerges as somewhere between 130,000 and 165,000. Extrapolating backward from 1764, Stampfer proposes a mid-seventeenth-century Jewish population of about 45,000, which is a rather large estimate for the number of Jews in the post-1648 Ukraine.

For Stampfer, the growth of Ukrainian Jewry by 1764 means that there clearly remained a significant Ukrainian Jewish population in the wake of the 1648 violence. In Stampfer's view, many Ukrainian Jews survived the violence by fleeing temporarily and, upon the cessation of violence, made their way back into the areas of their earlier habitation, resettled, and contributed to the remarkable post-1648 surge of the Jewish population in the Ukraine.

For our purposes, these numbers suggest something else. The violence of 1648–1649, as horrific as it was, by no means sparked a permanent exodus of Jews out of the Ukraine. Once again, a severe crisis does not seem to have provoked significant Jewish demographic displacement.

In the preceding chapter, we noted the reality of formal banishments of Jews from various areas of western Christendom. While acknowledging fully the reality of these expulsions and the disruptions in Jewish life they entailed, we noted that they were limited in time and space. For most of pre-modern Jewish history, Jews were untroubled by formal expulsions. In the present chapter, skepticism concerning involuntary Jewish population movement as a result of repressive governmental enactments or the threat of violence is far greater. We have come to question altogether hostile governmental edicts as factors in forcible Jewish migration. The situation with respect to flight from popular violence is a bit more complex. While it is clear that the twenty-first century shows unquestionable instances of migration forced by the threat of violence, our survey of pre-modern persecutions that stretched over sufficient time and space to allow Jewish victims to absorb fully the dangers they faced and to lay the extensive plans involved in long-term relocation did not reveal significant instances of forced Jewish population movement. While some forced Jewish movement of this kind is conceivable, it seems unlikely that such dislocation played any role of significance in overall pre-modern Jewish population patterns.

The emergence of large numbers of pre-modern Jewish refugees as a result of governmental banishments, deeply harmful governmental limitation of Jewish spiritual or material existence, or the threat of uncontrollable violence has not been established. Thus, overall the number of pre-modern Jewish refugees seems to have been quite limited. The reality of considerable Jewish population movement and new constellations of Jewish settlement is beyond doubt. The demographic distribution of Jews from early antiquity to the end of the eighteenth century shows recurrent and radical change. If these radical changes cannot be the result of enormous numbers of Jewish refugees on the move, then the alternative is enormous numbers of Jewish migrants on the move. We must now examine closely this alternative.

PART THREE

Jews as Migrants

SIX

Late Antiquity

Governmental expulsions of Jews became innovative realities late in pre-modern Jewish history, and violence so threatening to Jews as to necessitate flight may have on rare occasions taken place.[1] The drama of these events has conferred upon them extensive attention and significant impact on perceptions of pre-modern Jewish population movement. At the same time, traditional Jewish and Christian thinking assumed that Jewish exile inevitably involved persecution, suffering, and forced dislocation. The combination of inherent drama and fulfillment of biblical prediction thrust compulsory Jewish demographic displacement to the center of Jewish and Christian consciousness, creating the erroneous impression that Jewish population movement over the ages was consistently forced, harmful, and painful.

Forced displacement of Jews should not, however, obscure an alternative reality, clearly and regularly documented in past Jewish experience. Jews also relocated voluntarily, enticed by appealing opportunities and often encouraged by ruling authorities eager to attract them as new and useful settlers. These relocations were arduous but positive experiences, undertaken in search of better circumstances and often resulting in radically improved conditions. Since such voluntary migrations were not at all predicted in Scripture and lacked eye-catching drama, they have tended to be overlooked. The third section of this book examines closely Jewish population movement from late antiquity through the end of the eighteenth century, with a focus on often-neglected voluntary Jewish relocation; it offers a balanced assessment of the proportional relationship between compulsory displacement of Jews and voluntary relocation.

In order to enable the desired balanced assessment, we must begin by creating meaningful periodization of the centuries between late antiquity and the end of the eighteenth century. The periods we shall identify and analyze must be coherent in terms of the political, economic, and demographic conditions set by the majority societies within which Jews found themselves and the resultant coherence of Jewish circumstances. For our purposes, we shall treat pre-modern Jewish history in five segments. The usefulness of these five periods of Jewish experience flows from the coherence of the majority environment within which Jews found themselves, the related patterns of Jewish life, and thus the relative uniformity of the Jewish population movement.[2]

For these five periods, there are of course no demographic statistics of the kind to which we have become accustomed over recent decades. What we must do, in the absence of such statistics on population movement, is identify major changes in Jewish settlement patterns and attempt to account for these changes. In the process, we shall adduce evidence of governmental expulsions or wide-ranging violence that would explain why large numbers of Jews relocated and thus created new centers of Jewish life or reinforced older centers. To be sure, the absence of formal banishments or intense violence will in and of itself point to the likelihood of voluntary Jewish migration. In addition, we will attempt to identify positive aspects of the settings in which new Jewish settlements appear. Such positive characteristics will strengthen the case for voluntary Jewish migration.

The first of our five periods involves the centuries of late antiquity. During this lengthy time period, Jewish settlement continued to include a Palestinian Jewish community, flanked to its east by the well-established Jewish community in Mesopotamia and to its west by the growing Jewish community of the Mediterranean Basin. This configuration of world Jewish population was essentially the same as had been in evidence ever since the early history of biblical Israel. During the early centuries of late antiquity, Jews lived under the rule of the polytheistic Greek and Roman empires in Palestine and the Mediterranean Basin and under parallel polytheistic rule in Mesopotamia. In both settings, Jews had long been settled, had enjoyed recognition of their special monotheistic religious needs, and had gained important rights in acknowledgment of these special needs. During this entire period, Jews were a well-established element in the population in both areas, which translated into diversity of economic pursuits and relatively comfortable relations with the non-Jewish majority.

During the fourth century, a major change in governance of the Roman Empire took place, as the Christian Church—long feared and persecuted by the Roman authorities—ascended to power. The transition to living under monotheistic rule was fated to have long-term implications for Jewish life, but the process of change was slow at its outset. Consolidation of the Church's authority was protracted, and during the arduous course of this consolidation the Jews were hardly a high priority on the Church's agenda. Jews were accorded special recognition by the Christian authorities in a number of positive ways, although restrictions on Jewish life were slowly introduced.

The second period, which stretches from the seventh through the twelfth century, opens with the appearance of yet a third monotheistic religious faith—Islam—and its remarkably rapid spread. Beginning its history on the Arabian peninsula, Islam quickly established itself in this somewhat marginal area and galvanized a remarkable series of conquests in all directions—northeastward, northwestward, and due westward. By the 730s, only a century after the beginning of these conquests, Muslim armies had taken over in its entirety the venerable Mesopotamian empire, had stripped away major segments of the Byzantine Empire including Palestine, and had conquered from western Christendom all of North Africa, almost all of the Iberian peninsula, and portions of the Italian peninsula. The vast Islamic empire stretched from India in the east to the Atlantic Ocean in the west and incorporated within its borders the overwhelming majority—perhaps as much as eighty to ninety percent—of the world's Jews. Although this enormous empire eventually devolved into a series of separate political units, the entire area remained a coherent socioeconomic and cultural entity, with Arabic as its dominant language and with remarkable freedom of trade and movement throughout its borders.

The third period to be treated reflects the rise of western Christendom from its weak and backward position in the year 1000 to its position of growing power over the course of the ensuing centuries. This process of change involved nothing like the drama of military conquest that created Muslim hegemony during the first half of the Middle Ages. The processes that transformed western Christendom from powerlessness to power began in northern Europe, long a backward hinterland to the more fully developed south. Slowly northern forests were cut down, arable lands increased, population grew, trade and commerce strengthened, cities expanded, governance became more effective, and the Roman Church became better organized and increasingly dominant. Quickly, this northern European society began to spread its tentacles southward, reclaiming territories taken centuries earlier by the Muslims and even daring to penetrate into the Islamic heartland in an audacious albeit short-lived effort to reconquer the sacred sites of Christianity in the Holy Land.

The implications of these changes in western Christendom for Jewish life were enormous. The demography of the Jewish people began to change subtly but significantly. For the first time, Jews in numbers broke out of the borders within which they had lived from time immemorial—the borders defined in the east by Mesopotamia and in the west by the Mediterranean Basin. In the northern and most rapidly progressing sectors of Christian Europe of the second half of the Middle Ages, Jews were newcomers and suffered the liabilities normally the lot of newcomers. In these northern territories, Jewish economic activities were limited rather than diversified, and Jewish relations with non-Jewish neighbors involved a tension not notable in the older areas of Jewish settlement. Despite these problems, the Jews of medieval Christian Europe began slowly to dominate the Jewish world in the same way that the broader population and culture of Christian Europe was beginning to dominate the West in its entirety.

The fourth period opened toward the end of the thirteenth century. By this time, the maturation of Christian Europe had begun to alter the balance of power in the Western world altogether and had begun to shift the shape of Jewish life in the West as well. The Jews of Christian Europe, both the older Jewish communities of southern Europe and the newer and more rapidly growing Jewish communities of the north, were well on their way to dominating global Jewish life demographically, economically, and even spiritually and intellectually.

At the same time, by the end of the thirteenth century the maturing and increasingly well-organized states of northwestern Europe began to expel their Jews, initiating a new set of Jewish movements, most of which were forced upon the Jews. Significantly, the new Jewish settlers in northwestern Europe did not react to their banishment by abandoning western Christendom. Rather, they proceeded eastward into the less fully developed sectors of northern Europe, once again supported by rulers desirous of enhancing the economic development of their realms. The governmental authorities of north-central and northeastern Europe were now in the position of their earlier northwestern European confreres, that is to say desirous of the economic skills that Jews might provide. As a result, the pattern of governmental invitation and protection, Jewish settlement, and popular resentment that was seen earlier in the northwest was now repeated in the northeast, with an increasingly large Jewish community developing there by the year 1500 and continuing to grow steadily thereafter.

By the sixteenth century, major changes and the onset of a new period in European and Jewish history were palpable. These changes began at the outset of the sixteenth century with the Protestant Reformation and its shattering of the religious unity of Latin Christendom. The chaos that ensued slowly eventuated in grudging and de facto acceptance of a more pluralistic society, which had important implications for the Jewish outsiders in European society. Eventually, the de facto acceptance of religious pluralism moved toward de jure acceptance of religious pluralism, which was yet more significant for the Jews. Demographically, these changes translated from the movement eastward in Europe from 1300 to 1600 into Jewish movement back westward, which culminated eventually in the massive migration of Jews to the Americas, especially the United States, which lies beyond the purview of this study.

Looking back over the Jewish demographic changes that took place from late antiquity to the end of the eighteenth century, we find them staggering in their magnitude. Major Jewish populations developed in areas that were totally unknown to Jews in late antiquity—northern Europe and eventually the New World, while the venerable Jewish center in the Land of Israel was diminished and recast. Awareness of the magnitude of these Jewish demographic changes directs our attention to the patterns of demographic movement observable during this lengthy period, to the instances of compulsory population movement, to the reality of volitional Jewish relocation, and to the proportional relationship between these two styles of Jewish population movement.

Where precisely were Jews located during late antiquity? The center of Jewish life demographically, politically, and religiously had become once again the Land of Israel. Jews had been expelled from their homeland in the year 586 b.c.e. by the Babylonians and exiled into Mesopotamia. Not long thereafter, the Persians displaced the Babylonians as rulers of the large Mesopotamian empire, reversed the repressive Babylonian policies, and permitted Jews to return to their homeland. No clear-cut numbers are available, but it seems that at the outset only a small minority of the exiled Jews took advantage of the opportunity for return.[3]

The evidence furnished by the books of Ezra and Nehemiah for the mid-fifth pre-Christian century shows a relatively small and struggling Jewish community in the Land of Israel, supported in many ways by what seems to have been a larger and stronger community of Jewish exiles in Mesopotamia. These diaspora Jews had found effective ways of maintaining cohesion and identity in their exilic setting. Nehemiah and Ezra brought to the struggling Jewish community in the Land of Israel the powerful support of the Persian authorities. In the case of Nehemiah, this reflects ascent to a position of importance in the Persian court, in tandem with ongoing concern for the Jerusalem community and its sacred space. Nehemiah and Ezra—especially the latter—also introduced a set of religious reforms that suggest a thriving and Jewishly engaged Mesopotamian Jewry.

Over the ensuing centuries, the once struggling Jewish community in the Land of Israel solidified demographically and in every other way. Unfortunately, this process cannot be traced in any detail. However, as we begin to gain documentation during the second pre-Christian century, the picture that emerges is quite different from that portrayed for the fifth century in the books of Ezra and Nehemiah. The Jewish community of the Land of Israel appears at this point larger, better organized, and more vigorous than in the early centuries of the return. Numbers have expanded; community structure and effective leadership are prominent; the temple has assumed a role of centrality and importance. There is even evidence of significant and ultimately creative internal dissidence provided by the events that led to the Maccabean uprising. All this bespeaks constructive change that cannot be charted in any detail.[4]

Given the strategic location of the Land of Israel at the eastern end of the Roman Empire, this area, in which the Jewish population dominated, assumed considerable political importance to the imperial authorities. This meant that the Romans, who assumed control of Palestine and its Jewry during the first pre-Christian century, had to find effective ways to relate to the Jews of Palestine, thus assuring the ruling elite in Palestinian Jewry political importance within the Roman Empire. The Jewish community in Palestine assumed a position of political as well as demographic centrality, at least within the Roman Empire. Religiously, the Jerusalem Temple served as a central shrine for worldwide Jewry, with diaspora Jews visiting it to the extent possible and supporting it financially as well. The claims for the centrality of the Jerusalem Temple extended beyond the Roman sphere; the centrality of the Jerusalem Temple was projected as global.

Beginning in the fourth pre-Christian century, Jewish life in the Land of Israel, like life everywhere in the Near and Middle East, was roiled by the invasion of the Greeks and the introduction of Greek culture into traditional Near and Middle Eastern societies. The Jews of the Land of Israel, like their neighbors, had to wrestle with the disparities between traditional Near Eastern norms and values and the alternative Greek norms and values. Such wrestling was often painful and divisive; at the same time, it was ultimately constructive and creative. The Jews of Palestine engaged Greek culture vigorously, divisively, and productively. The alternative understandings of Judaism generated by the encounter with Greek culture are well attested within Palestine and were often transmitted from that base into the various diaspora communities. Out of this wrestling with Greek culture emerged new interpretations of the biblical legacy that would eventuate in classical Judaism and Christianity.

The role that migration from the diaspora communities—the Mesopotamian diaspora in the east and the Roman diaspora in the west—into the homeland might have played during the period between Nehemiah and Ezra in the fifth pre-Christian century and the early Christian centuries cannot be documented. To the extent that there was such migration and that it strengthened the Jewish community in the Land of Israel, it would in all likelihood have been volitional in nature, since there are no known banishments or persecutions in the two sets of diaspora Jewries during this lengthy and poorly documented period.

Outside the Land of Israel, there were two major Jewish diasporas—one in the east and one in the west. The eastern diaspora was, as we have seen, created by the Babylonian expulsion of Jews from their land in 586 b.c.e. as a result of a failed rebellion. Unlike the Israelites of the northern kingdom, the Judeans of the southern kingdom were able to sustain themselves as a community in exile. Eventually, they formed the demographic backbone for the Jewish resettlement of the Land of Israel and offered political support and religious guidance to the newly reconstituted Jewish community in its early days. Beyond the period of Nehemiah and Ezra illuminated in the biblical books, we know almost nothing of the fate of Mesopotamian Jewry for more than a millennium. The most that we can say is that it maintained itself in a way that enabled it to become the dominant center of Jewish life toward the end of late antiquity, a process to which we shall turn shortly.

The western diaspora was far more extensive spatially and thus less homogeneous than the eastern diaspora. By the middle of the first century, Jews were spread all across the Mediterranean Basin, on both the southern and northern shores of the sea. This broad expanse divided into a number of subcultures, united only by the overarching authority of Rome. Not surprisingly, Jewish population seems to have been largest in the eastern sectors of the Mediterranean Basin, which are closest to the Jewish center in Palestine, and to have thinned out further westward, in areas much removed from the Land of Israel. In any case, the unity provided by Roman control of the entire Mediterranean Basin and the ease of sea travel in those days facilitated the spread of Jews throughout the entire Mediterranean littoral.

Once again, we have no serious documentation that clarifies the spread of Jews across the Mediterranean regions. To a limited extent, the roots of some of this spread can be traced to the Judean uprising against Babylonia and its suppression. Some of the Judeans, fearful of Babylonian suppression of the rebellion, seem to have fled westward to Egypt to avoid the impending destruction and decimation. While this dislocation may have laid the cornerstone for some of the settlements in the eastern areas of the Mediterranean Basin, the number of Jews that moved westward in this way was surely limited. As the Jewish community of the Land of Israel strengthened during the fifth pre-Christian century through the first Christian century, it almost certainly became the source of growth for the western diaspora communities as well.

Volitional movement of Jews out of the Land of Israel into the diverse sectors of the Mediterranean Basin was facilitated by a number of factors. The first was the political unity of the entire area. Roman control of the shores of the Mediterranean Sea facilitated business ties throughout the area, which in turn stimulated population movement for all the peoples of the region, Jews included. The ease of sea travel reinforced the political and business cohesion provided by Roman rule. Finally, the attitude toward migration in the Mediterranean ambience was generally quite positive. In contradistinction to the biblical view of migration as a punishment, the diverse populations living in the Mediterranean Basin saw the creation of satellite communities emanating from an original center as a marker of vigor and vitality. To the extent that Jews might absorb these positive views, movement through the Mediterranean area was fostered.

For those choosing to move out of the Land of Israel and relocate in Roman territory, the most immediately accessible areas in the eastern Mediterranean would have initially made the most sense. Areas that are today Syria and Asia Minor would have been settled first, as would have Egypt and Cyrenaica as well. The importance of the Syrian cities and Asia Minor for early Christianity reflects nicely this pattern of settlement. Paul's origins in Tarsus in Asia Minor serve as an indication of this pattern of Jewish settlement, as does his subsequent preaching throughout this area subsequent to his conversion experience. Numerous sources indicate the presence of vibrant Jewish communities southwestward from the Land of Israel in the cities of Egypt and Cyrenaica.

An additional significant center of Jewish population was in the capital city of Rome itself. Josephus in describing regular Palestinian Jewish negotiations with the Roman authorities highlights the support of Rome's Jews to the diverse delegations dispatched from the various and often contending parties in the Land of Israel. Paul also, as depicted in Acts of the Apostles, was engaged in major—albeit negative—interactions with the Jews of Rome. That the hub of political and economic life throughout the Roman Empire would have attracted Jewish immigrants is not at all difficult to understand. The city of Rome would have acted as a magnet to Jews seeking economic opportunity. The lure of great political and economic centers is a theme we shall encounter recurrently throughout this and the ensuing chapters.

Our knowledge of Jewish settlement in the more westerly areas of the Mediterranean Basin is seriously deficient. Limited and uncertain evidence suggests the existence of Jews all the way westward to the Atlantic Ocean, but a clear grasp of the size and significance of these Jewish settlements is unavailable. Once again, however, the overall sense is that such Jewish settlements were formed out of voluntary Jewish movement from the major demographic center in the Land of Israel or from diaspora locations further eastward in the Mediterranean Basin. While these Jewish settlements in the western sectors of the Mediterranean Basin often claimed very ancient roots, these memories do not provide genuine and reliable evidence of the early development of Jewish life in these areas.[5]

Thus, as we commence our exploration of the extensive movement of Jews throughout the Western world, we begin with a relatively secure—albeit limited—sense of the existing centers of Jewish life at that point in time. The dominant demographic center of Jewish life prior to the outbreak of the rebellion of 66–70 was the Land of Israel. The disruption of Jewish life in Palestine in the wake of the earlier rebellion against the Babylonians had been reversed, and Palestinian Jewry was once more at the heart of worldwide Jewish life. An eastern diaspora had been established in Mesopotamia as a result of the Babylonian expulsion of Jews from the Land of Israel, and this diaspora community had been successful in maintaining its cohesion and identity, although the lack of sources precludes any concrete observations about the vicissitudes of its fate. Finally, there was a second diaspora westward of the Land of Israel, which stretched across the Mediterranean Basin. For this diaspora, we do have occasional source materials. The sense gleaned from these materials is a vigorous and growing set of Jewish communities formed by voluntary movement out of the homeland.

For our initial period, from late antiquity through the Muslim conquests, a major observation involves what did not happen, rather than what did happen. Despite traditional and popular conviction of a Roman expulsion of Jews from Palestine in the wake of suppression of the Jewish rebellion, there was in fact no such expulsion. Rome did not utilize this technique of punishing rebels, and the subsequent history of Palestinian Jewry indicated clearly ongoing and vigorous Jewish presence. This vigor resulted in the evolution of new patterns of Jewish religious life and communal leadership.

Toward the end of late antiquity, a major shift in the relationship between the formerly dominant Palestine center and the eastern diaspora Jewish community took place. Precisely when this shift occurred and what factors brought it about are both unclear. Sources for Palestinian Jewry for this period in late antiquity are limited, and sources for Mesopotamian Jewry are confined to the early strata of the Babylonian Talmud, which is notoriously unconcerned with demographic and social issues. Indeed, it is the Babylonian Talmud itself as a whole that provides the best gauge for the obscure changes that took place in the relationship between these two centers.[6]

In a general way, the broad environment of both Palestinian and Mesopotamian Jewry between the year 70 and the Muslim conquest was altered. In Palestine and the Roman Empire, the change was occasioned by the rapid spread of gentile Christianity throughout the empire. The efforts of the Roman authorities to halt this spread through persecution eventually proved ineffectual or even counterproductive. The willingness for martyrdom on the part of many profoundly committed Christians made a deep impression on polytheistic observers. Rather than being cowed by the spectacle of Roman persecution of Christians and thus frightened away from Christianity, many Romans were moved by the devotion and commitment exhibited by the Christian martyrs. As the chaos of the third century, with its succession of emperors and internal uprisings that did incalculable harm to the economy throughout the empire, continued into the fourth century, one of the contestants to the imperial throne embraced Christianity, in a departure from the norm. Emperor Constantine's new stance toward Christianity set in motion a protracted period of change, during which the Church and its leadership slowly gained increasing power within and control of the Roman Empire.[7]

For the Jews of the Roman Empire, this meant a radically new experience of living under the rule of an alternative and indeed a closely related monotheistic faith. During their prior experience of living under the domination of polytheistic empires, Jews had successfully wrested for themselves a set of special privileges required by the unique demands of their monotheism. Jews were regularly excused, for example, from state religious functions and obligations normally incumbent upon all members of society. Recognizing that such behaviors would be impossible for the monotheistic Jews, a sequence of empires over many centuries acknowledged this uniqueness and excused their Jewish subjects from such obligations. Now, a radically new situation was created, with monotheistic Christianity slowly ascending to political power in the far-flung empire.

Christianity had emerged as a sect within first-century Palestinian Jewry, but it seemingly made little headway among Palestine's Jews. Eventually, Jesus, the central figure in the movement, was condemned by the Roman authorities to crucifixion, which was the normal punishment for those suspected of insurrection. This might seem to suggest that Jesus was part of the insurrectionist faction within Palestinian Jewry, but he was portrayed in a totally different manner in the texts that became canonical within the Church, where he appears as utterly unconcerned with and uninvolved in contemporary political issues.[8]

With Paul and his conviction that Jesus was sent to the entire world and that gentile adherents of Jesus were free from the obligations of Jewish law, the Jesus movement took a decidedly new turn. Although the break with Judaism and the Jewish world was slow and fitful, the demographic change within the Church, as its constituency became heavily and then overwhelmingly gentile, made such a rupture inevitable. As a result of the break with Judaism and the Jews, the culprits in the crucifixion of Jesus were projected as the Jews in their entirety or at least as the leadership of the Jewish community of Palestine. Even though, technically, the crucifixion of

Jesus had been ordered by the Roman authority in Jerusalem and it had been carried out by Roman soldiers, the canonical Gospel accounts fixed blame for the execution of Jesus on the Jews, who were portrayed as insisting strenuously and implacably on his condemnation and execution. Thus, the canonical narratives—key to Christian history and belief—project a decidedly negative portrait of Judaism and Jews.

Nonetheless, as Christianity came to prominence and power in the Roman world, the harshness of the Gospel portrait was softened considerably. Certainly, the legacy of Judaism as a permitted religious faith that long antedated Roman authority and had been in force throughout the many centuries of pagan Roman rule played a considerable role in this mitigation. Consequential also was growing awareness that the embeddedness of Christianity in Judaism required protection of Judaism and Jews. Since so much of the Gospel case for the special role of Jesus was grounded in what the Church saw as his fulfillment of the predictions of Israel's early prophets, veneration for these prophets and the community of which they were a part became a necessity. Indeed, as the Church took an increasingly aggressive missionizing stance toward the polytheistic world around it, acknowledgment of the superiority of monotheistic Judaism over polytheism became obvious and useful.

In practical terms, this all translated into a formal Church stance that insisted on safe and secure existence for Jews within Christian society. In the view of Church leadership, most forcefully Augustine, God himself had ordained such safety and security, which was thus binding and could not be questioned. Furthermore, Jewish witness to the truth of the prophecies that Jesus was said to have fulfilled was exceedingly useful in missionizing among pagans and in correcting the errors of those Christians defined as heretics.

Church spokesmen claimed that both Jesus and the Church he founded fulfilled biblical prophecies. A striking example of this latter fulfillment of biblical prophecy by the post-Jesus Church was patent in the demographic realities in evidence by the fourth century. On one hand, the spread of Christianity far and wide in a position of power and authority served as convincing evidence of its fulfillment of the positive predictions of the prophets of Israel. At the same time, the dispersal of Jews far and wide in secondary and subjugated conditions constituted evidence of fulfillment of negative prophecies. This readily observable contrast seemed to provide tangible and accessible proof for the error of Judaism and thus, more important, the truth of Christianity. Divine fiat and maintenance of the Jews for their contribution to Christian truth constituted the cornerstones of the structure erected by Augustine for protecting and preserving Jewish life in Christendom.

While Jews were useful to Christians, they at the same time presented considerable dangers. First of all, they were also monotheists and thus threatened to drain off some of the polytheists attracted in a general way to rejection of the prevailing theologies of multiple deities. More important, Judaism was extremely close to Christianity, indeed was the matrix out of which Christianity had evolved. To a significant extent, Judaism and Christianity represented alternative readings of the Hebrew Bible. Jewish insistence on the divine roots of the Hebrew Bible served Christian missionizing purposes very well; Jewish readings of the Hebrew Bible were at the same time potentially threatening. To the extent that Christians might be attracted to Jewish readings of the Hebrew Bible, they would abandon their true faith; to the extent that they might simply question Christian readings, they would be religiously threatened. Jews thus constituted a serious religious danger to the ever expanding Church.

God had commanded safety for Jews, and preserving them served Christian purposes well. At the same time, barriers against adverse Jewish influence on Christian neighbors had to be erected, and they were. Perhaps the most important barrier involved elimination of any circumstances in which Jews might exercise power over Christian peers, since power always involves potential for influence. Jews were not to own Christian slaves, occupy political positions of authority, or marry Christian spouses. These concerns led ineluctably to limitation of contact between Jews and Christians, although this legislation would evolve slowly over the centuries, reaching final and extreme form only in the Middle Ages.

Thus, the Christianization of the Roman Empire, which was a protracted process, introduced significant change for Jewish life. In practical terms, the changes were initially fairly restrained. Jews were accorded the same rights to safe and secure existence they had enjoyed under polytheistic rule. To an extent, the safeguards were even enhanced, since this safety and security were projected as divinely commanded and at the same time useful to the Church. This safety and security included the right to practice Judaism freely and without constraint. To be sure, limitations were imposed on Jewish behavior, but during the closing centuries of late antiquity these limitations do not seem to have been unduly onerous.

One further aspect of Jewish life in the Roman world during these closing centuries of late antiquity deserves brief mention. As noted, the Jesus movement does not seem to have made much headway in the Jewish community that dominated first-century Palestine or among the lesser non-Jewish population of Palestine. Paul's successes with gentile adherents seem to have taken place largely outside the Land of Israel, in the Roman diaspora. Somewhat anomalously, a religious community that venerated a Palestinian figure and a set of events that took place in Palestine expanded and flourished in an alternative setting. With the accession of the Church to power in Rome, the possibility of identifying the sacred sites of earliest Christianity, erecting appropriate religious shrines on these sites, and more generally encouraging Christian settlement in the Land of Israel emerged. These developments, very much associated with Constantine's mother Helena, were not designed to impact ongoing Jewish life in Palestine. Conceivably, they to an extent did.

While the Jews of the Roman world living in both the Land of Israel and the western diaspora were experiencing the changes associated with the Christianization of the Roman Empire, somewhat parallel changes were taking place in Mesopotamia and thus impacting the eastern Jewish diaspora. As we have seen, Mesopotamia by the year 70 had long been under a succession of imperial rulers. The Assyrians had been replaced by the Babylonians, the Babylonians by the Persians, the Persians by the Greeks, and the Greeks by the Parthians. Each of these changes in rule affected the vast areas under imperial domination, although the differences were relatively minor. With respect to the Jewish minority in the eastern diaspora, the major change took place when the Persians unseated the Babylonians and replaced their harsh policy toward minority communities with a more lenient stance.

In the 230s, the Parthian Arsacids were replaced by the Persian Sassanians, who were devotees of Zoroastrianism, a dualistic faith that is difficult to place precisely on the spectrum of religions extending from polytheism to monotheism. There is good reason to argue its status as a polytheism and equally good reason to identify it as a monotheism.[9] In any case, the Zoroastrian authorities, like their peers in the Christianized Roman Empire, seem to have instituted occasional intrusions into Jewish religious life, without significantly altering the longstanding toleration of Judaism bequeathed from the prior imperial traditions.[10]

In this changing environment within the Roman Empire, with its central Jewish community in the Land of Israel and its western diaspora settlements, and within the Mesopotamian empire, with its well-established but poorly documented eastern diaspora, a major demographic shift seems to have taken place during the closing centuries of late antiquity. Slowly and in ways that cannot be closely charted, centrality in the Jewish world began to shift from Palestine to Mesopotamia. This shift seems to have involved at its core demography, with Mesopotamian Jewry expanding in number and Palestinian Jewry shrinking. Once again, details are lacking, and a precise timeline cannot be established. However, when sources begin to proliferate during the early centuries of Muslim rule, it is clear that the largest Jewish community in the world had come to be located in Mesopotamia and that this would remain the case all through the first half of the Middle Ages and into the second half as well.

The same shift is patent in the political and organizational spheres as well, although once again details are lacking. In Mesopotamia, an authority parallel to the Palestinian Patriarch emerged in the Exilarch. While the Patriarch had the prestige of Palestine behind him, the Exilarch claimed descent from the last kings of Judah, who had been exiled into Babylonia. This claim of Davidic descent was internally useful, although arguably secondary in significance to the support of the non-Jewish authorities enjoyed for many centuries by the Exilarchs. Radical diminution of the power of the Patriarchate by the Christian emperors of Rome in the early fifth century serves as a convenient marker of the shifting stature enjoyed by these two offices of internal Jewish leadership.

During the early centuries of late antiquity, as classical Judaism coalesced, with the Pharisaic rabbis exercising growing although hardly exclusive authority, the academies of the Galilee emerged as the central institutions of rabbinic Judaism, and it was from these academies that the first authoritative text of rabbinic Judaism—the Mishnah—emerged. Codification of the Mishnah was a double-edged sword for Palestinian Jewry. On the one hand, the Mishnah served as a tangible index of the centrality of the Galilean academies; at the same time, the availability of this authoritative corpus meant that its further analysis and expansion could take place in alternative locales. In the event, the academies of the Land of Israel became the scene of such analysis and expansion, which eventually coalesced as the Jerusalem Talmud. However, precisely the same kind of analysis and expansion was initiated in the increasingly active and increasingly independent academies of Mesopotamia, which led to the eventual compilation of the lengthier, richer, and ultimately more authoritative Babylonian Talmud. For subsequent Jewish history, *the* Talmud was the Babylonian Talmud.

The shift in centrality in Jewish life demographically, politically, and religiously is a reality, lack of detailed data notwithstanding, and it reflects considerable movement of Jews from Palestine to Mesopotamia. As we have seen, traditional Jewish and Christian thinking attributes this demographic movement to Roman force, although the imposition of such force is nowhere attested. In the face of a total lack of evidence of the Romans driving Jews from Palestine into Mesopotamia or anywhere else for that matter, we may reasonably surmise that the chaotic circumstances in the third-century Roman Empire had significant impact on Jewish population movement from Palestine to Mesopotamia, as Jews became aware of better living circumstances not all that far away. To be sure, this bespeaks rational assessment of alternative circumstances and volitional movement. Jews were moving freely and of their own accord, as migrants and not refugees.

The period from late antiquity to the rise of Islam shows considerable Jewish demographic movement. The western diaspora seems to have expanded somewhat, although details are lacking. More obvious is the expansion of the eastern diaspora. By the end of this period, the Mesopotamian Jewish community had usurped the position of Palestinian Jewry as the dominant Jewish community worldwide. In demographic, economic, and religious terms, Mesopotamian Jewry had assumed primacy. What factors seem to explain these changes?

During this period, there is no evidence of governmental edicts that influenced Jewish demographic movement. To be sure, both traditional and modern treatments of Jewish history assume that Roman suppression of the revolt of 66–70 and destruction of Jerusalem and its temple were accompanied by an Assyrian- and Babylonian-style expulsion of the rebellious Jews. There was in fact no such expulsion, either in the year 70 or in 135, at the point of Roman suppression of the second Jewish rebellion. Governmental edicts of banishment played no role in the migration of Jews during the period between 70 and 600.

There was, during this period, one major governmental edict that made Jewish life untenable. In the wake of the rebellion of 66–70, the Romans seemingly perceived the Jerusalem Temple as the locus from which the rebellion had been instigated, and they destroyed the sanctuary. In the wake of the second rebellion, which could not have drawn strength from a temple, the Romans seem to have concluded that observance of Jewish law would have to be quashed in order to seal off the wellsprings of Jewish rebelliousness. Emperor Hadrian thus proscribed key observances of Jewish law, an enactment that could have made Jewish existence untenable and could have triggered massive emigration from Roman-controlled areas. This legislation did result in a number of martyrdoms, but was not sufficiently implemented to occasion wide-ranging emigration.

Limited evidence of a second governmentally enacted decree that would seem to have made Jewish life untenable comes from seventh-century Visigothic Spain. Very limited sources mention royal decrees ordering conversion of Jews or banishment, but data about the execution of these decrees are nonexistent. Such governmental edicts do not constitute outright banishment of Jews, but rather the demand for religious change that would in effect nullify Jewishness. In any case, close recent analysis of these decrees has concluded that they were policy statements only and were not in fact carried out in any significant measure.[11] Neither edicts of banishment nor limitations on Jewish religious life caused major Jewish demographic change in late antiquity.

Perhaps most surprising of all is the lack of impact of the violence of 66–70 and 132–135 on Jewish migration. Roman suppression of two Jewish uprisings in Palestine was bloody and thorough, with massive destruction and major loss of life in the wake of both rebellions. Strikingly, this protracted violence did not alter the demography of Jewish life in late antiquity. Despite the upheavals of two rebellions and their suppression, Palestine remained the largest and dominant Jewish community down through the third century. The chaos of the third century, which did not involve anti-Jewish violence but rather broad instability throughout the empire, seemingly served to convince many Jews to relocate.

By and large, demographic change during this period of late antiquity was not in any significant way forced upon Jews; such migration as took place, which was considerable, was volitional. The major movement discernible, which took place between Palestine and Mesopotamia, involved Jews who were convinced that they would find in the more peaceful and more prosperous Sassanian Empire better living opportunities than in the strife-ridden and dissension-wracked Roman Empire. It is striking that the first seven centuries of Jewish population movement that followed the debacle of the year 70 should have been dominated by voluntary migration in search of better circumstances.

SEVEN

The Islamic World

During the early years of the seventh century, the Byzantine Empire and the Sassanian Empire continued to joust against one another, regularly invading, conquering, and then retreating. These empires housed the two largest sets of Jewish communities in the world, with the remaining set of Jewish communities located farther westward in the Mediterranean Basin, living under Western Roman rule. The two contending empires were blissfully unaware that a new danger was coalescing on the Arabian peninsula. Long a hinterland to the major civilizations of Mesopotamia and the Mediterranean Basin, this seemingly backward area was germinating a new and impressive monotheistic vision and a new and powerful monotheistic community.[1]

Muhammad, the prophet of Islam, was surely influenced by Jewish and Christian enclaves scattered across the Arabian peninsula. However, Islam did not emerge directly out of either a Jewish or Christian matrix, as Christianity had emerged out of Palestinian Jewry. Instead, Muhammad promulgated an innovative perception of the history of divine-human engagement. In his view, the one and only God in the universe had in his beneficence conferred upon humanity a sequence of revelations of his truth and will. The Jews had been the first recipients of these revelations; the Christians had been next; the third recipients of divine truth—this time full and final divine truth—were the Arab peoples. The partial revelations enjoyed by Jews and Christians entitled them to deep respect by Muslims, but God had conferred full truth only upon the latter. Galvanized by this vision, the heretofore fractious tribes of Arabia came together into a cohesive and potent religious community and political force.

The development of Islam reflects some Jewish precedents and some Christian precedents. Like biblical Israel, the Muslim community was simultaneously a religious, political, and military entity. Area after area of the peninsula was taken over by this religious/political/military force. Unlike biblical Israel and very much like the Church, entry into the community was with the passage of time open to all. Islam, born within the Arab population of the peninsula, fairly quickly embraced converts of all races and ethnicities. Emerging on the Arabian peninsula and rapidly dominating it, Islam swiftly moved beyond its point of origin. As control of the peninsula was increasingly assured, raiding parties set out beyond it in search of riches. Raids escalated into conquests, and raiding parties evolved into increasingly well organized and well equipped armies.

The Muslim conquests of the seventh and early eighth centuries were remarkable in their extent and rapidity. In a northeasterly direction, Muslim armies overran the Sassanian Empire and took it over entirely, absorbing it into the realm of Islam, indeed eventually making it the center of the realm of Islam. In a northwesterly direction, they conquered important sectors of the increasingly independent eastern half of the Roman Empire, including Palestine. They were, however, not successful in conquering all of the extensive imperial holdings, thus leaving the Byzantine Empire as an ongoing foe. In a more straightforwardly westerly direction, the Muslim armies conquered the southern and western shores of the Mediterranean Sea, tearing away vast sections of the western half of the Roman Empire. By the early eighth century, the Sassanian Empire had disappeared, absorbed into the realm of Islam, and much of the eastern and western halves of the Roman Empire had passed into Muslim control as well. Islamic armies had completed one of the great conquests in Western history and had fashioned one of the most powerful empires in Western history.

During the seventh and early eighth centuries, the armies of Islam proved themselves militarily formidable. Before long, the Muslim rulers proved themselves adept in other respects as well. They exhibited the ability to administer the vast areas they were conquering and to maintain the economies and living standards of these areas. With the passage of time, as the Muslim authorities became aware of the rich cultural legacy of Greco-Roman civilization, they encouraged preservation and adaptation of this legacy to the new circumstances. An imposing literature of translation from Greek and Latin into Arabic emerged, which was eventually to prove invaluable for Western civilization altogether. As Christian Europe began its own remarkable rise to power (which we shall treat in the next chapter), its cultural maturation benefited markedly from the recovery of the Greek and Roman cultural legacy through a new round of translations, this time from Arabic into Latin.

With the passage of time, more and more of the subject population in the vast Islamic world opted to join the faith of the rulers. Islam spread slowly but surely, without aggressive missionizing. The spread of Christianity had taken place largely as the result of proselytizing success. By contrast, the spread of Islam resulted from military conquest and societal control. This difference was important for the stances in both realms toward non-Christians and non-Muslims. In the Christian sphere, there was a strong commitment to intensive proselytizing among non-Christians; in the realm of Islam, the missionizing pressures brought to bear on non-Muslims were quite limited. This was especially the case with respect to Jews and Christians, projected as fellow monotheists and recipients of genuine divine revelation.

How did the remarkable Muslim conquests affect the Jewish world? The answer is simple and unambiguous: The impact was enormous, and it was felt in every sphere of Jewish life. Demographically, the overwhelming majority of world Jewry became part of the vast empire created by the Muslim conquests. The largest and most powerful Jewish community in the world at the end of antiquity was located in Mesopotamia, which was taken over in its totality by the Muslims. Thus, the dominant Jewish community in the early Middle Ages was ensconced at the very center of the enormous realm of Islam.

Much of the territory previously part of the Eastern Roman Empire came into Muslim hands as well. Perhaps most important, the Jewish community of the Land of Israel, which had lost its position at the center of the Jewish world but retained great importance nonetheless, passed into Muslim control. The same was true for the old and sizable Jewish community of modern-day Syria. To be sure, many Jewish communities under Byzantine control remained outside the orbit of Islam, continuing to live under

Eastern Christian domination. The same pattern is true for those Jews who had previously lived in the western half of the Roman Empire. The Jewish communities located on the southern and western shores of the Mediterranean became part of the world of Islam; a few areas of southern Europe along the northern shores of the Mediterranean, with rather small Jewish populations, remained in Christian hands. In an utterly new way, the vast majority of the world's Jews found themselves living under unified rule, that of the Muslims.[2]

For the very large number of Jews now encountering a new majority ambience, the situation was relatively benign. First of all, there was simple demographic reality—the Islamic empire housed a highly diversified subject population. The areas under Islamic rule included a rich mixture of races, ethnicities, religions, and cultures. This heterogeneity worked to the advantage of the Jewish population living under Muslim rule. Jews constituted but one minority community among many, and a relatively small one at that. Jews as a distinct minority group were by no means conspicuous—they were simply one of many such distinct groups.

Moreover, Jews constituted one of the two religious communities recognized as blessed with genuine divine revelation. For the Muslims, humanity was divided into three fundamental categories—the sphere of idolatry, which was composed of polytheists and could claim no basic rights; the sphere of the Peoples of the Book, including Jews and Christians, which had enjoyed divine revelation and which was therefore entitled to respect and secure existence within the Muslim world; and the sphere of Islam, which was the sphere of full truth.[3]

Of the two fully acknowledged Peoples of the Book, Jews tended to be favored by the Muslim authorities, for a simple reason. Whereas Christians in many areas of the Muslim world had lost ruling power, Jews had nowhere exercised political independence and political authority. There was therefore no reason to suspect Jews of harboring hopes of overthrowing the Muslim authorities and regaining hegemony. The key to winning the allegiance of the Jews was simply the quality of treatment meted out to them. Positive treatment of the Jewish minority—it was anticipated—would ensure ready acceptance of Muslim rule. The treatment accorded the

Jews was by and large quite positive, and the anticipated Jewish reaction was realized.

The general tendency of the medieval Muslim authorities to avoid aggressive missionizing worked to the advantage of their Jewish subjects, among others. There was considerable Jewish conversion to Islam, although it cannot be traced in any detail, but Jews in the medieval Muslim world did not endure the constant missionizing pressure suffered by their confreres in the medieval Christian world. Aggressive missionizing was a painful fact of Jewish life in Christendom; this was not the case in the medieval Islamic world.

In this Islamic setting, Jewish life flourished. The Jews living in the Islamic world were age-old inhabitants, whose presence much antedated the emergence of Islam; these Jews maintained their diversified economic outlets and their well-established social relations with non-Jewish neighbors; they continued to organize themselves effectively as a self-governing minority community; they pursued traditional Jewish intellectual activities and—stimulated by their creative environment—branched out in new spiritual and intellectual directions as well. In a world very much in motion, Jews traveled extensively, sometimes for trade and sometimes in search of knowledge, religious, scientific, or philosophic. In addition, Jews regularly relocated into areas that seemed to promise improved life circumstances. Demographic displacement was common for the Jews in the Islamic world and resulted in changing constellations of Jewish community life.

For the earliest centuries of Muslim rule, from the seventh through the ninth centuries, source materials are extremely limited. Slowly, literary creativity accelerated during the tenth century, offering the earliest albeit limited reflections of Jewish experience in the realm of Islam. The preservation of a most unusual collection of literary and documentary data has emerged from one of the ancient synagogues of Cairo. These unusual materials survived in a *genizah* in the synagogue and provide a remarkable opportunity to track multiple aspects of medieval Jewish life, including Jewish population movement.

A *genizah* is a traditional Jewish storage facility for texts whose sanctity demands that they enjoy reverent treatment when they can no longer serve in normal fashion. Often, such books, collected over an extensive period of time, underwent formal burial, which meant of course their physical disintegration. The Cairo Genizah was unusual in a number of ways. In the first place, the materials thrown into this storage facility included much more than the usual sacred texts. For reasons that are still not fully clear, this *genizah* became a repository for all sorts of material written in the Hebrew language or, even more unusually, simply in Hebrew letters. In this way, a treasure trove of quotidian materials in both Hebrew and Judeo-Arabic emerged. In addition, this *genizah* was never cleared out for burial and the resultant disintegration of materials. Finally, the dry climate of Cairo ensured the preservation of the materials in the Cairo Genizah in a way that would not have been possible in other settings. As a result of this concatenation of circumstances, twentieth- and twenty-first-century scholars have at their disposal an unparalleled corpus of documentation of everyday Jewish life in the medieval Islamic world.

Upon Western discovery of the Cairo Genizah in the early twentieth century, attention understandably focused on newly discovered literary texts. These included copies of biblical books much older than any previously available, Hebrew originals of texts from antiquity long known only in Greek translations, and medieval texts totally unknown. Items such as personal letters, dowry lists, and prescriptions hardly seemed of value. Slowly, the importance of these everyday documents began to be recognized. The key figure in the exploitation of these quotidian materials was S. D. Goitein. In his late fifties, Goitein began to immerse himself in these materials, and he devoted the remaining three decades of his life to collecting, transcribing, translating, cataloguing, and comprehending these rich and not easily understood documents. Eventually, Goitein published five monumental volumes, in which he depicted in exquisite detail the everyday lives of the Jews of the medieval Islamic world, in an unparalleled scholarly achievement.[4]

The very first volume of Goitein's masterpiece focused on the economic activities of the Jews of the medieval eastern Mediterranean Basin. This volume offered a strikingly innovative view of medieval Jewish economic activity. The regnant perception of medieval Jewish economic activity, based on the experience of the Jews of northern Europe that we shall engage in the next chapter, projected medieval Jews as confined largely to business and banking. The Cairo Genizah materials painted a dramatically different picture. The Jews of the medieval eastern Mediterranean filled every rung of the economic ladder, with the exception of agriculture. They stood at the very bottom of the economic scale, working as poorly paid unskilled laborers; they stood at very top of the economic scale, serving as highly skilled and highly sought-after physicians and as bankers at the head of corporate enterprises of great magnitude and wealth; they filled every conceivable economic niche between the extremes. Indeed, the diversity of Jewish economic activity revealed in the Cairo Genizah helped reconstruct some of the reality of Jewish economic life in late antiquity, since the Jews of the medieval Islamic world were in many instances continuing age-old Jewish economic patterns.[5]

The data preserved in the Cairo Genizah reveal a Jewish community that was extremely mobile. In general, the combination of traditional Near Eastern trade routes and the easy travel arrangements available via the Mediterranean Sea enabled Jews to move all across the vast Islamic realm, from Mesopotamia in the east to Spain in the west. The presence of Jewish settlements everywhere throughout this enormous area undoubtedly facilitated Jewish movement. Jewish traders and travelers had at their disposal reliable co-religionists at every point in their journeys. There is considerable evidence of Jews proceeding well beyond the confines of the Islamic world. Bands of Jewish traders are portrayed as moving all across backward northern Europe in search of raw materials and well into the Orient in search of luxury goods. The medieval Islamic world was open to movement all across it and beyond it.[6]

In this mobile world, significant demographic change clearly took place, although once again precise details as to timing are lacking. In tracking demographic change, we must remind ourselves of the configuration of Jewish population on the eve of the Muslim conquest. By the seventh century, the largest Jewish community was to be found in Mesopotamia; the formerly largest center of Jewish life in Palestine had declined somewhat, but was still quite significant; the Jews of the western diaspora had been split between the two increasingly separate sectors of the Roman Empire, with the

Eastern Roman/Byzantine Empire probably housing the larger of the two Jewish populations.

By the twelfth century, much had changed. Mesopotamia and its Jewry and Palestine and its Jewry were now part of the Islamic world. In effect, the two largest Jewish communities on the eve of the Muslim conquests became part and parcel of the realm of Islam. The rest of world Jewry was in effect split into three segments. One segment consisted of the eastern shores of the Mediterranean Sea, such as Syria and Palestine, and the southern and western shores of the Mediterranean Sea, all of which passed into Muslim hands; one segment consisted of Asia Minor and remained under Byzantine domination; and the final segment stretched from a sliver of northern Spain through southern France and Italy and remained part of much reduced western Christendom. This simple description reveals the extent to which the reconfiguration of majority power resulted in a thorough shift of the political ambience of world Jewish population, with the bulk of world Jewry concentrated in those areas conquered and ruled by the forces of Islam.

In our effort to delineate in somewhat more detail the configuration of Jewish population at the end of the first half-millennium after the Muslim conquests, we shall depend heavily on a remarkable document—the travelogue of a mid-twelfth-century European Jew named Benjamin. Benjamin set out from his hometown of Tudela in Spain, which had passed from Muslim control to Christian control earlier in the twelfth century. His journey took him across southern Europe into the Byzantine Empire and eventually to the heart of the Muslim empire in Mesopotamia. On his return to Spain, Benjamin added important stops in Egypt, which was under Muslim rule. In his travelogue, Benjamin offers interesting details about the general conditions of life in the various cities he visited. He often provides useful information on the size of the Jewish communities, their economic activities, and outstanding schools and scholars.[7]

Early on, Benjamin's travel report seemed utterly fanciful. However, as knowledge of the twelfth century has increased, details in Benjamin's travelogue have been increasingly confirmed, thus making it an invaluable resource for reconstructing the contours of worldwide Jewish life early in the second half of the Middle Ages. The one major uncertainty with Benjamin's travel report involves the precise limits of his journey. He describes himself as reaching areas of India in the east and—during his return trip—making his way into northern Europe. There is considerable doubt as to both these claims, and we shall not take them seriously, since in any case he does not offer significant information on Jewish demography in these two areas. We shall confine ourselves to the heart of his travels through the Mediterranean Basin and Mesopotamia.

Following is a list of the major and unchallenged places Benjamin visited in his travels, and his estimate of the Jewish populations he encountered. The sites are listed sequentially, and categorized under their ruling authorities: Latin Christendom, Byzantium, the crusading principalities, and the sphere of Islam. Precisely how Benjamin secured his numbers, especially the larger numbers, and thus what exactly they mean, is by no means clear. However, our interest is comparative, and the numbers he provides are highly illuminating in this regard.

- Latin Christendom
  - Narbonne—300 Jews
  - Lunel—300 Jews
  - Posquieres—400 Jews
  - Marseilles—300 Jews
  - Capua—300 Jews
  - Naples—300 Jews
  - Salerno—600 Jews
- Byzantium
  - Thebes—2,000 Jews
  - Salonica—500 Jews
  - Constantinople—2,500 Jews
- Crusader Palestine
  - Acre—200 Jews
  - Caesaria—200 Jews
  - Jerusalem—200 Jews
  - Ramleh—300 Jews
  - Ashkelon—200 Jews

The realm of Islam

Damascus—3,000 Jews
Aleppo—5,000 Jews
Mosul—2,000 Jews
Baghdad—40,000 Jews
Babylon—3,000 Jews
Hillah—10,000 Jews
Basra—10,000 Jews
Susa—7,000 Jews
Cairo—7,000 Jews
Alexandria—3,000 Jews

A few conclusions leap out of the fascinating numbers Benjamin provided here. Clearly, the religio-political sphere that had come to dominate world Jewry by the twelfth century was the realm of Islam. As noted earlier, the overwhelming majority of early medieval Jews were absorbed into the Islamic empire, and this remained the reality through the twelfth century, even as the Western scene had begun to show signs of change. Benjamin's figures for major cities in the Islamic world dwarf those of the cities in the eastern and western Roman spheres. In the Islamic world, cities with Jewish populations in the thousands are common; some reach ten thousand and more. None of the cities in Byzantium come close to these Jewish populations, and the cities of western Christendom lag far behind.

And then there is Baghdad, with its unique Jewish population of 40,000, a number that clearly left Benjamin aghast. Nothing he had seen elsewhere in the Jewish world came remotely close to this number. Explanations for this abnormality abound. In the first place, Benjamin's depiction of the city of Baghdad itself is breathless—it is clearly a city the likes of which he had never before encountered.[8] Then there is the reality of its political status. It was in many ways the power center of the West. Just as the city of Rome in late antiquity attracted a large Jewish population, in the same way the lure of Baghdad must have been nearly irresistible to ambitious Jews.

Next in size to the cities of the Muslim sphere were the areas dominated by Byzantium. In the Byzantine sector, the figures for Jewish inhabitants of

Constantinople and Thebes are impressive, but still far lower than for many cities in the realm of Islam. Byzantium clearly ranked a rather distant second to the realm of Islam in Jewish population. In western Christendom, the Jewish population figures are far less than those for Byzantium and paltry when compared to the Islamic sphere. The towns of western Christendom visited by Benjamin, all located in the southern sectors of Latin Christendom, housed relatively small Jewish communities, and we can safely hypothesize that the Jewish population of the northern sectors of western Christendom was minuscule. To be sure, three hundred years later, Jewish population distribution was well on its way to major change, as we shall see in the next chapters.

Moving from religio-political spheres to geographic areas within the realm of Islam, we note the contrastive fates of the two dominant Jewish communities of the early Middle Ages—the Jewries of Mesopotamia and Palestine. The former obviously flourished remarkably under Islamic rule during the first half of the Middle Ages. The first Islamic dynasty, the Umayyad, made its political center in Syria. When the Abbasids displaced the Umayyads, they transferred the center of their governance to Mesopotamia, with Baghdad emerging as the capital and with the passage of time an extraordinarily impressive city, as seen in Benjamin's exhilarated description. This meant that world Jewish life was predominantly focused in the center of power in majority Islamic society. Baghdad housed a Jewish community immeasurably larger and more influential than any other Jewish community seen by Benjamin. Moving beyond Baghdad, there is a broader sense of a large Mesopotamian Jewish population.

By contrast, the Jewish population of Palestine had declined precipitously. Benjamin's visit came more than a half century after the crusader conquests of the 1090s and early in the Muslim effort to dislodge the Europeans, which by the end of the thirteenth century achieved full success. The insecurities of the area and the disruption of its economy probably account for the striking decline depicted by Benjamin.[9] The Jews of Palestine in all likelihood found more appealing living options not all that far away in safer, more secure, and economically more viable sectors of the Islamic world.

We should note two lacunae in the information provided by Benjamin of Tudela. The less important of the two is useful information on northern Europe, which Benjamin may or may not have visited. In any case, he does not provide useful information about the still small, but rapidly growing Jewish population in the north at the midpoint of the twelfth century. It is highly unlikely that the numbers in these newly emergent Jewish communities would have been at all impressive at this still early point in time. These numbers would expand dramatically during the ensuing centuries, as we shall see shortly.

The more important lacuna involves the southern and western shores of the Mediterranean Basin. Benjamin visited Egypt, but did not proceed further westward and encounter the increasingly significant Jewish settlements along the North African coast. Likewise, he did not visit and report on the strong Jewish communities in Muslim Spain. While the Christians had begun the process of reconquest and had taken over important strongholds, like Benjamin's hometown of Tudela, the majority of the peninsula remained in Muslim hands and housed vibrant Jewish communities. Broad growth of the Jewish communities along the southern and western shores of the Mediterranean Sea served as the foundation for proliferation of major centers of Jewish learning all across this area. These centers produced a host of experts in Jewish law and important new commentaries and codes of Jewish legal material. Not surprisingly, these new experts developed a strong desire for independence from the venerable central Jewish academies of Mesopotamia.[10]

Abraham ibn Daud wrote his fascinating *Sefer ha-Kabbalah* at roughly the same time that Benjamin was making his trip eastward and provides some insight into Jewish life in the important areas of North Africa and Muslim Spain that Benjamin did not visit and describe. Ibn Daud's book is a very important exemplar of a major mode of medieval Jewish history writing—histories of Jewish Oral Law transmission. Jewish Oral Law faced internal challenges mounted by Jewish sectarians called the Karaites, who insisted on the indisputable sanctity of the Hebrew Bible and denied the authority of Jewish Oral Law; it faced parallel challenges from Christian and Muslim thinkers. In response to these potent challenges, rabbinic authorities from early on compiled histories of Oral Law, tracing purportedly accurate and authoritative transmission from teacher to teacher and center to center. Abraham ibn Daud's *Sefer ha-Kabbalah* is a major and widely cited example of this literary genre.

At the same time, it is something more. The first six chapters of the book are fairly traditional, progressing from the biblical period through the *geonim,* the authoritative post-talmudic sages of the Mesopotamian academies. The seventh chapter, titled by the modern editor "The Succession of the Rabbinate," traces the post-geonic progression of Oral Torah in the western diaspora, most pointedly in ibn Daud's native Spain.[11] This seventh chapter serves as yet another attack on the prior centrality of the Mesopotamian academies, arguing strenuously for the growing expertise and independence of the newer and more westerly centers of Jewish learning. In addition, the seventh chapter provides a broader sense of the maturation of Spanish Jewry under slowly diminishing Islamic rule.

Ibn Daud tells a charming tale to anchor the new centers of Jewish learning in older locales. His tale involves a Muslim privateer named ibn Rumahis, commissioned by the Spanish Muslim ruler Abd ar-Rahman to pillage Christian merchant ships. The privateer was moderately successful, capturing a vessel that contained inter alia four distinguished Jewish scholars setting out from the old center of rabbinic learning in Bari, Italy. Ibn Daud claims to know the names and fate of three of the four, which rightly or wrongly confers an impression of serious attention to reliable detail. Moving from east to west, ibn Rumahis allegedly sold a rabbi named Shemariah in Alexandria. From there, R. Shemariah proceeded to Cairo, where he became head of the academy. The privateer sold his second Jewish captive, R. Hushiel, in North Africa. R. Hushiel moved on to Qairawan, where he too became head of a major academy and father of a very distinguished rabbinic authority. The third captive, R. Moses, and his son were sold in Cordova. For this segment of his story, ibn Daud provides detailed information on the way in which the ex-prisoner, arriving incognito, dazzled the Spanish rabbis meeting in the Cordova academy with his mastery of rabbinic law, ascended immediately to its leadership, and began the process of elevating the level of study to parity with older centers.[12]

Abraham ibn Daud in his seventh chapter provides information that extends well beyond the walls of the talmudic academies. In his seventh chapter, he presents additional facets of the Jewish position in Muslim areas of the Iberian peninsula. Ibn Daud portrays the growing importance of a wealthy and powerful Jewish elite, well connected to the Muslim rulers and committed to utilizing its power and influence on behalf of the Jewish community at large. These Jewish courtiers promoted a wide range of Jewish interests, including religious and intellectual pursuits. This was a period of considerable uncertainty within Muslim ruling circles. On the one hand, political power was fragmenting internally, with smaller and less effective political units emerging; at the same time, the Christian push southward exerted increasing pressures on the Muslim ruling class. Out of this combination emerged augmented influence for the Jewish minority and its leaders.

In the face of the Christian threat, the Muslim rulers needed to mobilize their resources to the fullest, including the non-Muslim minority populations. These minority populations consisted essentially of Christians and Jews, the former utterly untrustworthy given the powerful Christian pressures being exerted from the north and the latter ostensibly trustworthy. Once again, Jews had no intrinsic stake in the outcome of the Muslim-Christian contest for control of Iberia. The issue for Jews was quality of treatment. It is possible that by this time Jews might actually have come to prefer Muslim to Christian rule. In any case, out of the complex circumstances of twelfth-century Spain emerged an ever stronger Spanish Jewry.

Overall, Jews clearly moved throughout the length and breadth of the vast Islamic world. Jewish population distribution by the days of Benjamin of Tudela and Abraham ibn Daud had changed considerably from what it had been at the close of late antiquity and the onset of the Middle Ages. The area in which this movement took place was essentially the same space where Jewish life had been centered from earliest antiquity. Jewish living and movement were concentrated in the broad region from Mesopotamia in the east through the Mediterranean Basin in the west, which had been the locus of Jewish settlement from time immemorial. Within this area of traditional Jewish habitation, Jews moved freely and often extensively. During the first half of the Middle Ages, when the bulk of this area fell under the unified rule of Islam, Jewish movement was a constant phenomenon, which resulted in the shifting fortunes of centers of Jewish population, with some expanding and some contracting.

Once again, we must ascertain the dynamic of this Jewish population movement. As was true for late antiquity, we know of no significant expulsions of Jews during the first half of the Middle Ages. Indeed, the pre-modern Muslim world had no tradition whatsoever of expelling Jews and no theological ruminations (such as became common in western Christendom) on the propriety of such expulsions. As noted, the Jews constituted an ancient population element throughout the Islamic world, were fully diversified economically, and were reasonably well integrated socially and culturally. The Jews were hardly a conspicuous element in the complex human tapestry of the Islamic world. In many areas of this Islamic world, for example Spain, invigorated western Christendom was beginning to exert serious military pressure, which transformed the Christians in society into potentially dangerous collaborators, heightened perceptions of the Jews as loyal allies, and resulted in positive overtures on the part of the Muslim rulers toward their Jewish subjects.

In general, the medieval Islamic authorities refrained from intrusion into the religious affairs of their minority populations, especially the religious affairs of the Christian and Jewish minorities. Serious proselytizing was rarely undertaken, and limitations imposed on Jewish religious practice were minimal. There is one rather bizarre exception to this generalization, an exception highlighted by Abraham ibn Daud. According to ibn Daud, the Almohade ruler of North Africa and parts of Muslim Spain instituted a policy of forced conversion, unique in the annals of medieval Islam. This purported policy of forced conversion resulted, according to ibn Daud, in the flight of Jews from the affected areas, with the relocation focused on—but by no means limited to—the expanding territories of Christian Spain. Ibn Daud's own family was purportedly part of this forced migration.[13] As we have seen, recent scholars have come to question the reality of this decree, especially as they have delved into the Islamic sources for the incident.

Anti-Jewish violence was hardly a significant element in Jewish experience in the medieval Muslim world. As a venerable and well-integrated element in the diversified population of the Islamic areas of the West, Jews rarely were the objects of majority attention and hatred. On occasion, Jewish magnates of the kind portrayed by ibn Daud could and did overstep their boundaries. Perhaps the most conspicuous of such courtiers was Samuel ibn Nagrela, originally of Cordova, depicted in rich and fascinating detail by ibn Daud. Ibn Nagrela was accomplished in multiple domains: He was a highly capable administrator, a successful general who led Muslim armies into battle, a traditional Jewish scholar, and a talented poet. As sometimes happens with such extraordinarily gifted individuals, Samuel lost his sense of proportion and especially his sense of the place of Jews in an Islamic society. His highhanded ways as vizier to the rulers of Granada triggered a violent reaction against his son and successor. Just as the Jews of Granada benefited hugely from Samuel's power, they suffered greatly from the popular backlash he inspired.[14] Again, however, this outburst was exceptional, and violence or the threat of violence did not play a significant role in Jewish relocations across the Islamic world.

Thus, the demographic changes reflected in Benjamin's itinerary, in Abraham ibn Daud's closing chapter of *Sefer ha-Kabbalah*, and in the obvious invigoration of North African and Spanish Jewish religious and cultural life were the result of volitional movement on the part of Jews seeking better circumstances. This volitional migration was sufficient to result in considerable evolution in the patterns of Jewish settlement from the Muslim conquest down through the twelfth century.

EIGHT

Medieval Northern Europe

Our focus on Jewish population movement puts us in a uniquely advantageous position to appreciate one of the most significant developments in Jewish history—a demographic turning point insufficiently recognized and appreciated, with enormous economic, social, political, and cultural implications for subsequent Jewish life. From the prehistory of Israel through the end of the first Christian millennium, Jews moved about extensively, but always within clearly defined boundaries. Throughout this lengthy period, Jews lived in the roughly rectangular space that begins with Mesopotamia in the east and proceeds through the Mediterranean Basin in the west. In this area, Jews constituted a small but well-established element in the general population. As control of this area evolved, new rulers encountered a well-ensconced Jewish population, diversified economically and integrated socially. Sketching out a status for the Jews was hardly a necessity for new ruling authorities. The framework of living for the Jewish minority was traditionally grounded and well known to all.

Even as a new religious and political force erupted out of the Arabian peninsula in the seventh and early eighth centuries, conquering most of the extensive area that Jews inhabited, little changed for these Jews who came under Islamic domination. Their circumstances and status were sufficiently well established and required no significant alteration. Jewish economic and social life continued comfortably along its well-worn tracks, and Jewish political and religious status was adapted to the theology of Islam without undue difficulty.

Toward the end of the first Christian millennium, Latin Christendom, the weakest of the three religio-political blocs in the West (the realm of Islam, eastern Christendom, and western Christendom), began a process of vitalization that was destined to transform it into the dominant Western power by the end of the Middle Ages and on into modernity. This vitalization was centered in northern Europe, which from time immemorial had constituted a backward hinterland to the Mediterranean south. After lagging behind for so long, northern Europe emerged as a robust and powerful area in all respects and eventually reached a position of leadership within Latin Christendom and on the world scene at large.[1]

This remarkable vitalization in general and the rise of northern Europe in particular were more radical than the changes associated with the rapid spread of Islam. The armies of Islam emerged precipitously out of the Arabian peninsula and conquered the established centers of Western civilization. In the process, the ruling elite was altered, but the geography of Western economy, military strength, and culture was not. The rise of northern Europe, on the other hand, transformed slowly but irrevocably the geography of the West. New territories all across the heretofore backward north—areas that became England, France, Holland, Germany, and Austria—emerged as centers of power and culture; previously minor towns—London, Paris, Amsterdam, Berlin, and Vienna—became the premier urban complexes of the late medieval and modern West.

The northern sector of Europe in the year 1000 did not house a Jewish population of any significance. This lagging area saw Jewish merchants crisscross it in order to purchase its products; prior to the year 1000, however, northern Europe offered no incentive for Jews to leave their homes in the more advanced areas of the Mediterranean Basin in order to pursue economic opportunities. As northern Europe surged forward, however, attractive opportunities emerged, and Jews gravitated northward to take advantage of these opportunities. A new Jewish population began to coalesce as an element on the northern European scene. Gradually, Jewish settlement in northern Europe expanded, and these Jews eventually came to dominate worldwide Jewish population in its entirety.[2]

The new Jewish settlers in northern Europe did not enjoy the traditional circumstances and status that characterized Jewish life in the older areas of Jewish settlement. Entirely new economic and social realities developed, and new status for the Jewish immigrants had to be articulated by the authorities of church and state. Since Jews were newcomers, and since newcomers are regularly resented by the indigenous populace, not surprisingly much of the new reality and new status was decidedly limited and limiting, inferior to the well-established reality and status enjoyed by Jews in their older areas of habitation. The newness of the Jews of the north stimulated innovative configurations of Jewish economic activity, altered popular imagery of Jews, created difficult social relations between the Jews and their non-Jewish neighbors, fostered altered Church stances toward Judaism and Jews, and fashioned new relationships between the political authorities and their Jewish clients.

For our purposes, it is important to note that this major alteration in patterns of Jewish settlement reflects nothing of the biblical predictions of divine punishment through forced wandering. There is no evidence of decrees of expulsion, of interference with Jewish material or spiritual circumstances, or of dangerous outbreaks of anti-Jewish violence in the older areas of Jewish habitation during the first few centuries of the invigoration of northern Europe. The adventurous Jews who relocated into the rapidly developing sectors of Latin Christendom, especially the areas of northern Europe, were drawn to these new locales by their attractiveness and promise. To be sure, settlers in new locales always elicit considerable opposition on the part of the indigenous population, and that opposition was strong, vocal, and sometimes violent in medieval northern Europe. Out of the complex relations among the Jewish immigrants, the evolving economy, the indigenous populace, the Church, and the ruling authorities, Jewish life in northern Europe took new and often problematic forms. Nonetheless, Jews voluntarily and in increasing numbers gravitated toward rapidly maturing western Christendom, especially its northern tier, eventuating in one of the most influential and underappreciated population relocations in Jewish history.

The vitalization of Latin Christendom early on took an aggressive turn. Perceiving the European lands conquered centuries earlier by the Muslims as rightfully Christian, the warrior class of Christian Europe, especially the warriors of the north, embarked at an early point in the vitalization process on a protracted effort to dislodge the Muslim conquerors and reclaim territories in continental Europe for Christendom. The major spheres of action in this effort were the two large Mediterranean peninsulas—the Iberian and the Italian. In both cases, there were almost immediate victories and achievement. The Muslims and the Byzantines as well were fairly quickly driven off the Italian peninsula. There were early important victories on the Iberian peninsula also, although the extent of Muslim control of Spain meant that the effort to reconquer the entire peninsula would require a number of centuries.[3]

Christian successes on the Iberian peninsula set the backdrop for the first stage in the expansion of the Jewish population of western Christendom. This early expansion involved Jewish decisions to stay put, rather than to move, which is our central focus. As Christian forces slowly reconquered the towns of Iberia, Jews, who had been long established in these towns and had lived comfortably under Islamic rule, faced a painful decision. Should they follow their Muslim overlords southward and thus remain in a religio-political ambience they knew well and from which they had benefited considerably? Alternatively, should they stay put and serve the new masters of their towns, the conquering Christian kings, and thus court the dangers of an unknown new order? This was of course not an abstract question; it was posed dramatically and inescapably by the accelerating change of hegemony in the towns of the peninsula.

The decision-making of these Jews was facilitated by the stance of the conquering Christian rulers. Determined to maintain the level of economic activity and urban stability in the conquered areas, the conquering Christian authorities sought to persuade the Jews of these newly Christian towns to remain in place and to contribute to the maintenance of economic and urban life. A number of charters issued by the conquering Christian kings to Jews have survived and are illuminating.

King Alfonso I of Aragon, for example, issued in 1115 an early charter to the Jews of Tudela, which was subsequently to serve as the home of the Jewish traveler Benjamin, whom we have already met. This charter took full note of the disruptions occasioned by warfare. The king was aware that many of the Jews of Tudela had fled in the face of the hostilities. He "commanded by his grace that all those who had left return to Tudela to live, with all their possessions and their goods." In this relatively brief charter, King Alfonso ordered that the homes of these Jews be inviolable and that no one quarter either Christians or Moors in them. Jewish taxes were to be paid in one term each year, and Jews were exempted from onerous tolls and customs. All this was clearly intended to persuade the Jews formerly resident in Tudela to return to the town and lend their support to the new order.[4]

While the addition of Jews to western Christendom through Christian conquest was of considerable significance, more important to the development of Jewish life in Christian Europe and more germane to our focus on Jewish wanderings was the decision of Jews to move from Muslim territories into Christian southern Europe and, even more radically and consequentially, from Mediterranean lands both Muslim and Christian into areas of the north previously inhabited by only minuscule numbers of Jews. This latter and more significant process has left very little evidence of its unfolding. There are a number of later versions of the claim that Charlemagne transferred a prominent Italian Jewish family to the Rhineland town of Mainz. This claim cannot be taken as historical reality, but it does reflect subsequent northern European Jewish awareness of southern European roots and of the role of the political authorities in the early settling of northern European Jews.

What was it that attracted Jews who had seemingly lived comfortably in the Mediterranean ambience for well over a millennium to leave their prior habitations and make the trek northward into unknown territories and circumstances? While we are not privy to the private thoughts of the Jews migrating into northern Europe, the overwhelming sense is that they were attracted by the economic opportunities available there and the overall dynamism of the rapidly developing young society. As was true for the areas of the Iberian peninsula conquered by the Christian kings, so too in northern Europe there was more than simply Jewish perception of opportunity. In this new area as well, the ruling authorities, keenly aware of deficiencies of human resources in their rapidly developing domains, were anxious to secure the talents of new settlers who would bring with them advanced economic and urban skills. That these new settlers happened in some instances to be Jews seems to have been beside the point to these rulers.

The limited sources available for reconstructing the earliest stage of Jewish migration into northern Europe during the eleventh century point to Jewish concentration in trade. The basic developments in northern European infrastructure, such as the cutting down of forests, the expansion of arable lands, and the enhanced food supply, all made possible the growth of trade. This in turn promoted the development of urban areas as centers for this burgeoning commerce. The Jewish concentration in business in northern Europe during the earliest period of vitalization was a reflection of economic needs that Jews and their governmental sponsors felt were pressing and could be usefully met by the new Jewish settlers.

Concentration in business on the part of the Jews attracted northward is reflected in the slim source materials available for the earliest stage of Jewish life in northern Europe, materials that lack the breadth and richness of the Cairo Genizah data. Especially useful for reconstructing the earliest period in the evolution of northern European Jewry is a unique combination of two sources that attest to the foundation of a new Jewish community in Speyer in 1084. One of these sources is a Jewish narrative depiction of the events of 1084; the second is the charter of invitation extended by Bishop Rudiger of Speyer to the Jews he had invited to settle in his town.[5] With respect to Jewish business activities, the bishop's charter of invitation stipulates that the newcomers have been accorded "the free right of exchanging gold and silver and of buying and selling everything they use—both within their residential area and, outside it, beyond the gate down to the wharf and on the wharf itself. I have given them the same right throughout the entire city." The sense conveyed by this permission is that the Jews settling in Speyer were predominantly—although not necessarily exclusively—merchants.

In the opening to his charter, Bishop Rudiger clarifies his thinking about the new Jewish settlers and explains his decision to invite them.

> When I wished to make a city out of the village of Speyer, I Rudiger, surnamed Huozmann, bishop of Speyer, thought that the glory of our town would be augmented a thousandfold if I were to bring Jews. . . .

Toward the end of the charter, Bishop Rudiger explains that he has chosen to facilitate Jewish settlement in Speyer through the generous terms he has stipulated in his charter.

> In short, in order to achieve the height of kindness, I have granted them a legal status more generous than any that the Jewish people have in any city of the German kingdom.

Valuing Jews for the economic contribution they might make and attracting them through generous settlement terms were standard for northern European rulers during the early centuries of vitalization. These perceptions and policies were critical to Jewish settlement in northern Europe during the initial period of vitalization and remained in place for some time. Many rulers perceived in Jewish settlers a valuable addition to the economy of their realms. Jewish immigration was encouraged by promises of support of all kinds, including guarantees of physical safety and business backing. Thus, the movement of Jews into northern Europe was fostered by the combination of Jewish perceptions of economic opportunity and societal dynamism on the one hand and the support of the ruling class on the other.

The evidence from Speyer is the fullest that has survived for governmental support of Jewish relocation into northern Europe. However, there are brief further noteworthy items that buttress the fuller evidence from Speyer. One comes from a Hebrew narrative that focuses on the exploits of a Jewish magnate of the early eleventh century. Faced with a most unusual demand for baptism of Jews purportedly initiated by the king of France, this Jewish magnate stepped forward, challenged the right of his overlord to enact such a radical edict, and insisted on traveling to Rome in order to clarify the issue at the papal court. The trip to Rome was undertaken, was purportedly successful, and elicited a formal papal bull that prohibited anti-Jewish violence and coerced baptism.

Subsequent episodes in the life of the Jewish magnate-hero are then briefly depicted by the Jewish author. "He returned to his family in Lotharingia and lived there for twelve years. Eventually, Baldwin, Count of Flanders, sent an invitation that the [Jewish] magnate come to him and bring with him thirty

Jews—known to and beloved by him [the Jewish magnate]—to be settled in his [Baldwin's] domain. He [the Jewish magnate] arose and went to him [Baldwin], and they received him with great honor."[6] Although full details are lacking, the process of invitation to Flanders corresponds nicely to what we have seen in the fuller material for the establishment of a Jewish community in Speyer.

Rulers such as the count of Flanders, the bishop of Speyer, and obviously many others as well encouraged Jewish settlement in their domains. They were surely motivated by desire for economic improvement of their realms. They may well have sensed that Jews were a particularly mobile element in society, alert to the advantages of relocation. The movement of the Jews into northern Europe during the first period of its vitalization thus seems to have resulted from a combination of perceived economic opportunity and valuable support extended by the ruling elite. This Jewish relocation into the north shows no evidence of forced Jewish movement of the kind predicted in the Hebrew Bible and claimed in traditional Jewish and Christian thinking and in modern post-theistic thinking as well.

During the course of the twelfth century, a new economic activity was opened up for the Jews of northern Europe. This new economic activity was no longer the result of the early immaturity of northern European society; by the twelfth century, the northern European economy had matured considerably. Rather, the new economic option for Jews was the result of an increasingly powerful Roman Church, which was one of the major features of the vitalization of western Christendom. As the Church became better organized and exercised increasing influence over everyday Christian life, it began to press vigorously for full observance of proper Christian behavior and thought, by both the clergy and the laity. Some of these campaigns were more or less doomed to failure, for example the campaign against prostitution. However, the vigorous campaign launched against the sin of Christian usury, the giving or taking of interest on loans between Christians, was reasonable and in considerable measure was successful.

The Church attack on Christian usury coincided with a marked increase in economic activity across northern Europe, as governmental, ecclesiastical, and private projects of all kinds necessitated a flow of capital that required banking and lending. To the extent that the Church achieved success in its anti-usury campaign, it was in fact opening an entirely new economic specialization for the northern European Jews, who were not bound by the ecclesiastical prohibition of Christians taking interest from or paying interest to another Christian. Evidence of moneylending as increasingly important to Jewish economic success abounds in both Christian and Jewish sources. The new economic specialization provided augmented economic opportunities for Jews already ensconced in the north and for those considering relocation.

Even more than for trade, governmental support for Jewish moneylending could be enormously helpful. It was to be sure possible to carry on Jewish lending without direct governmental involvement. This could be achieved through the depositing of items worth more than the principal of the loan and the anticipated interest as security against default. In this way, borrowers who failed to pay would not leave the lenders empty-handed. However, such pawnbroking was tedious and onerous; more important, this style of moneylending was generally limited to small loans. Items for deposit that would cover large loans were limited.[7]

To the extent that governments were willing to involve themselves in support of Jewish moneylending, loans for far larger sums could be disbursed. These loans would be secured through the promise of governmental enforcement of the obligation. In this way, very large sums could be lent, often with land used as collateral. Governmental promise of enforcement made utilization of land as collateral possible. For a period of time in the second half of the twelfth century and the first half of the thirteenth century, this system of governmental enforcement of Jewish loans worked to the advantage of both Jews and their overlords. Jews were able to lend large sums, and a cadre of wealthy Jewish bankers emerged. The authorities were well informed as to Jewish resources and were thus able to tax Jewish profits heavily. It was by no means gratuitous of certain churchmen to suggest that there was actually a Jewish-Christian partnership in the moneylending business. The new specialization in moneylending provided a lucrative new outlet for Jewish economic activity and reinforced the sense of Jewish utility within the ruling class. Again, expansion of the young Jewish population of northern Europe was fostered by the combination of economic opportunity and governmental support.

The vitalization of northern Europe did not take place evenly all across the north. The changes first manifested themselves in the northwestern sectors of the continent, in the territories that eventually coalesced into the kingdoms of England and France. The rapid vitalization of these two areas reflects the effectiveness with which broad demographic and economic improvements took place in these territories. The central sectors of northern Europe developed more slowly, and northeastern Europe lagged yet further behind. The rulers of these lagging areas were of course fully aware of the changes taking place to their west, and they aspired to fostering parallel improvements in their domains.

As we have seen, one of the key development techniques utilized by the rulers of the more successful sectors of northern Europe was invitation to and support of new settlers who could bring with them the business and urban expertise of the more advanced Mediterranean south. This development technique resulted in the support for the Jewish movement into northern Europe that we have tracked. Eventually, the rulers of north-central and northeastern Europe emulated their more westerly brethren and reached out to the Jews of northwestern Europe with similar invitations and support.

In 1244, Duke Frederick of Austria extended a charter of invitation to Jews who would settle in his diverse domains.[8] Comparison of this charter with the invitation extended to the Mainz Jews settling in Speyer offers some striking similarities and some equally striking differences. Both Bishop Rudiger and Duke Frederick wished to attract Jews and set out to achieve this objective by offering potential Jewish settlers meaningful inducements. The tone of both documents is warmly supportive of Jewish settlement. The major differences flow from the changes in Jewish economic activity and Jewish status over the century and a half that elapsed between 1084 and 1244. Close examination of the two documents allows us to identify key issues common to both, especially guarantees of Jewish physical security, judicial independence, and support for Jewish business. To be sure, these issues are dealt with in different ways, which reflect changes in general northern European life and in northern European Jewish life in particular.

Both charters provide Jews with physical security. In the earlier document, Bishop Rudiger extended this physical security by creating for the Jews a separate and walled-in Jewish neighborhood, in which they would feel safe. By 1244, feudal notions of the Jews as clients of rulers, in effect as "belonging" to these rulers, had fully crystallized. This meant that mistreatment of Jews would constitute an assault on the "property" of the ruler with penalties ranging in severity from fines to death, imposed by the rulers to whom the Jews belonged. While there was surely a demeaning element in this arrangement, it at the same time provided Jews with considerable security. Harming a Jew was considered a serious affront to the ruling authority and would be costly. The same was to be true for assaults on Jewish communal property, such as synagogues and cemeteries.[9]

In both documents, there was also concern for protecting Jews from a range of potentially hostile Christian courts. In effect, Jews were to appear only before their own courts or—if the case required a higher judicial venue—before the court of the reigning authority. No other court was to exercise jurisdiction over the Jews. In addition, the 1244 document reflects the maturation of the Jewish court system over the intervening century and a half. The specifications for the independent Jewish court system in 1244 are considerably more detailed. In both cases, however, the overarching objective is to assert the independence of the Jewish courts and the ultimate authority of the ruler's court.[10] In addition, the 1244 document introduced some judicial protections beyond court venue. Interesting is the opening stipulation that "no Christian shall be admitted as a witness against a Jew unless there is a Jewish witness along with the Christian."[11] This is a rather striking piece of judicial protection.

In both charters, there is an obvious intention to support Jewish business, but the business to be supported evolved markedly from 1084 to 1244. By 1244, the twelfth-century Church assault on Christian usury had fostered especially in northern Europe a Jewish specialization in moneylending. While that specialization had eventually developed in a highly sophisticated form in England and France, with the government recording and enforcing Jewish loans, in north-central and northeastern Europe the governmental sophistication for such support was lacking. Thus, the Jewish lending reflected in the 1244 document was of the decidedly primitive variety, with Jewish loans insured through the depositing of pledges equal or greater in value than the principal of the loan and the anticipated interest.

In the charter of 1244, there is but one reference to sophisticated moneylending involving documentation and its enforcement by the authorities. This stipulation comes late in the document and is relatively curt: "If a Jew has lent money to a magnate of the country on his possessions or on a note and proves this by a document, we will assign the pledged possession to the Jew and defend them [the possessions] for him [the Jew] against violence."[12] Given the highly sophisticated system for supporting Jewish lending in late-twelfth- and early-thirteenth-century England and northern France, including full-blown bureaucratic offices and mechanisms for enrolling and enforcing Jewish loans, the primitive quality of this lone stipulation is patent.

Protecting Jewish lending that involved the depositing of moveable goods as pledges is the dominant theme in the 1244 charter. There are more clauses devoted to such protection in the charter than to any other issue.[13] While deposition of pledges seems inherently simple, there are in fact serious potential complications. For example, there could be disagreement about the amount of the loan against which the pledge had been deposited or over whether the loan had been repaid and the pledge returned. Additionally, the Christian could claim that he had not in fact deposited the pledge, but that it had been taken from him by theft and then deposited. Moreover, Jews might lose pledges through theft or fire. In all these contentious situations, the duke promises to favor the Jewish claimant, which constituted considerable support for Jewish business. By 1244, the Church had introduced numerous limitations on Jewish moneylending, but of these the only one cited in the document involves limitation of the rate of interest that Jews might charge.[14] Overall, the support for Jewish moneylending of the pawnbroking variety is the dominant theme in the charter, and Duke Frederick extended potent support for this dominant Jewish business activity.

Thus the thirteenth century saw a second phase in the voluntary movement of Jews, this time across northern Europe. The Jews of northwestern

Europe—growing in numbers, restricted in economic outlets, and encountering increasing limitation and resistance on numerous fronts—were confronted with new opportunities in the more slowly developing sectors of northern Europe. In effect, the same dynamic that had earlier brought Jews to northern Europe was repeated. Jews perceived new economic opportunities that were reinforced by governmental support. Once again, Jews responded positively to the combination and relocated voluntarily. Slowly, the Jewish population of northern Europe, concentrated increasingly in the central and especially eastern sectors of northern Europe, began to move toward parity with the far older Jewish population of the Islamic sphere; eventually, it exceeded markedly this older Jewish population and became the largest center of Jewish habitation in the world.

The appeal of the burgeoning northern European economy was real; the inducements offered by the northern European authorities were meaningful; and Jews relocated voluntarily into northern Europe. The obstacles that lay in the way of the Jewish immigrants were, however, considerable. The first obstacle was the very newness of this area to Jewish settlement. In the traditional areas of Jewish settlement, Jews were an accepted part of the environment—they were perceived as residents of Mesopotamia and the Mediterranean Basin from time immemorial. In northern Europe, in contrast, they were obvious newcomers, and newcomers are almost never welcome in human societies. The newness of the Jews in northern Europe was exacerbated by a second feature of this developing area. In contradistinction to the Muslim sphere and its tapestry of racially, ethnically, and religiously diverse humanity, northern Europe was a monolithic environment. In multiple ways, especially religiously, the population was highly homogeneous, which made the Jewish newcomers yet more obvious in their distinctiveness.

With respect to the Jewish immigrants, religious identity and ethnic identity coalesced. Northern European Christians might be ethnically French, English, German, and more; Jews by virtue of their Jewishness were a clearly distinct religious group that was at the same time a clearly distinct ethnic community as well. In addition, the newly settling Jews were perceived as different culturally, with their own language for worship and religious study; as a highly urbanized group; and as a community deeply committed to business and subsequently banking. Thus, Jews were identifiably different from many perspectives. Their initial newness and Jewishness were reinforced in multiple ways, enhancing the sense of their distinctiveness.

As these Jews made their way into northern Europe, they were perceived as quintessentially "other." Their multifaceted distinctiveness exposed them from the outset to a profound perception of their otherness and thus to animosity, to limitation, and to danger. Like so much else in northern European Jewish life, the subsequent growth and domination of this Jewry has transformed its unique features into the paradigm for all of post-70 Jewish life. As we have seen, Jewish life in the traditional areas of Jewish settlement does not exhibit this majority perception of radical otherness. The temptation to transpose the special characteristics of northern European Jewish life into the standard for all Jewish experience must be steadfastly resisted.

The most important manifestations of resistance to Jewish newness and otherness across northern Europe came from the populace at large. People of all periods and places are negative toward newcomers, and the reactions of the indigenous population of northern Europe were standard. There was resistance to the Jewish settlers as new and totally distinct from the majority and occasional manifestations of local violence. The founding of a Jewish community in Speyer in 1084 was related in part to such local violence. As the Jewish chronicler of the new Speyer settlement indicated, the Jewish settlers were originally Mainz Jews, whose lives had been roiled.

> All the Jews' quarter and their street were burned, and we were in great fear of the burghers. At the same time, Meir Cohen came from Worms, bearing a copy of *Torat Cohanim.* The burghers thought it was silver or gold and slew him.[15]

Clearly, all of Mainz Jewry did not depart. However, some Mainz Jews were prepared to respond positively to the invitation of Bishop Rudiger of Speyer.

The papal call to the crusade in 1095 intensified the perception of Jews as outsiders and transformed for some northern European Christians the sense of Jews from outsiders to enemies. The slogan under which rogue crusaders assaulted Rhineland Jews is portrayed in the oldest of the extant Hebrew narratives of the 1096 violence in the following terms:

> They said to one another: "Behold we travel to a distant land to do battle with the kings of that land. We take our lives in our hands in order to kill and to subjugate all those kingdoms that do not believe in the Crucified. How much more so [should we kill and subjugate] the Jews, who killed and crucified him." They taunted us from every direction. They took counsel, ordering that either we turn to their abominable faith or they would destroy us from infant to suckling.[16]

This is a striking report on the grounding of the anti-Jewish violence, which is corroborated in the later Hebrew narratives and in some of the Latin narratives as well. The perception palpable here is that the Christian crusading warriors have set forth on an all-out war against the non-Christian world. This all-out war was intended to eventuate in total Christian victory. This perception of the crusading enterprise was very far removed from that enunciated by Pope Urban II and pursued by the mainstream crusaders, which did not include obliteration of all non-Christians and made no mention of Jews whatsoever.

Given the sense of a total battle against the non-Christian world, the Jews are projected as occupying a unique position in that non-Christian world. The other non-Christian enemies—which obviously means the Muslims—are guilty of not believing in "the Crucified"; the Jews are projected as more heinous in that they were responsible for making Jesus "the Crucified." To this initial *a fortiori* argument that Jews are more reprehensible than Muslims is added yet another *a fortiori* argument, namely that Jews are right here at home and thus far easier to engage than the far-off Muslims.

All this runs counter to formal and regularly reiterated Church doctrine. However, the emotional appeal of this slogan was profound in certain northern European circles. Jews were projected as the immediately adjacent enemies of Christianity who were at the same time the most heinous enemies of Christianity. These intensified anti-Jewish perceptions did not surface among the crusading militias that eventually succeeded in conquering Jerusalem in 1099 and were subsequently repudiated vigorously by Church leaders, especially by leaders of the later crusades. However, they once again reflect the special circumstances of Jews as newcomers and interlopers in the otherwise Christian society of northern Europe.[17]

During the twelfth century, the Church assault on Christian usury created yet another grounding for anti-Jewish sentiment across northern Europe, where the Jewish specialization in moneylending was most pronounced. Moneylending—like newcomers in society—has never been popular. In northern Europe, where the lenders were newcomers, religious dissidents, and ethnically other to boot, the animosities aroused by Jewish moneylending was intense. Jewish moneylending became perceived in many quarters as more than simply obnoxious; it was seen as a way in which Jews vented their hostility against the Christian society that hosted them and sought to inflict harm upon that Christian society. Anti-usury sentiment was fanned by Church opposition to aspects of Jewish moneylending that it saw as harmful to its Christian constituency, especially to the poor and vulnerable in Christian society. Again, the Church repudiated anti-Jewish violence grounded in opposition to Jewish usury, but its concerns over Jewish lending stimulated deeply negative feeling that on occasion erupted into violence.

As we proceed through the twelfth century, a period during which the pace of change in western Christendom accelerated and thus a period of enhanced sense of dislocation as well, many of the inhabitants of Christian Europe—again especially its northern sectors—felt threatened and identified major sources of danger within society. As noted by R. I. Moore, a series of problematic groups were highlighted—heretics, lepers, and homosexuals among others. Within this cluster of groups perceived as dangerous, the Jews were highly conspicuous, in fact arguably the most prominent outsider group of all.[18]

This sense of the Jews as threatening and dangerous drew enormous strength from both past and present. As we have seen in the rogue crusading slogan, recollections of the Jewish role in the Crucifixion were prominent, transforming Jews into a group that did harm in the past to Jesus and does harm in the present to Jesus' followers. Given the growing visibility of Jews in the always unpopular business of moneylending, the sense of past Jewish enmity and harmfulness was much reinforced by perceptions of contemporary Jews as steeped in hostility and committed to wreaking havoc on their Christian neighbors.

This sense of historic and contemporary Jewish enmity eventuated in the emergence of a series of damning popular images—Jews as murderers of Christians, especially Christian youngsters; Jews as crucifiers of Christians, again especially Christian youngsters; Jews as committed to the utilization of Christian blood for their religious ritual; Jews as poisoners of wells; Jews as desecrators of the sacred host. In effect, the early popular resistance to Jewish settlement in northern Europe morphed into perceptions of Jewish malevolence that would carry over into modernity and cause untold misery for modern Jews.[19] Popular resistance to and animosity toward the new Jewish settlers constituted a major impediment to successful Jewish integration into western Christendom.

The Church played a major role in the maturation of western Christendom during the second half of the Middle Ages, and its impact on Jewish life was extensive and complex. There has been a tendency in modern history writing to depict the medieval Church negatively, which is an offshoot of the emergence of the modern historical enterprise out of the Enlightenment, with its negativity toward religion in general and the medieval Church in particular. This tendency has been fully absorbed by historians of the Jews, who have regularly identified the Church as the villainous element on the medieval scene.[20] In fact, the realities were far more complex. The medieval Church did great harm to the Jews in some ways and was powerfully supportive and protective in other ways.

By time that Jews began to make their way into medieval northern Europe, the Church had adumbrated a complex doctrine concerning the place of Jews in Christian society, a doctrine that was both protective and limiting. At the same time, many general ecclesiastical policies and programs that had nothing to do with Jews ended up affecting medieval Jews profoundly. As a result of both the specific policies on Jews and their place in Christian society and the more general programs and policies that affected Jews indirectly, the medieval Church played a major role in European Jewish life in general and in the evolution of the young Jewish community of northern Europe in particular.

We have already seen two instances of innovative Church programs that were formulated with no thought of Jews and no intention of affecting them, but that exercised enormous impact on medieval Jewish life. The more significant was the Church assault on Christian usury, set in motion with no concern for Jews whatsoever. In the event, however, the new ecclesiastical initiative opened an innovative, important, and problematic channel for Jewish economic activity. The impact of this ecclesiastical initiative on northern European Jewry was immense—for both good and ill. It created new options for Jewish economic success and economic contribution to society in general and to the ruling class in particular. At the same time, it reinforced markedly the negative popular sentiment toward the new Jewish settlers. We have also noted the innovative papal call to crusading, which was clearly issued with no implications announced or even intended for Jews, but which served to fan anti-Jewish animosities, in sectors of northern Europe at least. These ripple effects were of great significance to the development of Jewish life in medieval western Christendom.

In a more focused manner, the medieval Church was heir to a rich tradition of doctrine and policy concerning Jews and their place in Christian society. This policy was balanced, insisting on safety and security for Jews, on limitations that would preclude Jewish harmfulness to Christians and Christian society, and on the obligation to preach peacefully, reasonably, and sympathetically the message of Christianity to Jews and in this way to win them over to the true faith. Given the multifaceted dimensions of this policy, the impact of the Church on medieval Jewish life in western Christendom cannot be distilled simplistically into either the positive or the negative. The elements in Church policy were complex, and the impact of this policy was necessarily complex as well.

For a variety of reasons, the Church Fathers adumbrated a policy of protection for Jews in Christian society. This policy was regularly repeated all through the Middle Ages. We have noted the strange incident in early-eleventh-century northern France of an attempt at forced conversion and the intervention of a major Jewish leader, who insisted that forced conversion was illegitimate. This wealthy and powerful Jew supposedly demanded and received permission to travel to Rome to make his case at the papal court. The meeting with the pope was purportedly successful. The Jew purportedly spelled out what he perceived to be Church policy; the pope is portrayed as considering the matter carefully and eventually agreeing with the Jew's understanding of Church policy. The pope then supposedly composed a bull that announced officially this clarified Church policy. This policy stipulated "that no Christian is permitted to kill a Jew for any reason, nor to injure him, nor to take his property, nor to force him to leave his faith."[21]

The Hebrew narrative is rich in folkloristic elements and does not inspire great confidence. However, there is striking congruity between this purported early-eleventh-century papal stance and the subsequent *Constitutio pro Judeis*, proclaimed by many popes from the twelfth century on. The *Constitutio* assures Jewish physical and spiritual safety in the following terms: "We decree that no Christian shall use violence to force them to be baptized, so long as they are unwilling and refuse. . . . Moreover, without the judgment of the authority of the land no Christian shall presume to kill or wound any of them or rob them of their money or change the good customs that they have thus far enjoyed in the place where they live."[22] The stipulations of this well-documented papal bull make the Hebrew narrative somewhat less implausible, since the core of the Hebrew account corresponds nicely to Church teachings previously known from late antiquity and subsequently proclaimed all through the Middle Ages.

This commitment to Jewish safety was scrupulously maintained throughout the Middle Ages, in the face of outbreaks of popular violence, some of which were touched off by Church initiatives. The call to the First Crusade, which surely included no reference whatsoever to Jews, was interpreted by some marginal crusaders as justifying attacks on Jews. These rogue crusaders offered their Jewish victims the alternatives of baptism or death. During the course of the First Crusade, this strange byproduct of the call to arms against the Muslims holding the sacred sites of Christianity in the Holy Land elicited no formal Church attention, although a number of Rhineland bishops made every effort to protect the endangered Jews.

Early in the preparations for the Second Crusade, anti-Jewish agitation was once again manifest in the Rhineland, which had been the scene of the serious assaults fifty years earlier. As a result, the key spiritual leader of the Second Crusade, Bernard of Clairvaux, addressed the issue forcefully and unambiguously. While his earliest letters urging the warriors of western Christendom to take up the cross lacked any reference to Jews, once alerted to the danger Bernard added an important warning in his later letters. He announced in no uncertain terms that Jews played no role in the crusade and that anti-Jewish violence was utterly illegitimate. When rumors of anti-Jewish violence continued to circulate, despite the position he had proclaimed, Bernard made his way directly to the affected area in order to intervene personally and obviate any damage.[23]

We have also noted the spate of anti-Jewish allegations that were sounded across northern Europe, beginning during the twelfth century and proliferating during the subsequent two centuries. The leadership of the Church publicly denied most of these allegations and went to considerable lengths to dissuade the Christian faithful from accepting them. This was especially the case with the claim that surfaced in the 1230s that Jewish religious practice required the utilization of Christian blood. Pope Innocent IV in 1247 addressed a lengthy papal missive to the archbishops and bishops of Germany, in which he reported the appearance of the new slander and asserted that it was thoroughly unfounded. According to Innocent IV, the notion that Jews would use Christian blood for the purpose of their ritual is unthinkable, given Jewish faithfulness to the laws of the Hebrew Bible, which prohibit utilization of blood of any kind.[24] Shortly thereafter, Innocent IV reissued the *Constitutio pro Judeis*, with an important new protection: "Nor shall anyone accuse them of using human blood in their religious rites, since in the Old Testament they are instructed not to use blood of any kind, let alone human blood. But since at Fulda and in several other places many Jews were killed because of such a suspicion, we by the authority of these letters strictly forbid the recurrence of such a thing in the future."[25] All through the subsequent medieval centuries and into modernity, the Church maintained its opposition to this and other slanders, although the success of these denunciations was limited.

The Church's commitment to Jewish safety was genuine. At the same time, it was also committed to ensuring that the Jews resident in Christian society inflict no harm upon that society. The basic form of such harm was Jewish religious influence exerted on Christian neighbors. Precisely because Christians and Jews shared a common sacred literature and core religious values, the potential for Jewish religious influence was deemed significant from antiquity onward. The first concern in this regard was to ensure that Jews not occupy positions of power over Christian peers, since power inevitably confers the potential for influence.

In medieval Christian Europe, there was striking progression from precluding Jewish religious influence by prohibiting Jews from positions of power to limiting Christian-Jewish contact altogether. The most significant step in this new direction was the stipulation in the Fourth Lateran Council of 1215 that Jews be forced to wear some kind of distinguishing garb that would immediately alert others around them to the fact they were Jews.

> Whereas in certain provinces of the Church the difference in their clothes sets the Jews and Saracens apart from the Christians, in certain other lands there has arisen such confusion that no differences are noticeable. Thus it sometimes happens that by mistake Christians have intercourse with Jewish or Saracen women and Jews or Saracens with Christian women. Therefore, lest these people, under the cover of an error, find an excuse for the grave sin of such intercourse, we decree that these people [Jews and Saracens] of either sex and in all Christian lands and at all times shall easily be distinguishable from the rest of the population by the quality of their clothes.[26]

This 1215 innovation was fated for a very long history in Christian Europe. Jews fought the imposition of distinguishing garb on the grounds that it exposed them to constant danger of assault, and occasionally some Jews were able to secure special dispensations freeing them from the obligation. However, while the danger of physical violence was real, there was in fact a broader and more pervasive harm associated with the imposition of distinguishing garb. Such distinctiveness always implies inferiority as well, and so it was on the medieval scene. The distinguishing garb, in the form of badges or hats or whatever, signified clearly to the Jews and their Christian contemporaries Jewish inferiority.

There were yet further leaps in the interpretation of Jewish harmfulness. The original understanding of Jewish harmfulness focused on the sphere of religious influence. Ironically, with the Church crackdown on Christian usury and the resultant gravitation of Jews to moneylending, Church leadership became increasingly concerned with the harmful impact of Jewish moneylending on Christians and Christian society. Thus Jewish usury became in the eyes of the Church a new and different form of Jewish harmfulness. Church leaders agitated for a number of reforms relative to Jewish moneylending, all intended to lighten the burden of Christian indebtedness to Jews.

The most well known stipulation regarding Jewish moneylending was enacted in the same Fourth Lateran Council that decreed distinguishing Jewish garb.

> The more the Christian religion refrain from the exaction of usury [a reference to the successful Church campaign against Christian usury], the more the Jewish perfidy becomes used to this practice, so that in a short time the Jews exhaust the financial strength of the Christians. Therefore, in our desire to protect the Christians in this matter, that they should not be excessively oppressed by the Jews, we order by a decree of this synod that, when in the future a Jew under any pretext exact heavy and immoderate usury from a Christian, all relationship with Christians shall therefore be denied him [the Jew] until he shall have made sufficient amends for his exorbitant exactions.[27]

Ecclesiastical disquiet over Jewish moneylending eventually played a role of significance in the loss of support of their Jews on the part of key secular authorities in the westerly sectors of northern Europe.

During the middle decades of the thirteenth century, new concern with Jewish harmfulness emerged. A convert from Judaism to Christianity claimed that rabbinic literature, which was key to Jewish religious identity, blasphemed Christianity, taught hatred of Christians, and should not be tolerated in Christian society. A trial was convened in Paris; the Talmud was examined and found guilty; large quantities of Talmud manuscripts were publicly burned. A few years later, Pope Innocent IV moderated the anti-Talmud policy of the Church. The Jews were to be allowed to have and use their Talmud, albeit with offensive passages removed.[28]

Thus the stance of the Church was anything but simple and straightforward, and its impact on the burgeoning Jewish population of Latin Christendom was complex. The medieval Church remained true to the policy first established by the Church Fathers that stipulated the Jewish right to a safe and secure existence in Christian society. This policy was regularly reiterated, and—more importantly—it was insisted upon in practice, with major churchmen stepping forward to protect Jews from danger. At the same time, the Church was ever alert to damage that Jews might inflict upon their Christian hosts and was equally zealous in protecting Christians and Christian society against such damage. In the process, the Church efforts served to curtail aspects of Jewish life and to exacerbate the negative sentiment against the Jewish newcomers in Christian Europe.

Ultimately, the key to success or failure in Jewish settlement rested with the temporal authorities of northern Europe. The feudal structure of medieval Christian Europe meant that all groupings in society were related in one way or another to their feudal overlords. However, by and large these relationships were very much constrained by well-established custom. For the Jewish newcomers, such custom did not exist, allowing maximum flexibility for the temporal authorities of northern Europe in structuring the relationship between themselves and the Jews. The lack of traditional norms in governmental treatment of Jews and the deep dependence of the new Jewish settlers on the political authorities for their physical security and often for their business success made the relationship between the ruling class and the Jews of northern Europe especially malleable and especially susceptible to manipulation by the stronger element in the dyad—the northern European rulers.

In simplest terms, the temporal authorities supported their Jewish dependents in a fundamental quid pro quo. The rulers would provide safety and business backing, in return for which the Jews would through their business enrich the general economy—recall Bishop Rudiger's sense of Jewish immigrants improving the business environment of Speyer—or through tax contributions to the ruler's coffers. This simplistic model, however, does not do justice to the complex realities of the medieval scene. In supporting and benefiting from their Jewish dependents, the temporal authorities had to be constantly sensitive to the policies and demands of the Church and to the reactions of the Christian populace. Negotiating the interactions of Jewish needs, Jewish contributions, Church demands, and popular opposition involved convoluted reckonings, and the result was complex and shifting policies on the part of the rulers of medieval northern Europe.

From the Jewish perspective, the key element in the relationship with the authorities was physical safety. By and large, this was relatively uncomplicated for the temporal rulers. In this respect, the policies of the rulers and the Church dovetailed perfectly, as both were committed to ensuring stability in society in general and Jewish physical security in particular. While medieval Europe is often perceived as the scene of constant persecution of its Jewish inhabitants, such was not in fact the case, at least through the period of the eleventh through thirteenth centuries, upon which we are for the moment focused. Crusade-related violence is often adduced as the index of consistent anti-Jewish violence. However, the outbreaks of crusade-related anti-Jewish violence were, despite their great drama, extremely limited, thanks to the generally strong and energetic Church and governmental opposition to crusade-related and all other forms of anti-Jewish violence.[29]

By and large, the rulers of northern Europe during these three centuries were likewise effective in their support of Jewish business activities, although here the story becomes somewhat more complicated. Presiding over the economic expansion that formed the foundation of the overall vitalization of northern Europe, the rulers of the north sought to encourage economic advancement in whatever ways possible, including the attraction of human resources that could contribute to the burgeoning economy. Jews who might be enticed into relocating and contributing the knowledge and skills they had amassed were viewed as useful to the broad advancement these rulers sought to support. These Jews, it was assumed, would improve the economic climate of the towns in which they settled.

With the passage of time, governance matured across the western sectors of northern Europe, and the Jewish economic specialization evolved from trade into moneylending, largely as a result of the Church campaign against Christian usury. Once again, Jews were deemed useful in terms of their stimulation of the general economy. At the same time, the Jewish money-lenders offered yet a further boon to the temporal authorities. To the extent that Jewish moneylending became more sophisticated and profitable through the backing of the secular rulers, these rulers gained enhanced knowledge of the details of Jewish lending and thus could exploit it increasingly effectively. Jews profited handsomely from the new-style lending business, and so did their sponsors and protectors.

The revenue realized by northern European rulers from their Jewish subjects was often quite significant, which entailed considerable danger. Eventually, a concern developed for protecting this revenue, which meant in effect limiting Jewish movement from domain to domain. Especially as Church-sponsored limitations on Jewish lending won governmental backing, the possibility that such constraints might tempt Jews to relocate to more congenial domains in which the limitations were not in effect made northern European rulers very sensitive to maintaining control of their Jews and the revenue realized from them. Out of this concern emerged sensible steps, including the simultaneous initiation of anti-usury legislation jointly on the part of many holders of Jews and introduction of the metaphorical language of Jewish serfdom as a way of highlighting the right of rulers to restrain Jewish movement.[30]

In addition to the threat of excessive control of Jewish movement by the ruling class, there was also the danger of over-exploitation of Jewish resources. Medieval governments were, like most governments, constantly strapped financially. With a readily available and exploitable resource like the Jews, the temptation to tax beyond reasonable bounds was high. Robert Stacey has argued convincingly that, during the 1240s, the financially beleaguered king of England taxed his Jewish subjects to the point that he destroyed the economic foundation of the Jewish business ventures from which he was benefiting.[31]

The concern with Jews on the part of the ruling authorities of northern Europe revolved around economic issues—general stimulation of the economy and governmental revenues. While exercising considerable latitude in their treatment of their Jewish clients, the rulers of northern Europe were not entirely free of constraints. A major influence on governmental treatment of the Jewish newcomers was traditional Church teaching, which was complex and could be bent in a number of alternative directions. Europe's feudal lords enjoyed great latitude in dealing with their Jewish subjects, but had to be mindful at all times of the Church and its demands. Periodically, the authorities of the Church harshly chastised Christian rulers deemed insensitive to Church policies. On occasion, these ecclesiastical critics berated rulers for persecuting their Jews; at other times, churchmen castigated rulers who seemed to allow their Jews too much latitude.[32]

In less tangible ways, the populace at large, which was by and large hostile to the Jewish newcomers, exercised impact as well. The rulers of medieval Christian Europe were insistent on the maintenance of law and order in their realms. This meant governmental suppression of all tendencies toward anti-Jewish violence. Such violence threatened an important resource of the ruling authorities. Even more importantly, such violence endangered public welfare and governmental power in a more general way. Unchecked anti-Jewish violence could easily spread in broader directions. The ruling class bore responsibility for maintaining order, even if the targets of popular animosity were the unpopular Jewish newcomers. At the same time, the authorities had to be cognizant of such unpopularity and factor it into their considerations when adumbrating policies vis-à-vis the Jews.

If we step back to the beginning of the time frame covered in this chapter, to the beginning of the second Christian millennium, the changes in Jewish demography by the year 1300 were stunning. During the twenty centuries of Jewish history that preceded the onset of the second Christian millennium, Jewish settlement was confined to roughly the same area, from Mesopotamia in the east through the Mediterranean Basin in the west. There were, to be sure, shifts in the constellation of the various components in this Jewish population. Occasionally, Jews went beyond these boundaries, but the number of such adventuresome Jews was small, and they never affected the overall distribution of worldwide Jewish population. The first major breach in this longstanding Jewish population configuration took place as the result of the vitalization of northern Europe, which attracted Jews into this rapidly developing area and which alerted major rulers to the potentially positive impact of Jewish settlers.

Much attention has fastened on the negative aspects of this Jewish migration into northern Europe—the popular resentment and occasional violence, the ecclesiastical limitations, and the eventual banishment from sectors of medieval Christian Europe, which we shall engage shortly. Not enough attention has been accorded to the positive aspects of this movement. For better and for worse, Jews made their way into areas of Europe that were fated to eventually dominate the West. The first stage of this movement took place against the backdrop of the vitalization of northern European civilization during the early centuries of the second half of the Middle Ages.

In terms of the history of Jewish population movement, the migration of Jews out of the traditional Jewish comfort zone was truly momentous. Its stimulus lies once again in Jewish desires for betterment. We have discerned no evidence of the imposition of force on these intrepid Jews; their peregrinations were self-generated, often abetted by forward-looking political authorities seeking to improve the economy of their domains. In ways not sufficiently noted and emphasized, the history of the Jewish people was reshaped and redirected by these Jewish migrants of the early second millennium.

NINE

Movement Eastward

During the period of 1300 through 1600, world Jewry remained centered in its traditional sites, although the growing Jewish population of the northern sectors of western Christendom was on the verge of changing the configuration of overall Jewish demography. The new Jewish settlements of northern Europe were beginning to constitute an increasing percentage of worldwide Jewry. Before too long, these Jews would become the majority of world Jewish population.

Within newly emergent northern European Jewry, these three centuries saw a decided move eastward. This movement eastward was initially yet another stage in the voluntary migration that had brought Jews to northern Europe altogether. The lagging areas of north-central and northeastern Europe and their economic horizons beckoned, and the Jewish sense of opportunity was reinforced by governing authorities that—like their earlier northwestern-European predecessors—perceived in new Jewish settlers stimulation for economies poised on the cusp of development. Toward the end of the thirteenth century and on into the fourteenth, the more advanced polities of the northwest began to limit and then expel their Jews, the first governmentally decreed displacement of Jews since the Babylonian exile of 586 b.c.e.[1] North-central and northeastern Europe absorbed these expellees and thus laid the foundation for becoming the largest reservoir of Jewish population during the modern period.

Strikingly, the Jews expelled from England and France did not opt to return to the Mediterranean Basin, from which their ancestors had originated. The migration of these banished Jews eastward across northern Europe reflects the extent to which the one-time Jewish newcomers had come to identify with their adopted ambience. They clearly saw themselves as embedded in the new civilization that had its beginnings in the vitalization of northern Europe during the late tenth and early eleventh centuries. The process of settling into the new environment of northern Europe had been complicated and in many respects difficult. Segments of northern Europe society had resisted the new immigrants and limited them in numerous ways. Nonetheless, these Jews chose to remain in the north, and despite the impediments encountered they succeeded in building a successful and increasingly large outpost of the Jewish people, fated to evolve eventually into the dominant branch of worldwide Jewry.

Over the course of the medieval centuries, many of the innovative features of northern European Jewish life slowly made their way southward. These included: a skewed economic profile; popular antipathy and increasingly extreme anti-Jewish imagery; an expanding set of ecclesiastical constraints; enhanced exploitation by the ruling authorities; the new governmental policy of expulsion of Jews. This last eventually influenced the rulers of Iberia to follow suit and banish their Jews, under somewhat different circumstances and for somewhat different reasons.

The expulsions from Spain in 1492 and Portugal in 1497—it might seem—should not have been all that distressing to Jews, following as they did the banishments from England, France, and multiple locales in north-central Europe. Yet the Spanish expulsion had enormous impact on Jewish thinking, and the reason is simple. This was the banishment of an age-old Jewish community, one that saw itself and was seen by non-Jews as profoundly rooted in European soil. Spanish Jews had lived on the Iberian peninsula from time immemorial, arriving long before the birth of the ruling religion, Christianity.[2] Thus the impact of the banishment from Spain resonated throughout the Jewish world, strongly reinforcing the traditional sense of Jews as doomed to endless displacement.

On a more practical level, the expulsion from Iberia introduced radical change into the old and established Jewries of the Islamic world. These long-settled communities both benefited and suffered from the intrusion of Jewish newcomers, who constituted an innovative and dissonant element in their complex composition. Spanish exiles took leadership roles in these older Jewish communities, with the result that in present-day parlance these

Jewish communities are often mislabeled as Sephardic—that is, descendants of Iberian Jews. Thus, both the newer and older segments of world Jewry saw considerable forced relocation and resultant change over the closing centuries of the Middle Ages.

The early movement of Jews eastward across northern Europe was—like the movement into northern Europe altogether—voluntary. Before too long, however, Jews were forced eastward across northern Europe in the very first instances of post-586 b.c.e. compulsory population movement. Our close examination of the intervening two millennia of Jewish life between the return from Babylonian exile and the end of the thirteenth century has shown no significant evidence of forced Jewish displacement in any of its forms. We have discovered no governmental banishments of Jews. We have noted occasional interference with Jewish spiritual existence—in the wake of the Bar Kokhba rebellion, perhaps briefly by the Visigothic rulers of Spain, perhaps by some early northern European rulers, and perhaps briefly by the Almohade rulers of Spain and North Africa. Even if these questionable incidents genuinely occurred, they clearly did not lead to serious Jewish population dislocation. Likewise, anti-Jewish violence prior to the thirteenth century does not seem to have triggered significant forced Jewish migration. Limited anti-Jewish assaults occurred in the new Jewish settlement areas of northern Europe, were largely related to the early stages of the crusading enterprise, and do not suggest significant involuntary Jewish relocation. Jewish settlements occasionally visited by anti-Jewish violence were by and large quickly rebuilt and repopulated.

Almost nineteen centuries elapsed between the massive governmental expulsion of Jews ordered by the Babylonian emperor Nebuchadnezzar early in the sixth pre-Christian century and the first major European expulsion, the decree of banishment from England enacted in 1290. This lengthy period devoid of governmental expulsions or significant forced population movement of any kind hardly corresponds to the frightening Mosaic portrayal of relentless forced displacements of Jews and to the standard Jewish, Christian, and modern perceptions of compulsory Jewish population movement as a dominant feature of Jewish life.

That Jews should have lived for almost two millennia without suffering forced relocation can be readily understood in the light of Jewish demography as we have seen it. As noted recurrently, up until the end of the tenth Christian century Jews continued to live within the well-defined set of territories that stretched from Mesopotamia to the Mediterranean Basin. While there was considerable Jewish population movement during this lengthy period, it took place voluntarily within this traditional area of Jewish habitation. Throughout these territories, Jews viewed themselves and were viewed by their neighbors as permanent residents, settled long before the advent of the dominant new religions of Christianity and Islam. Expelling such long-term residents could hardly be contemplated. Northern Europe—the locus of entirely new Jewish settlement—was obviously quite different. If this newly developing area had existed from time immemorial without Jews, then the removal of these Jewish newcomers was hardly unthinkable.

Despite the limited impact of the expulsion by King Philip Augustus of France in 1182, followed by his fairly rapid recall of the Jews, this precedent was significant. The notion of expelling Jews, ostensibly in order to protect simultaneously the Christian faith and the Christian populace of northern Europe, was embraced by numerous northern European rulers throughout the latter part of the thirteenth century and eventuated in the major expulsions from England in its entirety in 1290 and then from royal France in its entirety over the course of the fourteenth century.

The accelerating crescendo of these expulsions reflects growing discomfort with Jewish moneylending all across northwestern European society. The Church played a leading role in articulating and fanning this growing discomfort. The sense solidified in ecclesiastical circles that Jewish moneylending had become profoundly damaging to Christian society and that—minimally—protections had to be erected against the suffering endured by the Christian populace. Some churchmen went further, questioning the traditional conviction that Christian law granted Jews the right to take interest from Christians. The ecclesiastical discomfort with Jewish usury resonated with the populace at large and exercised considerable impact on the ruling class. This discomfort may well have been facilitated by the economic maturation of these areas, which made Jewish moneylending increasingly less necessary and useful.

At the same time, popular imagery of the Jewish newcomers, which was never very positive, became increasingly extreme in its negativity. By the latter decades of the thirteenth century, widespread conviction of Jewish enmity toward Christianity and Christians intensified. Jewish usury was perceived as one modality through which Jews sought to harm their Christian contemporaries. By the late 1200s, most of the major new calumnies were fully in place across northern Europe. Jews—it was widely believed—murdered Christians, especially Christian youngsters, gratuitously; Jews dispatched their Christian victims ritually via crucifixion, thereby recapitulating their historic sin; Jews utilized Christian blood in their Passover ritual; Jews regularly blasphemed the sacred host wafer, once again as a recapitulation of their historic sin. These widely disseminated beliefs very much intensified the animosity toward Jews as non-Christians, toward Jews as newcomers, and toward Jews as usurers.

The rulers of northern Europe—prodded by ecclesiastical pressure—took a series of steps to limit significantly the damage purportedly inflicted by Jewish moneylending. Certain classes of the population were prohibited from borrowing from Jews; certain items were eliminated as pledges deposited with Jews; the interest rate on Jewish loans was limited; compounded interest, which could result in the rapid escalation of indebtedness, was outlawed.[3] Eventually, some rulers—most prominently the pious king of France Louis IX—prohibited Jewish moneylending altogether. Saint Louis seemingly offered the Jews of France the alternatives of finding other economic outlets or leaving his realm. Although these steps were taken with serious intent, it seems likely that they proved difficult or perhaps even impossible to enforce. Methods for subverting the new rules were available and were seemingly utilized.

When these efforts at limiting or even eradicating Jewish usury proved ineffective in England and likewise in France, the conclusion was that the only way to end the pernicious Jewish practice was to expel the offending Jews, who were unwilling to abandon their lending business. To be sure, other considerations were involved in the English and French decisions to banish the Jews, but terminating Jewish usury was advanced as the legal and moral basis for these expulsions. The role of Jewish usury and the failure of the efforts to eradicate this blight were advanced by King Edward I of England as justification for his decree of expulsion, enacted in 1290.

King Edward began his decree by noting the problem of Jewish usury and the efforts undertaken in 1275 to eradicate it.

> We, moved by solicitude for the honor of God and for the well-being of the people of our realm, did ordain and decree that no Jews should thenceforth lend to any Christian at usury upon security of land, rents, or aught else, but that they should live by their own commerce and labor.

This laudable initiative was foiled by the insidious cleverness of the Jews.

> The said Jews did thereafter wickedly conspire and contrive a new species of usury more pernicious than the old, which contrivance they have termed *curialitas* [ostensibly a gift, but actually a subterfuge for usury] and made use of the specious device to the abasement of our people on every side, thereby making their last offense twice as heinous as the first.

Out of concern for God and his people, the king had attempted to remove the blight of Jewish usury from his land. The Jews had wickedly subverted his noble plan. There remained but one option for the monarch devoted to his faith and his people.

> Therefore we, in requital of their crimes and for the honor of the Crucified, have banished them from our realm as traitors.[4]

The same sequence of events took place in France, although over a more protracted period of time. King Louis IX prohibited Jewish usury in much the same way and using much the same language as noted in England. Precisely how the Jews of France were able to subvert this edict is not altogether clear, but it is obvious that they did. By the 1270s, the point when King Edward I was prohibiting Jewish usury, Jews in France were once again engaged in their moneylending business. Like the king of England, so too the king of France—Philip IV—expelled his Jews. This banishment lacked the flowery imagery of a "most Christian king" supplied by Rigord of St. Denis for the expulsion of 1182 or the high-blown rhetoric of Edward I in 1290. The emphasis in this expulsion was on disposition of Jewish property and Jewish loans. While royal profit may well have played a major role in the expulsion from France of 1182, its place in the banishment of 1306 is more obvious.[5] Indeed, failure in realizing the full profit anticipated stimulated an invitation to return to royal France in 1315, with the king and the returning Jews sharing the proceeds of tracking down debts owed to Jews.[6] In 1394, a thoroughly depleted French Jewry was expelled with finality from France.

Jews continued to enjoy in theory the right to live safely and securely in Christian societies, and even the alleged harm inflicted by Jewish moneylenders did not justify anti-Jewish violence. However, threatened Christian societies could legitimately protect themselves by removing peaceably and responsibly Jews whose economic activities were deemed harmful to their Christian neighbors. In this way, the Christian populace of England and subsequently France would be shielded from Jewish depredations. This is of course a far cry from the expulsions of antiquity by the Assyrians and Babylonians, determined to wipe out political opposition by destroying the cohesion of a potentially rebellious people. The expulsions from thirteenth- and fourteenth-century northwestern Europe—specifically England and France, its economically and politically most advanced areas—were not intended to destroy the Jewish communities banished, but only to remove the dangers purportedly posed by these Jews.

The relatively small principalities of north-central Europe were not sufficiently advanced economically and not sufficiently well organized politically to emulate the decisive actions of the thirteenth- and fourteenth-century kings of England and France. Nonetheless, expulsions from these various lands became standard features of Jewish life in this area over the closing centuries of the Middle Ages, often followed by subsequent recall of the banished Jews. The theory remained essentially the same. Jews were entitled to live safely and securely in Christian societies, so long as they brought no harm to Christians. Jewish moneylending could be readily construed as harmful, thus justifying banishment of the Jews.

The major Jewish population movement identified thus far for the period between 1300 and 1600 took place in the newly settled northern Europe and proceeded from west to east. In its initial stages, this movement was voluntary, but by the closing decades of the thirteenth century it became compulsory, with major and eventually lesser rulers formally banishing their Jews. We have earlier suggested two further potential modalities of forced Jewish displacement—limitation of Jewish material and spiritual life so severe as to provide for Jews no alternative but to leave and violence so threatening as to require flight. Does either of these modalities play a role in the forced Jewish population movement of the latter centuries of the Middle Ages?

We have already noted the effort of King Edward I of England to ban Jewish moneylending, which seems to have constituted the backbone of the thirteenth-century English Jewish economy. Edward's edict of banishment suggests that the effort was a failure. This means that English Jews neither abandoned Jewish usury nor abandoned England. King Louis IX of France provides yet further evidence of efforts to eliminate Jewish usury—efforts that were clearly unsuccessful. Significant Jewish relocation as the result of governmental efforts to curtail Jewish economic life does not seem to have taken place.

King Louis IX provides evidence of efforts to deprive Jews of the sources required for their spiritual existence as well, and these efforts likewise seem to have had no significant impact on Jewish population movement. In 1236, a convert from Judaism to Christianity gained access to the papal court and leveled serious charges against the Talmud, claiming that it contained blasphemous references to Jesus and Mary, condoned and in fact demanded anti-Christian behaviors on the part of Jews, and was rife with teachings that were infantile and demeaning to religion in general. If substantiated, these allegations would have resulted in the banning of the Talmud, which would have made Jewish religious life impossible and should thus have stimulated relocation into areas in which Jewish religious life could be carried on freely.

Pope Gregory IX was sufficiently impressed with these allegations to send the accuser, a shadowy figure named Nicholas Donin, to major kingdoms of western Christendom in an effort to examine fully the charges. The key center from which this campaign was to be coordinated was Paris, which is revealing. Strikingly, the charges were in fact not rigorously investigated anywhere but in Paris, where the trial of the Talmud was conducted with the faculty of the great university serving as the examining body. The ecclesiastical jury substantiated the Donin charges, and as a result, carloads of Talmuds were publicly burned under royal auspices in the center of the capital.[7]

This condemnation and burning of the Talmud constituted a major disaster for the Jews of thirteenth-century Europe, and they gathered their resources to combat this threatening new development. Key rabbinic leaders were successful in meeting with the new pope, Innocent IV, and securing from him amelioration of the extreme anti-Talmud stance that had emerged in Paris. The Talmud was to be regularly examined and censored, with offending passages deleted. However, the non-offensive portions of the Talmud, which meant the bulk of the vast compendium, were permitted to Jews for their religious use. Once again, King Louis IX espoused a more radical position: total prohibition of the Talmud. This remained the policy of royal France thereafter. In theory, this might suggest the need for Jews to leave royal France; in practice, they clearly did not leave. Once again, it seems likely that execution of the prohibition was simply not enforceable.

What then of anti-Jewish violence as contributing to forced Jewish migrations? Toward the middle of the fourteenth century, all of Europe was struck by the bubonic plague. The death toll from this gruesome calamity was extraordinary. Estimates suggest that anywhere from one-quarter to one-third of the European population perished during the two years of virulent plague. Jews suffered along with everyone else from the pestilence. In addition, Jews suffered a second and related blow. As the frightened European populace sought to identify the agents of the plague, considerable attention focused on the Jews, perceived at this time by the Christian majority to be steeped in animosity toward their Christian neighbors, and in fact regularly guilty of murdering these neighbors—especially the young and defenseless—whenever opportunity might present itself. Mobs in many European cities, convinced that local Jews had poisoned the town water supply and thus brought about the plague and its casualties, massacred these Jews. This was a situation in which the negative considerations that suggested leaving current places of residence were intense. However, since the plague was a pan-European phenomenon, alternative locales for relocation did not readily suggest themselves. There was little that the Jews of Europe at this point could do to escape the dangers to which they were exposed.

Forced Jewish population movement in the form of governmental expulsion was a reality across late medieval northern Europe. Forced relocation as the result of governmental edicts that made Jewish life untenable either materially or spiritually does not seem to have taken place. Indeed, it was precisely the failure to halt Jewish usury that was adduced by northern European rulers as grounds for their decrees of expulsion. Likewise, despite the reality of major mid-fourteenth-century anti-Jewish violence, it is unlikely that this resulted in forced Jewish population movement. Governmental decrees of expulsion occasioned the departures from northwestern Europe during the late Middle Ages.

The most striking characteristic of rapidly developing northeastern European Jewry was simply its remarkable demographic growth, emphasized by Salo Baron in his pathbreaking 1928 essay. Baron noted the extent to which European Jewish population growth (which largely involved northeastern European Jewry) outstripped non-Jewish population growth during the sixteenth through eighteenth centuries. From this reality, Baron concluded that there could not have been debilitating anti-Jewish violence during this period. Shaul Stampfer pointed to the same population growth in his study of the violence of 1648–1649. While Baron's inference from this reality certainly seems reasonable, in a broader way the present stage of medical science does not provide adequate comprehension of this unusual population growth. Perhaps someday medical science will illuminate such patterns of population expansion. In any case, the constantly growing population certainly created new and altered patterns of life for the Jews of northeastern Europe.

The first result of the Jewish population growth was a measure of economic diversification. The Jews moving eastward brought with them the skewed economic profile of northern European Jewry, the specialization in moneylending. We have noted the charter of 1244, issued by Duke Frederick of Austria, which reflected moneylending as the core Jewish economic activity and reinforced governmental protections for Jewish moneylenders in multiple and important ways. This charter from 1244 was widely adopted and adapted across northeastern Europe during the thirteenth century and beyond. In 1264, Duke Boleslav of Greater Poland utilized the charter as the basis for a charter of invitation to his domain. He repeated—with only minor variations—the thirty stipulations of the Austrian document and then appended six further protections for the Jews—largely Jewish lenders—whom he was attempting to attract to Greater Poland.[8] This document of 1264 created a foundation for the growth of the Jewish community of Greater Poland and more broadly northeastern Europe altogether.

The growing Jewish population of northeastern Europe necessitated two kinds of diversification, since any locale could absorb only a finite number of moneylenders. In the first place, immigrating Jews had to move beyond the limited number of urban settings initially available to absorb them. We have already noted the tendency to diffuse beyond major urban centers in the earlier movement of Jews northward in Europe. Since northeastern Europe was considerably less urbanized than the earlier northwestern European areas that absorbed Jews, diffusion of Jewish population meant a movement into villages and the countryside. With that movement came inevitable changes in Jewish economic activity.

In a more general way, the growing Jewish population in northeastern Europe required Jews to find new ways to support themselves. Since northeastern Europe was less urbanized than earlier northwestern Europe, there was less of an urban populace to resist Jewish economic diversification. Jews were thus able to move into new economic activities in a way that had not been possible in the earlier stages of northern European Jewry. This does not mean that resentment of Jewish moneylending and the new Jewish economic activities was reduced. The resentment remained intense. What was different was the ability of the resentful to limit Jewish economic diversification.

The problematic relations between the new Jewish settlers and the settled population of northeastern Europe were intensified by the perceptions that Jews brought with them of their new ambience and their attitudes toward it. These immigrating Jews were keenly aware of the fact that they were moving from an area of higher civilization to an area of lower civilization. To a significant extent, this sense was mirrored in the welcoming stance of the rulers of northeastern Europe, who saw in these new Jewish settlers a useful new economic force. Although this had been also true for the earlier rulers in northwestern Europe, the Jews immigrating into northeastern Europe during the fourteenth through sixteenth centuries themselves absorbed deeply this sense of moving into a new and lesser environment.

While the Jews migrating into northeastern Europe maintained a sense of moving from a higher to a lower civilization, their predecessors who moved into northwestern and north-central Europe during the earlier centuries of the second millennium quickly shed their negative perceptions. A striking gauge of this difference is the language adaptation of the two waves of Jewish migrants. In a striking way, the new Jewish settlers of northwestern and north-central Europe quickly abandoned the language culture they brought with them and absorbed the languages of their new homes. The new leaders of Jewish intellectual and religious life in northern France and Germany exhibit this absorption. As is well known, the great exegete Solomon ben Isaac of Troyes (Rashi) clarified difficult biblical and talmudic terms in his commentaries by supplying the vernacular French equivalents. The language adaptation of the Jews migrating into northeastern Europe was radically different. They chose to maintain the language culture they arrived with, medieval German. In this way, medieval German became the foundation for the new Jewish language of Yiddish.

This new language reflects the attitudes with which the new Jewish settlers arrived, and it established a pattern of social distance that would become a hallmark of northeastern-European Jewish history. This sense of northeastern Europe as an essentially backward area predisposed its Jews to an unusual level of mobility, an unusual level of willingness to relocate voluntarily. When changes farther westward opened opportunities to move in that direction, the Jews of northeastern Europe were fully prepared to take maximal advantage.

The movement of Jews eastward across northern Europe—both voluntary and involuntary—resulted in new patterns of Jewish life in northeastern Europe, much as the movement from the south to the north had done three centuries earlier. These new patterns of Jewish life are interesting in and of themselves; at the same time, they will prove important for understanding major aspects of the next stage in Jewish population movement, which began during the sixteenth century and intensified thereafter. This new stage of Jewish migration—which we shall analyze only through the end of the eighteenth century—saw Jews moving back across northern Europe into areas once closed to them and now slowly opening. Eventually, this movement westward centered on a sector of the globe unknown to Europeans until the end of the fifteenth century and thus often designated as the New World. By the end of the nineteenth century, which is beyond the temporal limits of this study, the movement of northern European Jews westward would trigger the largest Jewish migration in history, popularly perceived as precipitated by violence and hence involuntary, but in fact stimulated by economic factors and voluntary.[9]

By the end of the fifteenth century, one of the older centers of Jewish life—the major monarchies of the Iberian peninsula—saw the introduction of the northern European innovation of governmental expulsion into the south. The perceived Jewish harmfulness underlying and legitimating expulsion of the Jews from Castile, Aragon, and subsequently Portugal was quite different from that projected in the north. In the north, the ecclesiastical and political concern focused on Jewish usury; in the south, the focus was on the traditional Church unease about potential Jewish religious impact on the Christian majority, which took a very special form.

The circumstances of this potential Jewish religious impact in Spain were unique. In 1391, significant conversion of Jews had taken place in the face of wide-ranging anti-Jewish violence. When the violence subsided and life more or less returned to normal, assimilation of these converts proved extremely difficult, for multiple reasons. In the first place, much of the conversion was insincere. Many of the Jews converting were correctly convinced that conversion by force was illegitimate according to official Church doctrine. Unfortunately for these insincere converts, they were incorrectly convinced that, with the return to normalcy, their conversions would be invalidated, as had previously happened in the wake of such forced baptisms. Permission to return to Judaism was denied, and the converts were forced to remain in their new faith. Thus the community of converts from Judaism to Christianity included many who had no genuine desire to become Christians.

There was a second problem as well, and that was simply the large number of converts entering the Christian fold at one and the same time. In general, conversion from one identity to another is a disorienting and difficult process. Conversion from one religious faith to another in the Middle Ages was especially problematic. When the number of converts was small, as was generally the case with medieval Jews converting to Christianity, absorption of the new converts was fairly smooth. The Christian majority was normally delighted with the conversion and committed to accepting the converts. The converts themselves were totally cut off from their prior community and social circle, with no real choice but to amalgamate themselves into their new Christian ambience.

In the wake of the 1391 mass conversions, all these circumstances were different. The Christian majority did not see these conversions as victories for Christian truth and was not therefore fully committed to absorption of the many new converts. The converts themselves were sufficiently numerous to form their own social circle, which enabled them to keep their distance from the Old Christian majority. Indeed, the sense of Old Christians and New Christians—this language quickly emerged—is revealing. In traditional and ecclesiastically correct terms, there were no such categories as Old and New Christians—there were only Christians. The ubiquity of this new terminology indicates that social barriers were erected between those historically members of Spanish Christendom and the newcomers.[10] Considerable resistance to accepting the converts emerged in Old Christian society, which had to evoke resentment on the part of the New Christians, especially those who had accepted their new faith with genuine intentions of embracing it. The result of all this was backsliding into Jewish belief and practice on the part of some of the formerly Jewish New Christians.

This backsliding was a complex phenomenon, but important voices began to urge that the Jews of Spain were enticing their former co-religionists to abandon their new faith and return to their ancestral religion. Thus—it was argued—so long as Jews remained a part of Spanish society, the vital task of absorbing the New Christians into the Church and Christian society would never be successfully completed. The expulsion of 1492 from Castile and Aragon and the related expulsions from elsewhere on the peninsula were legally grounded once again in claims of Jewish harmfulness. However, in this instance, Jewish harmfulness took the form of purported religious influence on (New) Christians.

The formal justification of the expulsions from Iberia in 1492 and thereafter sprang from different concerns than those that had been utilized for justifying the earlier banishments from areas of northwestern and north-central Europe. In our analysis of those earlier expulsions, we have looked beyond the justifications toward the underlying motives of the rulers expelling their Jews. While the formal grounding for the 1492 expulsion lay in the problem of assimilating the formerly Jewish New Christians into full Christian identity, many students of medieval Iberian history have suggested a broader and bolder motivation on the part of the Spanish royal authorities. In this view, the underlying desire was to create a more monolithic Spanish society, grounded in shared Christian identity.[11] If this was in fact the case, then such royal motivation constitutes yet one more way in which developments in the north filtered down into southern Europe. In expelling their Jews, the ruling authorities in northwestern Europe had in effect fashioned a more homogeneous Christian society in their realms, and this homogeneity may well have influenced the rulers in Spain to follow suit.

As had been true in northern Europe, so too in the south the direction taken by those Jews banished from Iberia was eastward.[12] There were, however, few available refuges in the Christian sectors of Mediterranean Europe. The most immediate and simplest refuge for the banished Jews of Spain was neighboring Portugal, and many of the Jews who chose expulsion over conversion relocated there. The Portuguese refuge relatively soon turned negative, as 1497 was set as the date of expulsion from Portugal. Strikingly, the Jews settled in Portugal—both long-standing Jewish inhabitants and the newly arrived Spanish refugees—were precluded from making their exit, in effect forcibly converting them and thus creating a new and even more determined pool of crypto-Jews, destined to play a significant role in the next phase of Jewish migrations.[13]

Elsewhere in Christian southern Europe, there were few options for Jewish resettlement. Southern France was closed to Jews as a result of the final royal expulsion from France decreed in 1394. Potential Jewish settlement in Italy was limited. A few small Italian states were open to the Iberian Jews, but their numbers were limited and their absorptive capacity slim. The major refuges for these displaced Spanish Jews lay farther eastward in the rapidly developing Ottoman Empire, emerging as a major economic and political power. For the Jews expelled from Spain, the Mediterranean territories of the Ottoman Empire were climatically and physically familiar and thus congenial. Even more important, these Spanish Jewish refugees were welcomed by the Ottoman authorities. In effect, the dynamic we have already encountered a number of times was repeated once again. Rulers aware of the economic needs of their realms—in this case the Ottoman rulers—saw in potential Jewish settlers a valuable resource for the growth of the economy over which they presided. Once more, there was a sense that introduction of Jewish settlers from better developed areas would aid significantly in closing the gap between areas lagging economically and their more advanced rivals.

As the Spanish Jews made their way eastward into the Ottoman realm, their circumstances were far easier than the circumstances of the original Jews moving into northern Europe or their descendants making their way into northeastern Europe. In the first place, the Ottoman Empire housed a more heterogeneous population than did northern Europe. As they settled in the Ottoman Empire, the Spanish Jews simply became another element in the diverse humanity of the realm. Part of that humanity included well-established Jewish communities. New Jewish enclaves did not have to be created; the immigrating Spanish Jews simply attached themselves to the Jewish settlements already in place. This arrangement diminished considerably popular attention to and resentment of the new arrivals.

The Spanish Jews were added on as a new layer of Jews to an already diversified Jewish population of the Ottoman Empire. In some areas, the previously settled Jewish nucleus consisted of formerly Byzantine Jews, whose language and culture had been Greek; in other areas, the previously settled Jewish nucleus consisted of Jews from the earlier Islamic sphere, whose language and culture had been Arabic. Onto these prior Jewish elements were grafted the Spanish exiles. In a striking reflection of the dominance achieved by western Christendom during the second half of the Middle Ages, the Spanish refugees quickly rose to positions of leadership in this multifaceted Jewry. They constituted the wealthiest element in the diversified Jewish communities; they had the closest relationship with the ruling authorities; they set the cultural tone and norms for the Jewish communities in their entirety. This dominance is reflected in the subsequent tendency to identify all Jews from the early-modern Ottoman Empire as Sephardic or Spanish Jews. Since the ancestors of the majority of these modern-day Jews never set foot near the Iberian peninsula, the misleading nomenclature reflects the extent to which the new layer of Spanish refugees came to dominate Jewish life in the Ottoman realm.

The Ottoman Empire provided an effective refuge for the banished Spanish Jews. The economic opportunities and support of the ruling authorities combined with much reduced resistance to create relatively comfortable circumstances for the immigrating Jews. These comfortable circumstances were reflected in a surge of spiritual and intellectual creativity. In central spheres of Jewish culture and spirituality, there were major innovations that indicate successful accommodation by the refugees to their new environment.

Again it is not possible to identify either governmental edicts limiting Jewish material and spiritual life or outbreaks of violence as forcing the Iberian Jewish population displacement. There was, to be sure, a wave of devastating violence all across Spain in 1391, and it is often suggested that the Jewish communities of Spain never truly recovered. However, the recent findings of Mark Meyerson have provided an alternative perspective. Meyerson has suggested that, working in tandem, the Jews of Spain and their royal overlords moved effectively toward rebuilding the seriously depleted Jewish communities, debilitated by the killings, conversions, and overall destruction inflicted on Spanish Jewry in 1391.[14] It was governmental expulsion only that created major Jewish population movement on the Iberian peninsula.

Unlike the banishments of Jews in early antiquity, the medieval expulsions from western Europe were directed against a religious minority, were intended to remove a religiously grounded threat to the Christian majority, expelled Jews without specifying areas of resettlement, and were not intended to destroy the offending Jewish community. The world had changed radically from early antiquity to the Middle Ages, and so had forcible relocation of Jews.

The northern expulsions created pain and sadness for those banished, and empathy and concern on the part of Jews who learned of these banishments but were not directly affected by them. The extant literature, however, shows no sense of shock and disbelief. Moreover, the expulsions in the north did not set in motion major new developments on the Jewish spiritual and literary scene. Jews in the north moved eastward, suffered from the forced population movement, but quickly resettled themselves in their new northeastern European settings and began rebuilding, a process of reconstruction that proceeded more or less smoothly, grounded on the foundations laid in earlier northern European Jewish experience.

In this respect, the Spanish expulsion was radically different. It had an air of the unthinkable about it, and many in the Christian majority and the Jewish minority were convinced—up until the last moment—that it could not happen. The reason for this conviction lay in the lengthy history of the Jews in Iberia. The Jews of northern Europe constituted a relatively new phenomenon, and as such it was not hard to imagine the new settlement being undone. But this was hardly the case in Spain. Spanish Jews could trace their presence in Spain far back into antiquity; they were present in Spain before the birth and arrival of Islam and even prior to the emergence of Christianity as well. Spanish Jews saw themselves and were seen by most of their non-Jewish peers as a time-honored and ineffaceable element on the Spanish scene.

The sense of shock at the removal of this long-standing Jewry extended beyond the event itself. The expulsion of 1492 triggered major upheavals in Jewish religious and spiritual life. Among other developments it sparked was a new focus on the long history of Jewish suffering over the ages.[15] This unique response to banishment serves as one last index of the differences between the older centers of Jewish life and the new northern European center of Jewish life that—despite the banishments it had suffered—was rising to dominance on the worldwide Jewish scene.

Little could those Jews resettling in northeastern Europe or those relocating in the Ottoman Empire imagine that enormous changes were in the offing in northwestern Europe. These changes would set in motion new waves of voluntary Jewish population movement and once more reshape the demography of the Jewish world. Large numbers of Jews in northeastern Europe and a more modest number in north-central Europe would undertake the difficulties of leaving their home environments in search of better lives. Once again, the process would be far from easy. These Jewish migrants would once again encounter potent resistance, grounded in the normal human response to newcomers and reinforced by some of the characteristics the new Jewish migrants brought with them. The results, however, were momentous for subsequent Jewish history.

TEN

Return Westward

The expulsions from late-medieval Europe were the first suffered by Jews in almost two millennia and were grounded in an innovative set of justifications—the damage Jews purportedly did to the material and spiritual well-being of Latin Christendom. These expulsions were quintessentially medieval. That is to say, they were rooted in the medieval conviction of a fundamental and essential linkage between church and state. In this relationship, secular rulers bore responsibility to support fully the ecclesiastical authorities in a joint effort to foster materially and spiritually a truly Christian society.

When the major Iberian expulsions of the 1490s took place, there was little or no awareness of the possibility that the old order would shortly begin to change and that a new European society would eventually emerge, once again especially in the western sectors of the north. This new order, founded on an altered sense of the relationship between state and church, would have momentous significance for Jews, triggering massive new Jewish population movement—this time from east to west—and in the process refashioning once more the global distribution of the Jewish people and major aspects of Jewish life.

The Jewish population of northern Europe had been created by important changes in medieval Christian Europe that began at the end of the first millennium. These invigorating changes attracted Jews into northwestern and north-central Europe. Some of these Jews were then enticed eastward to take advantage of new economic opportunities in northeastern Europe; subsequently the Jews of northwestern Europe were forced eastward by the innovative expulsions that took shape during the thirteenth though fifteenth centuries. With the onset of the change across northern Europe, the Jews of northeastern Europe sensed new opportunities back in north-central and northwestern Europe and slowly began a voluntary population movement back in a westerly direction.

This movement took place in two stages, as the states of northwestern Europe, especially the Protestant states, began to adopt new and more positive perspectives on population diversity. During the first stage, from the sixteenth through the eighteenth centuries, there was slow and grudging de facto acceptance of greater religious diversity in the European population; during the second stage, from the late eighteenth century on, a new theory of the state emerged, a theory that formally endorsed the separation of church and state and thus the de jure acceptability of diverse religious groupings, including Jews, within European and eventually Atlantic society.[1]

Demographic change in world Jewry picked up in pace during the late medieval and early modern centuries, as the prior Jewish movement eastward in Europe was reversed and Jews began to take advantage of new patterns of economic and political thinking in the more advanced principalities of western Europe. In growing numbers, Jews began to leave northeastern Europe and settle themselves in areas of north-central and northwestern Europe increasingly open to them. The shift was slow but inexorable, as the Jewish population of northeastern Europe was growing steadily and sought new outlets for expanding numbers. The Jewish population in the western countries of northern Europe, which were in the process of fashioning new notions of societal organization and of the functions of the political authorities, grew, at first slowly and then with accelerating rapidity.[2] These changes culminated during the late nineteenth and early twentieth centuries in the largest migration in Jewish history, which moved Jews in unprecedented numbers from northeastern Europe to northwestern Europe and most of all to the new areas of Jewish settlement in the Americas.[3]

The new European notions of societal diversity and organization were set in motion initially by the Protestant Reformation. When Martin Luther successfully challenged the authority of the Roman Catholic Church, he in effect shattered the religious homogeneity that had been the hallmark of medieval European civilization. While the European population remained predominantly Catholic, significant enclaves of Protestant population emerged. Not surprisingly, the old notion of church-state relations remained in force. This translated into efforts by Catholic regimes to stifle Protestants living under their authority, efforts by Protestant governments to suppress Catholics living in their realms, and the commitment of both sets of authorities to battle one another on the international scene. The result was a period of intense religious conflict, at the cost of enormous bloodletting and economic turmoil.[4]

Quietly and sporadically, some areas loosened their commitment to religious homogeneity. In such instances, small numbers of Jews appeared in one way or another and paved the way for acceptance of larger numbers of Jewish settlers. For the Jews relocating, the appeal was once more economic, although there was considerable desire for more comfortable living circumstances as well. For the majorities slowly and grudgingly accepting these Jews, the appeal was again largely economic.

In the earliest stage of this movement westward, the initial Jewish immigrants often arrived as Christians—as strange as that may sound. Once more, the backdrop to this curious phenomenon lies in the special circumstances of the Iberian peninsula. There, large numbers of Jews had converted, often forcibly, during the violence of 1391. The fate of these New Christians, as they were generally designated, was complicated in the extreme. On the one hand, as Christians they could now participate freely in the economic, social, and intellectual advances in society. Broad sectors of the economy were open to them, as were Spain's universities. All this was positive, and in material terms the New Christians of Spain benefited from their new circumstances.

On the other hand, there were potent negatives as well. As these former Jews became increasingly successful, they aroused considerable popular antipathy. Old Christians became resentful of the successes of their New Christian contemporaries and were determined to constrict the opportunities available to them. Laws were enacted that would limit those who could not produce evidence of "pure blood," a history of unbroken family attachment to Christianity. In addition, there was evidence that, even after many decades in the Christian fold, some of the Spanish New Christians rejected

Christianity in favor of their former Jewish faith. As a result, the threat of the Inquisition hung heavily over the heads of many of Spain's New Christians.

A further complication was added by the fate of the Jews in neighboring Portugal. The Jews of Spain in 1492 were given a choice between conversion and expulsion, and many chose the latter. For those unwilling to accept Christianity, the simplest refuge available was nearby Portugal. The ruling authorities in Portugal were only too happy to add these productive Jews to their domain. A few years later, however, as King Manuel sought the hand of the daughter of the Spanish monarchs Ferdinand and Isabella, pressure to adopt the Spanish policy of excluding Jews was exerted. Manuel succumbed to the pressure, but in a bizarre way. Like the monarchs of Spain, he decreed that Jews must either convert or leave his realm. However, he in effect made leaving Portugal impossible, by closing the ports, essentially forcing the Portuguese Jews into the Church.[5]

Helpfully for these forced converts, there was no Inquisition in Portugal yet, allowing many of the Portuguese forced New Christians to maintain their attachment to Judaism more or less secretly. Eventually, in 1547, a Portuguese Inquisition was established, which made the situation of those Portuguese New Christians who were crypto-Jews extremely difficult. In both Spain and Portugal, there were New Christians who were genuine Christians. In both kingdoms, there were also New Christians who secretly practiced Judaism, but the number of such crypto-Jews was considerably higher in Portugal than in Spain, partly as a result of the forced nature of the conversion of 1497 and partly because of the long history of relatively unfettered crypto-Judaism in Portugal.

Many of the Iberian New Christians, especially those of Portugal—both those genuinely Christian and those yearning to return to Judaism—were responsive to the possibility of relocation that would take them to a new setting, a setting in which they could utilize their advanced skills without suffering societal discrimination and the danger of prosecution. As some of the states of northwestern Europe became more successful in the international trade unleashed by the new maritime discoveries and the exploitation of the riches uncovered through them, these skilled but troubled and often endangered New Christians were attracted to the flourishing and freer environments.

A number of New Christians opted to leave Iberia voluntarily and settle themselves in promising areas of northern Europe. Often, when inquisitorial proceedings began against one member of an extended family, the rest of the family would emigrate en masse, out of well-grounded fear.

The modalities of acceptance of these new settlers varied from area to area. Some of these New Christians chose to settle in nearby southwestern France, in the Bordeaux-Bayonne area. While royal France was a staunchly Catholic realm, the southern sectors of France had a lengthy tradition of religious questioning, of opposition to the religious narrowness in the north, of outbreaks of what the Church defined as heresy, and of violent suppression of these outbreaks. Thus, the southern French Christian majority was inclined toward toleration of the peculiar religious behaviors of the newly arriving Iberian New Christians.

Some Iberian New Christians chose to settle in southern France simply in order to escape the social discrimination and danger of prosecution that had been their lot in Iberia. At the same time, other Iberian New Christians elected to settle in southern France in order to return to their original Jewish faith. This latter group of New Christians settled as Christians and in fact continued to maintain a public pose as Christians. Among themselves, however, they returned privately and quietly to the Jewish faith of their ancestors. Their Christian neighbors, imbued with the religious rebelliousness of southern France, by and large chose to turn a blind eye to the reality of this deceptive posturing and to the emergence of a small community of Jews in their midst. These southern French Christians represent a new, albeit curious example of growing European tolerance for religious diversity. To be sure, this unique community of crypto-Jews could not serve as the foundation for the acceptance of subsequent and overtly Jewish immigrants.

Yet another venue of refuge for the New Christians of Iberia was increasingly powerful Protestant England. Again, some of the New Christian settlers had no desire to return to Judaism; they were simply seeking more comfortable living circumstances. Once more, however, there was an element among these relocating New Christians that sought the opportunity to return to Judaism. In England, as in southern France, small groups of such returnees to Judaism emerged. On occasion, they were discovered and prosecuted. With the passage of time, however, some of these groups were able to secure and maintain de facto acceptance. In good English fashion, these now obviously Jewish immigrants were allowed to remain, to pursue their useful economic activities, and to carry on unobtrusively their Jewish activities. For a long time, the English authorities conferred upon this reality no formal acknowledgment. Rather, it was simply quietly accepted, and through silence became legitimized.

The most prominent of the refuges for the Iberian New Christians who desired to return to Judaism was newly independent Protestant Holland. The Dutch had battled long and hard to achieve independence from Catholic Spain and its intolerance. What emerged with Dutch independence was an intermediate stage of religious toleration—more overt than in southern France and England; less open than the subsequent acceptance in principle of religious diversity in Enlightenment thinking. On one hand, Holland created an established church; at the same time, however, there was deep sensitivity to the plight of those who did not belong to that church and who sought freedom to express their religious identity in alternative ways. As a result of its special circumstances, Holland was committed to an unusual level of religious toleration, which made it an ideal site for those Iberian New Christians who were seeking a venue in which they might abandon Christianity and return to Judaism.

The settlement of Iberian New Christians in the Netherlands began in the same way as their migration into southwestern France and England. They came ostensibly as Christians. Rather quickly, however, some of them returned to Judaism in a more overt manner than in southwestern France and England. They began to worship publicly and to establish the standard institutions of organized Jewish life—synagogues, cemeteries, and schools. These public institutions created the need for an explicit response to the new reality of a functioning Jewish community, and the authorities in the Netherlands, unlike those in southern France and England, slowly provided one.

As public recognition was increasingly achieved, new Jewish communities could emerge more openly and more effectively in major Dutch urban settings. These new Jewish communities created for themselves all the necessary accouterments of Jewish communal life, eventually even bringing to Holland fully trained rabbinic leaders. These Jewish communities flourished in every way. Their Jews were highly successful economically, which suggested to their Dutch contemporaries and observers elsewhere throughout northwestern Europe the advantages of a Jewish presence. These successes also alerted Jews living farther eastward to the advantages of relocating to the Netherlands. Although the nucleus of the Jewish population of Holland consisted of former Iberian New Christians, and this group continued to dominate the imagery of Dutch Jewry, in fact fairly quickly the number of northern European Jewish immigrants living in Holland outstripped the number of original New Christian settlers and their offspring. Dutch Jewry was perceived as a southern European–Sephardic Jewish community, even though its actual population was increasingly northern European and Ashkenazic.[6]

The situation of Dutch Jewry's most illustrious member, Baruch (Benedict) Spinoza, illuminates a number of important aspects of the seventeenth-century history of the community.[7] Spinoza came from an originally Portuguese New Christian family that had settled in Holland and returned to Judaism. His father and his father's uncle and first father-in-law (although not Baruch's grandfather) had been successful businessmen and pillars of the Jewish community, serving as officials within the communal organization. The young Spinoza received a thorough Jewish education in the well-structured Jewish schooling system. All of this reflects the cohesive and self-contained Jewish community and its effective educational system. As Spinoza's innovative and radical thinking became known within the Jewish community, the Jewish authorities mobilized their forces and excommunicated him effectively, which serves as further evidence of its organization and power.

Yet at the same time, Spinoza's life story reflects a different aspect of Dutch Jewish experience. In the first place, his groundbreaking ideas were stimulated in considerable measure from more open communication between Jews and Christians of a scientific and philosophic bent. The barriers that separated Jews from Christians in medieval Christendom were lowered considerably in seventeenth-century Holland. Moreover, Spinoza's post-excommunication experience is instructive as well. In earlier centuries, excommunication was a devastating blow, necessitating either reconciliation with the Jewish community or total abandonment of it through conversion. For Spinoza, there was no need for choosing one of these stark alternatives. In seventeenth-century Holland, a neutral society had begun to emerge. Spinoza left Amsterdam, resettled in the quiet town of Rijnsburg, plied his trade, and continued his studies and his writing. He was part of a congenial network of radical thinkers and felt no need to reintegrate into the Jewish community. The neutral society of which he was a part was a key feature of the changing European scene and held great future meaning for Europe's Jews.

As a result of the de facto acceptance of Jews in England and their more open acceptance in the Netherlands, yet one more new locale for Jewish settlement was opened during the seventeenth century, and that was across the Atlantic Ocean, especially in the area of the New World that would eventually become the United States. Since the Dutch and the English were the dominant colonial powers in this sector of North America, their policy vis-à-vis Jews in the homeland became the norm for the colonial territories as well.

Once again, the first settlers were Sephardic Jews. By the middle of the seventeenth century, however, the new Jewish settlers were no longer arriving as ostensible Christians. Instead, they were former New Christians who had fully returned to the Jewish fold in England or Holland and who thus arrived in the colonies as openly declared Jews. Acceptance of these new settlers was hardly an issue, thus creating a firm foundation for the accelerating population movement that eventually ensued and for the creation of the large American Jewish community of the twentieth century. Once more, the earliest Jewish settlers were descendants of Spanish or Portuguese New Christians; again, however, the immigrating Jews were increasingly coming from the vast reservoir of north-central and northeastern European Jewry.

The growing toleration of Jews in southwestern France, England, the Netherlands, and the North American colonies all represented one or another form of de facto acceptance of Jews. Meanwhile, active minds were beginning to question in more theoretical ways and in greater depth the underlying structure of European society, a structure that had led to incessant religious persecution in Europe and ongoing warfare and bloodshed between its states. The issue that agitated those concerned with these political realities and better possibilities for the future was whether they might discover and promote an alternative governmental structure that would create more stable and more peaceful circumstances for the persecution-ridden and war-torn people of Europe.

The cornerstone of medieval and early modern European political thinking was the inextricable bond between church and state, between the religious authorities in society and those who exercised political power. The long-accepted consensus was that the most exalted calling of the ruling class and the highest objective of political power consisted of support for the dominant religious vision. Ensuring a uniform belief system and homogeneous patterns of religious behavior was—it was agreed—the most important responsibility of Europe's rulers. In enforcing this conformity, the rulers of Europe were justified in utilizing every coercive resource at their command.[8]

The sense was that the Church was committed to peaceful suasion, while the ruling class did the grimmer and harsher work of enforcement. Thus, for example, religious dissidence was met by churchmen with preaching and argumentation. If these initial efforts were unsuccessful, the Church had a small but powerful set of courts that could and did investigate charges of heresy. When ample evidence of heresy on the part of an individual was accumulated and this heretic refused nonetheless to recant, he or she was "turned over" to the secular authorities for execution. Enforcement of Church policy was regularly projected as the responsibility of the rulers of medieval and early modern Europe. In similar fashion, the Church could and did enlist the secular authorities to go to war against allegedly heretical neighboring states. Responding to this demand was viewed as the highest calling of the political authorities.

The implications of this system for non-Christian groupings within European society were significant and clear. As noted recurrently, the Church had early on recognized the right of Jews to live peacefully in Christian societies, with secondary status, to be sure, and in ways that would inflict no harm on the host Christian society. Eventually, this same recognition was extended to Muslims as well. Ultimately, the ruling class was charged with the responsibility of carrying out Church policy vis-à-vis these non-Christians. Once again, the Church established the policy—in this case for non-Christian dissidents, and the rulers of medieval and early modern Europe bore the responsibility of executing the policy.

Given the disintegration of medieval Christian religious homogeneity as a result of the Reformation, by the mid-seventeenth century the system had become increasingly dysfunctional, which challenged political thinkers to find a reasonable alternative. The alternative that emerged involved rethinking the nature of both church and state and the relationship between them. Thinkers like Spinoza and the Englishman John Locke wrestled with the foundations of authority for both church and state and the powers that these foundations legitimized for both. In consonance with general tendencies among Enlightenment thinkers, those probing the political realities of early modern Europe distanced themselves from the earlier insistence that the powers of church and state were divinely ordained. Rather, the innovative analyses tended to be empirical and naturalistic, focusing on human history and experience.

Locke's formulation was especially influential. He urged that the objectives of church and state were not interlocking; to the contrary, Locke projected the two as operating in wholly differing spheres and with alternative methods. For Locke, the purpose of the state was to regulate relations among members of society in a way that would ensure the fullest possible realization of human well-being. In his view, the state was the protector of the material interests of members of society, which Locke defined as "life, liberty, health and indolency of body, and the possession of outward things, such as money, land, houses, furniture, and the like."[9] For Locke, the state existed solely on the terrestrial level. In order to carry out its important terrestrial functions, the state had to exercise coercive powers, and these powers were legitimated by their importance in enabling the state to achieve its human-oriented objectives.

For Locke, churches were committed to utterly different objectives and utilized completely different methods in achieving their goals. While states operated entirely on the horizontal inter-human level, churches were focused on the vertical relationship between humanity and the divine. In this sphere, the exercise of coercive power was utterly inappropriate and unacceptable. In a sense, Locke incorporated the medieval sense of the Church operating through rational and moral suasion. However, whereas the medieval Church fell back on the coercive powers of the state when such persuasion did not achieve the desired results, Locke insisted on scrupulous maintenance of the distance between the two. Invocation of the power of the state in support of spiritual objectives was—for Locke—utterly illegitimate. The church and the state occupy two different spheres, and the boundaries between them had to be carefully maintained.

Interestingly, John Locke—while moved to his analysis of the relationship between church and state by the realities of the religious heterogeneity among the Christian population of seventeenth-century Europe—was able nonetheless to press his analysis to the point of raising the question of the openness of the state as he projected it to non-Christians. According to Locke, "if we may openly speak the truth, and as becomes one man to another, neither pagan, nor Mahometan, nor Jew ought to be excluded from the civil rights of the commonwealth because of his religion."[10]

This striking new formulation of the nature of politics and religion had enormous implications for northwestern Europe's slowly growing Jewish population. While mercantile thinking had encouraged certain forms of Jewish migration and had eventuated here and there in de facto toleration of Jews and Judaism in northwestern Europe, the new system slowly being advanced by European thinkers opened an entirely new place for Jews throughout European society. If European states were to tolerate a range of religions within their midst, then the entire scaffolding of rules and restrictions that had heretofore governed Jewish settlement and Jewish activity in Europe suddenly became outdated and illegitimate. Jews, like Catholics and Protestants, had a fundamental right to an equal place in European society, at least to the extent that they were willing and capable of shouldering the responsibilities of citizenship borne by all.

Toward the end of the eighteenth century, two new societies were fashioned on the foundations erected by Enlightenment thinking. In the first case, the American Revolution that began in 1776 was essentially a colonial uprising against the authority of the English monarchy. In the American colonies, the Enlightenment principles of governance had been more or less in effect prior to the revolution.[11] While the American Revolution and its aftermath resulted in formal adoption of the new theory of governance and society modeled on Enlightenment thinking, this new theory required no wholesale realignment of societal arrangements.

The situation in France was radically different. Pre-revolutionary France was a bastion of the old order, with the Catholic Church exercising enormous power; the society was still organized along the lines of the medieval synthesis of church and state. Enlightenment thinking had, to be sure, made its way into French intellectual circles and spawned an immense and influential literature, but the ruling forces in French society were still committed to maintenance of the medieval order. Thus, when the revolution ensued, it resulted in the overthrow of the old regime and the creation of an entirely new social order grounded in Enlightenment principles as to the nature and role of government and the nature and role of religion. In the wake of the revolution, there was a need for specification of the underpinnings and practices of the new order, in a way that was not required in post-revolution America. The differences between the two revolutions entailed major differences in post-revolutionary thinking about Jews.

As the issue of Jewish rights surfaced in post-revolutionary France, a vigorous debate ensued. Few voices argued that only Christianity, even in its diverse forms, was a valid religious faith for the new French state. Rather, the serious debate focused on the question of the potential of Jews for active and positive citizenship in the new France. Assessment of Jews as they were then known in France lay at the core of the debate, and this assessment was extremely complex, since there were alternative communities of Jews upon which judgments about their potential for citizenship might be grounded. To the extent that the perception of Jews involved those of north-central and northeastern Europe, for example the Jews of Alsace-Lorraine, conclusions as to the potential of Jews for productive citizenship tended to be negative; where it involved southern European or Sephardic Jews, such as those of Bordeaux and Bayonne, the conclusions tended to be extremely positive.

Jews had been formally banished from royal France in 1394, and that edict of banishment had never been rescinded. Thus, Jewish presence in eighteenth-century France was prohibited, and in almost all areas of France there was in fact no formal Jewish settlement on the eve of the revolution. There were, however, a few areas in which overt Jews were nonetheless to be found. The permission for such overt Jewish settlement was based largely on the fact that these areas had not been part of royal France in 1394. Rather, these territories had been attached to other principalities, which had permitted a Jewish presence. Thus, at the point when these areas came under French rule, the French authorities had debated the issue of Jewish presence, had considered the option of expelling these Jews and thus making the new area parallel in policy with the rest of France, and had decided to permit Jews ensconced in these areas to remain. This permission was accompanied by the clear understanding that permission to reside in these newly acquired territories did not establish the grounds for Jewish settlement elsewhere in France. Jewish settlement was limited to these areas and these areas only.

There was one very prominent area of overt Jewish settlement in pre-revolutionary France. Alsace-Lorraine had been taken over from Germany and had housed a fairly large and traditional north-central European Jewish community. The Jews of Alsace-Lorraine showed all the characteristics of north-central and northeastern European Jewish life. These Jews were limited in their economic activities and lived in highly segregated circumstances, much removed from the Christian population. Their sense of France and French identity was limited to nonexistent. As post-revolutionary France debated the issue of the Jewish place in French society, the largest group of Jews on the scene—those of Alsace-Lorraine—played a major and largely negative role in the unfolding debate.

There was, however, a rather different group of Jews in pre-revolutionary France, which was regularly adduced as well in the debate. We have already encountered the strange Jewish community of southwestern France, composed of former Iberian New Christians. As we have seen, some of the New Christian immigrants remained Christian, while others exploited their new circumstances to revert unobtrusively to Judaism. In this way, a community of Jews emerged, although maintaining the fiction of ongoing Christian identity. These Jews were deeply involved in international trade, were well integrated into southwestern French society, and were highly acculturated. During the argument over the place of Jews in the new France, this group was often cited, alongside and in contrast to the rather different Jews of Alsace-Lorraine.

In evaluating the Jewish potential for useful citizenship, much of the post-revolutionary argumentation was a reflection of the Jews who were foremost in the minds of the evaluators. For those opposed to citizen rights for Jews, the Jews of Alsace-Lorraine were uppermost in mind; for those advocating for Jewish rights, the Jews of the Bordeaux-Bayonne area were indicative of what Jews might become, given the right opportunities. Indeed, early in the deliberations of the French National Assembly (1789–1791), charged with drawing up the details for the new social order, the Jews of Bordeaux and Bayonne were quickly granted citizenship. They were clearly perceived as likely to become well integrated and constructive members of the new French society.[12]

As the members of the National Assembly began to debate the issue of citizenship for the remaining Jews, the Jewish potential for useful citizenship became the major line of argumentation of those opposed to Jewish rights in post-revolutionary France. Their opposition was largely grounded in the perceptions of the Jews of Alsace-Lorraine and their characteristics. Ultimately, this argument was successfully countered by the claim that distancing from prior European society had been imposed upon these Jews, not chosen by them. Thus, denial of rights to Jews would be unfair and indeed unconscionable. Jews had been distanced from European life by the Christian majority, which would then use that very distancing as the grounds for yet further and doubly unfair exclusion. Those who argued for Jewish rights anchored their argument in the standard liberal conviction that, if accorded equal rights, Jews would quickly change their ways and prove themselves useful and creative members of French society.

While the debate over the Jews lasted almost to the end of France's Constituent Assembly, ultimately the liberal position won out, and Jews were accorded citizen rights.[13] The equality of Judaism and Jews was now a de jure possibility throughout the new Europe ushered in by the French Revolution—a possibility that would slowly evolve into a reality in state after state. In terms of Jewish population movement, the Jewish reaction to the new equality is revealing. The entire prior edifice of demographic limitation was dismantled, and Jews could live wherever they might wish. Immediately French Jews streamed into Paris, the center of French business, government, and the arts, and quickly made it the predominant locus of Jewish settlement in France, which it has remained down to the present.

As increasingly large sectors of Europe accepted the new societal system embodied in the French Revolution, more areas became open to unfettered Jewish settlement, and Jews from the large Jewish population centers of northeastern Europe made their way westward into Germany, France, the Low Countries, and England. By the late nineteenth century, the overwhelming majority of Jews worldwide made their homes in Europe. The largest subgroup of European Jews remained in the more backward economic and political circumstances of eastern Europe, but the Jewish population of the more advanced sectors of western Europe was growing at a rapid pace.

Eventually, the movement westward proceeded beyond the barrier of the Atlantic Ocean into the New World. Eastern European Jews, limited by the backwardness of eastern Europe in general and by their special circumstances as Jews in particular, began a massive migratory movement. During the course of our review of Jewish migrations from late antiquity onward, we have encountered no movement that compares in numbers with the one that brought eastern European Jews westward across the Atlantic Ocean from the early 1880s through World War I. The magnitude of this migration is traceable to a number of factors, including the new openness of many western hemisphere countries to Jewish settlers, the large Jewish population of eastern Europe seeking a better life, the technological improvements that made transoceanic travel safer and cheaper than had previously been the case, and the improvements in communication that enabled eastern European Jews relocating in the New World to remain in contact with those they had left behind and to encourage them to make the same move.

With the realization of Enlightenment ideals of organization of state and church and the separation of the two realms, the circumstances that encouraged Jewish population movement westward were fully in place. The largest Jewish population by the seventeenth and eighteenth centuries was centered in northeastern Europe, suffered from the backwardness of this area, and was fully prepared to respond to the exciting new opportunities available in the new societies farther west. The largest migration in Jewish history—which lies beyond the boundaries of this study—ensued. This migration was certainly sparked by deep Jewish dissatisfaction with circumstances in northeastern Europe; it was, however, a voluntary relocation, with Jews making the difficult decision to uproot themselves and settle in a new setting.[14]

Toward the end of the Middle Ages, Jews suffered a new form of forced migration that removed them from the most advanced areas of western Christendom that were also the most advanced areas of the West. Slowly, as changes in societal structure opened the possibility of greater societal diversification, Jews mired in the backwardness of northeastern Europe began to sense the option of moving back in a westerly direction and availing themselves of the opportunities offered by these more advanced sectors of Europe. Initially, Jewish opportunities for relocation in the more advanced areas of north-central Europe and northwestern Europe were haphazard and not officially sanctioned. With Enlightenment thinking and the creation of states grounded in its principles, Jewish opportunities for resettlement became more stable, and the numbers of Jewish migrants became far larger, eventuating in the largest migration of Jews in history.

Epilogue

Over the ages, Jews have relocated regularly, becoming an unusually mobile human community. Have they done so primarily as refugees or primarily as migrants? The common view, grounded in the Hebrew Bible and expressed with variations in traditional Jewish, traditional Christian, and modern non-supernatural formulations, projects Jews as overwhelmingly refugees, with their population movement unfailingly involuntary, painful, and hurtful. In contrast, the present examination of Jewish population movement over the past two millennia has shown Jews to have been primarily migrants, relocating by and large voluntarily in search of a better life and with generally positive results. There have been to be sure displacements that were forced upon Jews and that were indeed painful and hurtful. Such involuntary relocation, however, constitutes the exception in Jewish population movement and was limited to specific times, places, and circumstances.

Throughout the first millennium, Jews migrated extensively, moving back and forth voluntarily and regularly within the boundaries of prior Jewish habitation, which stretched from Mesopotamia in the east through the Mediterranean Basin in the west. There is a widely accepted impression of Roman exile of Jews from the Land of Israel in the wake of suppression of the revolt of 66–70, but there was in fact no such expulsion. Nor did Roman suppression of the Jewish rebellion of 132–135 result in banishment of Jews from Palestine. Despite the human losses occasioned by both unsuccessful revolts and the disappearance of the Jerusalem Temple as a potent symbol of the centrality of the Land of Israel for all of world Jewry, the Jewish community of Palestine continued to dominate the world Jewish scene for a number of centuries following the year 70. Voluntary Jewish migration, stimulated by the general difficulties of life in the chaotic Roman Empire of the third century, not by Roman-Jewish conflict, began the elevation of Mesopotamian Jewry to a position of centrality and leadership within world Jewry.

The Muslim conquests of the seventh and eighth centuries consolidated the new configuration of world Jewish demography. As a result of these conquests, almost the entirety of world Jewry lived within the sphere of Islam. The emergence of Mesopotamia as the center of Islamic governance and culture reinforced the centrality of Mesopotamian Jewry as the largest, most powerful, and most influential Jewish community on the world scene. At the same time, as other sectors of the Islamic world, for example all across North Africa and into Spain, developed, the Jewish settlements in these areas become ever larger and increasingly more creative. By the end of the first millennium, important Jewish population centers were spread all across the traditional areas of Jewish habitation.

The second millennium brought with it major changes on the world scene, and these changes in turn stimulated important alterations in Jewish demography, triggered by innovative Jewish migration. The broadest changes on the Western scene involved the unanticipated emergence of once backward northern Europe into a major locus of vigor and power. Up until the end of the first millennium a backward hinterland to the southern areas of the continent, the northern sectors of Europe unexpectedly underwent remarkable vitalization, surging in population, economic productivity, political stability, and cultural creativity. By the end of the fifteenth century, newly ascendant western Christendom had become the strongest force in the West, leading the way in the discovery, exploration, and exploitation of far-off lands and poising itself to dominate the modern West.

The emergence of northern Europe as a vibrant new center of Western civilization encouraged enterprising and venturesome Mediterranean Jews to migrate northward, thus moving beyond the previous boundaries of Jewish settlement and creating a new venue for Jewish life. Some of the forward-looking rulers of northern Europe reinforced this Jewish migration by extending supportive invitations to Jewish settlement. The motivation of these rulers paralleled that of the Jews themselves. For both, economic considerations were paramount. Jews migrated in search of new economic opportunities, and the northern European rulers were attracted by the economic stimulation that such Jewish settlers might provide for their domains. Both sides enjoyed considerable success in achieving their objectives.

At the same time, there was major resistance to the new Jewish settlers. The very first element in this resistance was the simple newness of these Jews. Human societies rarely reach out with open arms to newcomers, and northern European society of the early second millennium was no exception. The indigenous inhabitants of northern Europe looked askance at the Jewish newcomers simply because they were new. This fundamental resistance was much enhanced by the religious homogeneity of the society that the Jews were entering. Whereas the religious composition of the Islamic world was diverse, so that the Jewish minority was by no means conspicuous, northern Europe's religious uniformity translated into the sense that the newcomers were religiously very different and thus additionally problematic.

The basic economic profile of the Jewish immigrants and the initial resistance of the northern European populace to them set in motion further complications. While Jews in the Mediterranean world, both its Islamic and Christian sectors, were longtime inhabitants and diversified in their economic outlets, only certain sectors within the Jewish population were in a position to benefit from the opportunities offered in rapidly developing northern Europe. Only Jews who enjoyed the mobility provided by trade and business were in a position to migrate into northern Europe. Thus from the outset the Jewish population of northern Europe was limited in its economic profile. The earlier Jewish economic diversity gave way in northern Europe to a skewed Jewish economy.

Given the initial popular resistance to the Jewish newcomers, the populace of northern Europe was unlikely to open broader economic outlets to them, and it in fact did not open such broader outlets. Further economic horizons did emerge for the new Jewish immigrants in northern Europe, however. As a result of the vigorous twelfth-century Church campaign against Christian usury, the Jews of northern Europe, already focused on trade and business, found a new, lucrative, and unpopular economic outlet in banking and moneylending. While exchange of capital is vital to all societies, especially societies in the throes of rapid development like those of medieval northern Europe, the people who provide these crucial services have over the ages been resented and vilified. Thus, the initial resistance to the Jewish immigrants evolved into a second level of distrust, with negative imagery of Jews as businesspeople and bankers supplementing the earlier perception of them as newcomers and religious dissidents. Negative perceptions of the Jews intensified, rather than ameliorating.

There was yet another secondary negative development for the new Jewish population of northern Europe. From the outset of Jewish settlement, the political authorities had played an important role in supporting these immigrants, as a result of the initial resistance of the indigenous population. As the twelfth-century Jews immersed themselves increasingly in the unpopular activity of moneylending, they again required considerable support from the ruling class. Once more, the authorities were willing to provide the requisite assistance, out of their desire to improve the general economy and to enrich their treasuries. The close alliance between the Jews and their baronial and royal protectors created two further problems for the Jewish immigrants. On the one hand, those in society resentful of the political authorities found yet another source of dissatisfaction with the Jews, perceived quite accurately as clients of these often unpopular authorities. In addition, the overwhelming role the authorities played in Jewish life opened the way for eventual exploitation of this role. Thus, for example, the medieval instances of formal expulsion of Jews, which began in twelfth-century northern Europe, almost always involved considerable profit for the authorities decreeing the banishment.

Perched between the popular resistance to the Jewish newcomers and the largely supportive political authorities was the Church, an increasingly powerful force in northern Europe and in western Christendom more generally. The broad lines of Church policy vis-à-vis Jews had been established long before the migration of Jews into northern Europe. From the early stages of its history onward and despite the negative portrayal of the Palestinian Jewish contemporaries of Jesus in the Gospels, Church policy had insisted on the rightful and indeed useful place of Jews in Christian society. In the Church view, Christian societies were obligated to protect scrupulously Jewish life and religious identity. Anti-Jewish violence was prohibited. At the same time, Jews were obligated to comport themselves in ways that would occasion no harm to the Christian societies that hosted them. The Jewish immigrants in northern Europe benefited from the Church's protective stance and were constrained by its insistence on limitations of Jewish impact on Christian host societies. With the passage of time, the threats from which Christians had to be protected and the Jewish dangers that had to be minimized or eliminated could and did evolve.

The emergence of northern Europe as a potent force in the West spawned a new set of Jewish settlements and eventually an entirely new branch of the Jewish people. In time, this new branch came to dominate worldwide Jewry in much the same way that the host society in which it embedded itself was dominating the West overall. As a result of this dominance, the patterns of life in this line of the Jewish people have often and mistakenly been perceived as the norms for all of Jewish history. Thus, for example, Jews are widely believed to have been businesspeople and bankers from time immemorial, which was not at all the case. The older Jewish settlements of late antiquity and the first half of the Middle Ages show thorough diversification of Jewish economic activity. Likewise, Jews are assumed to have aroused the animosity of their neighbors all through their lengthy history. Yet this too has not at all been the case. The older Jewish communities of late antiquity and the early Middle Ages—long resident in the heterogeneous Middle East and the Mediterranean Basin—enjoyed rather quiet and amicable relations with their non-Jewish contemporaries.

Toward the end of the twelfth century, northern European Jews began to suffer formal expulsion. These expulsions recurred throughout the closing centuries of the Middle Ages, eventually spreading southward and affecting the older Iberian center of Jewish life. This limited reality, spawned initially out of the unique circumstances of northern Europe, has reinforced the broad sense of Jews as overwhelmingly refugees, of involuntary displacement as a standard feature of historic Jewish existence, which it in reality was not.

Anthropologists have reached the conclusion that prehistoric humans, beginning from their point of origin in Africa, set forth and eventually spread across the globe. To an extent, the stimulus to this movement was the search for sustenance, but in addition the anthropologists also suggest an inherent human drive toward exploration of the new, a conclusion buttressed recently by geneticists as well. Human beings from time immemorial seem to have wandered.[1] Yet, clearly the propensity for migration has varied from human community to human community.

The traditional and popular views of Jewish history project an image of extensive wanderings and provide a simple explanation for the high level of Jewish population mobility. In these popular views, Jews moved around the globe at an unusual rate as refugees, meaning that they were forced to do so, although there is disagreement as to the nature of the forces that compelled unusually extensive Jewish population movement. In the traditional Jewish and Christian supernatural views, it was God who moved the Jews incessantly around the globe; in modern non-supernatural views, a variety of factors are invoked as forcing regular Jewish displacement. In both sets of views, however, there is agreement on Jewish population movement as extensive and as overwhelmingly involuntary.

The present review of Jewish relocation over the past two millennia has challenged these views of unusual Jewish mobility as involuntary; we have found that Jews have largely migrated voluntarily. This alternative view thus requires a different set of explanations for the unusual levels of Jewish mobility. The broadest and most significant factor underlying voluntary Jewish demographic movement involved the unusual nature of Jewish ethnic identity. Whereas ethnic identity generally involves very close ties to given locales, these constraints were removed as a result of the unique features of Jewish ethnic identity, thus freeing Jews from their close association with a given geographic area. This freedom enabled Jews to respond at an unusual level to shortcomings in their home ambience or to opportunities perceived elsewhere and to relocate.

Ethnic ties with given locales among the polytheists of antiquity were reinforced by the nature of polytheistic religious belief. The many gods of antiquity were very much associated with particular places, thus markedly reinforcing the geographic element in ethnic identity. Ethnic-religious identity related to specific locales limited the mobility of these polytheists; it did not eliminate their ability to relocate, but it did constrict them. Both Christianity and Islam rejected the multiplicity of gods and were committed to the notion of one deity only. However, both of these monotheisms broke all ties with specific ethnic identity. Thus the ethnic identity of Christians and Muslims was severed from the universality of the two monotheistic faiths. English Christians were very much tied to England, and French Christians to France. Both polytheist ethnics and Christian and Muslim ethnics were strongly rooted in specific geographic settings.

The Jewish situation was unique in combining specific ethnic identity with theological universality. Jews very much shared the conviction of one deity in the world, but held a different perspective on ethnicity and its territorial dimension. For Jews, the one God had indeed created the universe and controls it. For reasons shrouded in divine mystery, the one God chose one human family, which eventually evolved into one human community as his partners, revealing to them essential truths, protecting them, but making demands on them that could result in failure and punishment.

This relationship between the universal deity and the specific ethnic community of Israel involved as well a particular territory. For reasons as unfathomable as the choice of Israel as God's human partners, God also singled out a specific territory on the eastern shores of the Mediterranean Sea as the unique land of the people he had chosen. Like the well-being of this chosen community in general, this special territory could be temporarily lost as a result of Israel's transgressions. History was a contingent process, with its vicissitudes wholly dependent on Israel's fulfillment or non-fulfillment of its covenant with the one and only deity. Fulfillment of divine demands would bring blessing in the special land; failure to fulfill divine demands would entail punishment, beginning with suffering within the special territory and eventuating in expulsion from it.

Removal from the special land, however, would by no means signal the end of the ethnic identity or religious commitments and obligations of Israelites/Judeans/Jews. We have examined in some detail the horrific Mosaic predictions of divine punishment for neglect of the covenant, capped by expulsion from the Land of Israel and incessant wandering. As noted, these terrible developments would not end the ethnic and religious identity of the Israelites. At the point of true repentance, God would once again embrace them and bring them back from wherever they might find themselves.

God revealed all this to his early and later followers, beginning with the Patriarchs and then on to the Israelite nation led from exile and servitude to the Promised Land by Moses, and then—through prophetic messengers—to the Israelites settled in the Promised Land, and these teachings lie at the core of the biblical corpus that Jews revere as divinely communicated. God emphasized throughout these messages the element of contingency in Israel's fortunes. Israelite fulfillment of the demands of the covenant would assure safe and secure existence in the Land of Israel; failure to fulfill the demands of the covenant would result in suffering in the Promised Land or even exile from it. The exile might be brief or lengthy, but it would conclude eventually with the Jews properly ensconced in the land promised to them as their own.

The history of Israel and the Jews could fluctuate between two alternative stages—a positive phase that would result from fulfillment of the covenant and would involve divine favor, and a painful phase that would result from failure to fulfill the covenant and would involve divine displeasure and punishment. Key to this two-tier sense of history is the assurance that the first of these phases constitutes the norm of Jewish history and its ultimate end, with the second of these phases aberrational and temporary. However long the aberrational phase of Jewish history might last, it would eventually give way to the normative, that is to say to the happy return to safe and secure existence in the land promised by the God of the entire universe to his chosen people. In somewhat curious ways, this complex view of history freed Jews over the ages to migrate more readily than most other human communities. Migration was not projected as simple cosmopolitanism; it was an integral part of the covenantal relationship between God and Israel, with many of its implications carefully spelled out.

Most of the extensive guidance provided by God to his chosen people was universal, involving obligations of belief and practice that were binding everywhere, both in the homeland and in exile. There were to be sure covenantal obligations that were unique to the homeland phase of Jewish history, especially revolving around the temple that could be erected only in the sacred precincts of Jerusalem, once again a divine mystery like the choice by the universal God of one specific family/nation and one specific territory.

Less obvious but present nonetheless are guidelines for exilic existence. These guidelines appear less regularly, since so much of the biblical corpus is focused on the approach of the Israelites to the Promised Land and then their checkered history in that land. Nonetheless, valuable—and complicated—guidance is occasionally provided. Perhaps the most widely noted and cited guidance is provided by God through the prophet Jeremiah to Jews already a part of an early phase of the removal of Judeans from the Land of Israel.

The historical circumstances of Jeremiah's life and preaching were special.[2] The punishment he predicted unfolded over a substantial period of time. Thus, Jeremiah's messages were addressed to Judeans before the onset of Babylonian measures against Judea and during a period of intensifying Babylonian oppression. This meant that, while continuing to exhort his Judean listeners to repent and thus halt the accelerating punishment, there were also Judeans who had been sent into exile whom he could usefully address.

In part, Jeremiah, like Moses and the other prophets, assured those Judeans already in exile that their punishment would be temporary and that God would return them to their homeland and to the normalcy of Judean existence therein.

> When a full seventy years have passed over Babylon, I shall take up your cause and make good my promise to bring you back to this place. . . . I shall restore your fortunes; I shall gather you from all the nations and all the places to which I have banished you, says the Lord, and restore you to the place from which I carried you into exile.[3]

Babylonian persecution might easily be misinterpreted as normal imperial action, and the exile as a humanly engineered event. Jeremiah insisted that this was not at all the case. The Babylonians, in exiling the Judeans, were serving as God's agent in imposing divine punishment on errant Israel. Indeed, the very same God that set the punishment in motion would bring it to a close. Punishment was predicted and had begun. Those suffering the initial stages of this punishment could rest assured that it would eventually conclude with those whom God had chastised returning to their homeland. This is clear evidence of the two-tiered nature of Israelite/Judean/Jewish history—the genuine period of normative history in the homeland and the aberrational period of history in exile.

Much of the covenant was not constricted to the homeland and the period of normalcy therein. Since the God of Israel was the God of the entire universe, his non-localized demands were in force everywhere. Were there then specific living instructions for the aberrational period? Jeremiah in fact—before promising return to divine favor and the homeland—provides some.

> To all the exiles whom I deported from Jerusalem to Babylon: Build houses and live in them; plant gardens and eat the produce; marry wives and rear families; choose wives for your sons and give your daughters to husbands, so that they may bear sons and daughters. Increase there and do not dwindle away.[4]

The pain of exile should not be permitted to engender mass hopelessness and disruption of the normal rhythms of life. The exile was to last for a period of time, and those in exile were bidden to maintain life and continuity, in order to be prepared for the divinely provided return to the homeland and normalcy.

In addition, Jeremiah also provides guidance for relating to the non-Judean society in which the exiles find themselves.

> Seek the welfare of any city to which I have exiled you, and pray to the Lord for it. On its welfare your welfare will depend.[5]

While life in exile will be aberrational in terms of the ultimate trajectory of Israelite/Judean/Jewish history, life during the exilic phase of this history must go on nonetheless. Normal biological needs must be met, and this necessitates relating to the larger environment where those in exile find themselves. Their relationship to this larger environment must be healthy and positive.

Jeremiah's guidance to Judean/Jewish life in exile was widely noted and regularly quoted by subsequent Jews. His message was reinforced by the few biblical works that explicitly indicate their exilic provenance. The books of Ezra and Nehemiah, while focused on the resumption of Jewish life in the Land of Israel, through their core narrative buttress much of the Jeremiah urging. The central figures—Nehemiah and Ezra—are both Jews who have clearly immersed themselves fully in their exilic environment. Jewish life and Jewish identity have flourished in Babylonian exile. Indeed, Nehemiah is portrayed as having followed Jeremiah's advice to the point of reaching a very high station in the Persian imperial court. This constitutes much more than simple loyalty to and prayer for the non-Jewish authorities; it constitutes active immersion in the realities of non-Jewish governance and outstanding achievement in this domain.

A widely read late book of the Hebrew Bible is the book of Esther.[6] Viewed by modern biblical scholars as an ahistorical and imaginative novella, the book played a central role in a major annual Jewish celebration, the holiday of Purim, and was thus widely recited and pondered. The book is a simplistic paean of praise to the God that cares for exilic Jews and protects them from dangers. The human figures that dominate the tale once again have immersed themselves to the full in the life of the society in which they find themselves. This is the case for the central female figure of Esther, whose beauty brings her to the attention and eventually the harem of the ruler; it is even more obvious for the central male figure, her uncle Mordechai, who like Nehemiah rises to a position of eminence in imperial circles. Once again, these narrative figures follow the advice of Jeremiah, living life to the fullest in the new environment where they have found themselves. More important, the Book of Esther asserts that God's concern for his special people extends outside the Land of Israel as well. In their annual celebration of the festival of Purim, Jews over the ages have imbibed this message of living fully outside the Land of Israel and the concern of the universal God for his people wherever they might be.

Thus, the Jewish sense of ethnic identity and relation to ethnic territory is anything but simple. Jews do not view their exilic existence as simply a period away from the homeland, with carte blanche to live as they might wish and to exploit the temporary environment in which they might find themselves. Life in exile was regulated in much the same way as life in the Land of Israel. The obligations of living in exile included normal human activities in support of individual and group health and life. They also included a positive relationship to the larger environment. An unusual level of Jewish migration was facilitated by a conviction that living outside the Jewish homeland was part of the divine plan for Israel and that Jews were obligated to live according to the demands of the covenant during this less than auspicious phase of Jewish history. Jews were to maintain themselves as well as possible and to contribute effectively to the larger society in which they might find themselves.

The biblical message to Jews was unequivocal. They might well find themselves outside the special territory promised to them. Under these unfortunate circumstances, they did not cease to be Jews and were not free of the broad obligations of human existence and the special obligations imposed upon them as Jews. This meant that the normal constraints imposed on ethnic groups—the loss of ethnic identity by virtue of distancing from the ethnic territory—did not exist for Jews. Indeed, they were ordered to live life fully wherever they might find themselves. The ongoing sense of identity and obligation and the directive to full living combined to facilitate and to an extent encourage Jewish mobility. The special combination of ethnic particularity and religious universality proved problematic to Jews in modern societies; this combination played a major role in the unusual level of pre-modern Jewish mobility.

Finally, we might ask about the results of the special Jewish propensity for migration, especially the more extreme form that took Jews long distances from their homeland and even far from the broader expanse of lands they had populated all through antiquity. On the individual level, Jewish migration would seem to have been quite successful. The very fact that the Jewish population of northern Europe continued to grow and eventually evolved into the largest branch of the Jewish people implies individual success. Even when northern European Jews were expelled from the advanced northwestern territories, the banishments did not drive these Jews back to the older sectors of Jewish population. Northern European Jews banished from the northwest moved eastward, opting to remain in the northern corridor of the continent.

What then of the Jewish people as a group? Here views might diverge, largely because they involve assessment of recent and contemporary realities and present-day differences of Jewish opinion with respect to these assessments. Again, the Jewish immigrants into northern Europe encountered acceptance and rejection. The acceptance was sufficient to support ongoing immigration and continued growth of the Jewish communities of northern Europe. The rejection morphed into a set of destructive perceptions that inflicted damage all through the Middle Ages and into the early modern centuries. In the nineteenth century, these negative attitudes coalesced into the destructive stereotypes of modern anti-Semitism, and in the twentieth century they fueled the unimaginable tragedy of the Holocaust.

We have followed with some care the dire biblical predictions of divine punishment that would be meted out to errant Israel and have found them horrific—natural calamity in the Land of Israel, conquest of the Land of Israel, expulsion from the Land of Israel, endless and painful wandering across the face of the globe. The possibility of genocide, an effort to wipe out the Jews in their entirety, was not conjured up by the fertile imaginations of the biblical authors. Does the reality of the resistance to the Jewish newcomers evolving into genocide suggest that the results of the Jewish propensity for migration were ultimately negative? Does this tragedy ultimately outweigh all the positives introduced by the Jewish peregrinations we have tracked?

There is surely agreement both within the Jewish world and outside it as to the uniqueness of the Holocaust in Jewish history and perhaps in all of human history. Within the fragmented contemporary Jewish world, horror over the Holocaust has led some to question key aspects of the Jewish past and to chide their predecessors over alleged short-sightedness. While Jewish migration has not been cited specifically in the context of this criticism, which has by and large come from Zionist circles, some of the critics of diaspora Jewish life would likely project the Jewish migrations we have been tracking as a massive error in Jewish thinking. It seems fair to say, however, that this view would be held by only a minority of contemporary Jewish observers. The majority would insist on the benefits, certainly not thorough and untarnished, of the historic Jewish willingness for demographic change.

Indeed, we might also ask about the impact of the Jewish migrations on the larger Western society to which Jews attached themselves. Here too there is a difference of opinion. For the anti-Semites of the nineteenth century, the Nazis of the twentieth century, and their sympathizers, the Jewish peregrinations were an unalloyed disaster, introducing into the West the most destructive force imaginable, a force responsible for all that has been disruptive and harmful in the modern West. Happily, this seems to have become very much a minority view, overshadowed by the sense that the Jewish migrants we have been studying have enriched enormously Western life over the ages and especially since their entry into northern Europe—through their Nobel laureates, their Marxes, Freuds, and Einsteins, and their overall stimulation of Western economy, technology, political thinking, scientific inquiry, social sensitivity, and cultural creativity.

NOTES

Prologue

1. This study covers late antiquity through the extended Middle Ages. Late antiquity is defined as the period that began with the conquests of Alexander. At this time, Jews became part of the unified West that included the entire area from Mesopotamia in the east through the Mediterranean Basin in the west. The extended Middle Ages proceed though the end of the eighteenth century. This represents acceptance of the Annales School sense that—despite the onset of modern thinking during the sixteenth and seventeenth centuries—the Western world remained organized according to pre-modern ideals down through the end of the eighteenth century. Patterns of Jewish displacement over the past two centuries lie outside the scope of this study. As for geography, Jews have been dispersed throughout the Western world. Through the end of the first Christian millennium, Jewish population was limited to the rectangular territory from Mesopotamia through the Mediterranean Basin. Following the end of the first millennium, a new branch of the Jewish people developed in northern Europe. We shall follow Jewish population movement throughout both areas, exercising care not to neglect either.

1 Traditional Jewish and Christian Perspectives

1. The narrative sections of the Hebrew Bible portray the emergence of the covenant idea as extremely early. Modern scholars project this development as prolonged over time, with the narrative sections of the Hebrew Bible in fact composed at a rather late date, thus making the prophetic writings earlier than the narrative sections. See inter alia Mark S. Smith, *The Early History of God: Yahweh and the Other Deities in Ancient Israel* (San Francisco: Harper and Row, 1990). There are

many fine introductions to the Hebrew Bible. The one I have found the most incisive and useful is John J. Collins, *Introduction to the Hebrew Bible* (Minneapolis: Fortress, 2004).

2. For a valuable introduction to this first wave of prophets, see Collins, *Introduction to the Hebrew Bible*, chapters 15 and 16. I have also regularly consulted the relevant volumes on each of these prophets in the Anchor Bible. For a discussion of the multiple Isaiahs, see ibid., 307–309.
3. Isaiah 1:5–9. I shall cite English translations of passages from the Hebrew Bible in the Jewish Publication Society of America translation, *Tanakh: A New Translation of the Holy Scriptures According to the Traditional Hebrew Text* (Philadelphia: The Jewish Publication Society, 1985).
4. The Assyrians imposed the same punishment on all ethnic communities that resisted their drive toward hegemony. See Bustenay Oded, *Mass Deportations and Deportees in the Neo-Assyrian Empire* (Wiesbaden: Dr. Ludwig Reichert Verlag, 1979).
5. For a dating of Deuteronomy, see Collins, *Introduction to the Hebrew Bible*, 162–164.
6. Deuteronomy 28:49–50.
7. Deuteronomy 28:63.
8. Deuteronomy 28:64–68.
9. Deuteronomy 30:1–5.
10. For recent perspectives on the revolt of 66–70, see Martin Goodman, *The Ruling Class of Judea: The Origins of the Jewish Revolt Against Rome, A.D. 66–70* (Cambridge: Cambridge University Press, 1987), and Mladan Popovic, ed., *The Jewish Revolt Against Rome* (Leiden: Brill, 2011).
11. Daniel 2.
12. The sequence of empires is often reconstructed in different fashion by Christian exegetes and modern scholars.
13. Daniel 7:7.
14. The role of Jewish ritual in Jewish historical memory is emphasized by Yosef Hayim Yerushalmi in *Zakhor: Jewish History and Jewish Memory* (Seattle: University of Washington Press, 1982).
15. T.B., Rosh Ha-Shanah 18b.
16. Genesis 4:1–16.

2 Modern Perspectives

1. A comprehensive introduction to the Enlightenment in all its ramifications can be found in the remarkable trilogy by Jonathan I. Israel, *Radical Enlightenment: Philosophy and the Making of Modernity, 1650–1750* (Oxford: Oxford University Press, 2001); *Enlightenment Contested: Philosophy, Modernity, and the*

Emancipation of Man, 1670–1752 (Oxford: Oxford University Press, 2006); *Democratic Enlightenment: Philosophy, Revolution, and Human Rights, 1750–1790* (Oxford: Oxford University Press, 2011).

2. For illuminating examples of the contrasts between pre-Enlightenment and Enlightenment thinking, see the superb study by Christopher de Bellaigue, *The Islamic Enlightenment: The Modern Struggle Between Faith and Reason* (London: The Bodley Head, 2017). At a number of points, de Bellaigue presents from specific settings side-by-side nineteenth-century European Enlightenment perspectives and nineteenth-century Islamic pre-Enlightenment perspectives. The contrasts are of course stark.
3. See the careful and illuminating study of Geoffrey G. Field, *Evangelist of Race: The Germanic Vision of Houston Stewart Chamberlain* (New York: Columbia University Press, 1981).
4. See Jacob Katz, *The Darker Side of Genius: Richard Wagner's Antisemitism* (Waltham: Brandeis University Press, 1985).
5. Houston Stewart Chamberlain, *Foundations of the Nineteenth Century*, trans. John Lees, 2 vols. (New York: Howard Fertig, 1968).
6. Ibid., 1:335.
7. This lengthy and complex story is laid out in ibid., 1:352–493.
8. Ibid., 1:344–345.
9. S. D. Goitein, *A Mediterranean Society: The Jewish Communities of the Arab World as Portrayed in the Documents of the Cairo Genizah*, 6 vols. (Berkeley: University of California Press, 1967–1993), vol. 1.
10. Again note the Goitein reconstruction of a diversified Mediterranean Jewish economy.
11. On the eventual maturation of the Jewish communities of western Christendom, see Robert Chazan, *The Jews of Medieval Western Christendom, 1000–1500* (Berkeley: University of California Press, 2006).
12. Deuteronomy 23:21.
13. While a focus on moneylending seems to have begun in the young Jewish communities of northern Europe, the tendency eventually spread into the older Jewish communities of the south as well. See Yom Tov Assis, *Jewish Economy in the Medieval Crown of Aragon, 1213–1327: Money and Power* (Leiden: Brill, 1997).
14. Chamberlain, *Foundations*, 1:330.
15. Arthur Hertzberg, ed., *The Zionist Idea: A Historical Analysis and Reader* (Garden City: Doubleday, 1959), 105.
16. The writings of Leon Pinsker in English translation were collected and introduced by B. Netanyahu in *Road to Freedom: Writings and Addresses by Leon Pinsker* (New York: Scopus, 1944).
17. Mishnah Avot, 1:14, cited in ibid., 74.
18. Ibid., 75.

19. Ibid., 77–78.
20. Ibid., 84.
21. Ibid., 89.
22. Israel, *Radical Enlightenment;* Israel, *Enlightenment Contested;* and Israel, *Democratic Enlightenment.*
23. In his valuable study of the medieval roots of modern European nationalisms, Patrick J. Geary devotes his opening chapter to the role of nationalism in the evolution of modern historiography. See *The Myth of Nations: The Medieval Origins of Europe* (Princeton: Princeton University Press, 2002).
24. In the programmatic statement of a new "Science of Judaism," drawn up by a number of young German Jews in 1822, Immanuel Wolf projected a three-part enterprise—a textual study of Judaism, a history of Judaism, and then a philosophy of Judaism. The overarching syntheses were intended to serve the third purpose. See Paul Mendes-Flohr and Jehuda Reinharz, *The Jew in the Modern World: A Documentary History*, 3rd ed. (New York: Oxford University Press, 2011), 244–245.
25. On Heinrich Graetz, see the introductory essay by Ismar Schorsch in Heinrich Graetz, *The Structure of Jewish History and Other Essays*, trans. Ismar Schorsch (New York: Jewish Theological Seminary, 1975), and Michael Brenner, *Prophets of the Past: Interpreters of Jewish History* (Princeton: Princeton University Press, 2010), chapter 2.
26. Although Graetz was allowed to study at the University of Breslau, as a Jew he could not receive his degree there. Thus the degree was conferred by the University of Jena.
27. Graetz, *The Structure of Jewish History*, 125.
28. Ibid.

3 Innovative Recent Perspectives

1. Salo Baron, "Ghetto and Emancipation: Shall We Revise the Traditional View?" *The Menorah Journal* 14 (1928): 515–526.
2. Ibid., 526.
3. Recall Graetz and his sense of a new era dawning in the late eighteenth century, as noted above. On the uncertainty in the Baron sentence, see David Engel, "Crisis and Lachrymosity: On Salo Baron, Neobaronianism, and the Study of Modern Jewish History," *Jewish History* 20 (2006): 243–264, and Robert Chazan, "A New Vision of Jewish History: The Early Writings of Salo Baron," *AJS Review* 30 (2015): 27–47.
4. Robert Liberles, *Salo Wittmayer Baron: Architect of Jewish History* (New York: New York University Press, 1995).
5. Baron, "Ghetto and Emancipation," 516. Striking here is the readiness of the very young Baron to take on the iconic figures of the early twentieth-century Jewish

intellectual establishment. Also noteworthy is his reference to a range of Jews—rabbis, accorded first place in his list; scholars; and laymen.

6. Ibid.
7. Ibid., 516–521.
8. Ibid., 521–524.
9. Ibid., 524–526.
10. The lack of footnotes reinforces the sense of the 1928 essay as popular and polemical, since Baron was famous for his lengthy and comprehensive footnotes.
11. This footnote appears at the bottom of 516.
12. The very influential Annales School has formulated a sense of the "long Middle Ages," which ended only with the close of the eighteenth century, and this perspective is adopted here.
13. Baron, "Ghetto and Emancipation," 516.
14. Ibid.
15. Baron analyzed in much the same way three more specific aspects of late medieval and early modern Jewish life—serfdom, ghettoization, and the Inquisition. Baron sets all three, generally adduced as evidence of Jewish suffering, into their historical context, and that contextualization strips them of the horrific overtones that they normally evoked. For full details, see Chazan, "A New Vision of Jewish History."
16. Baron, "Ghetto and Emancipation," 521.
17. Ibid., 522.
18. On this momentous appointment and its complexities, see Liberles, *Salo Wittmayer Baron*, chapter 2, and Paul Ritterband and Harold S. Wechsler, *Jewish Learning in American Universities: The First Century* (Bloomington: Indiana University Press, 1994), chapter 7.
19. Salo Wittmayer Baron, *A Social and Religious History of the Jews*, 3 vols. (New York: Columbia University Press, 1937).
20. Again recall Graetz, as described in the previous chapter.
21. Baron, *Social and Religious History* (1937), 2:31–32.
22. Ibid., 2:31.
23. Ibid., 1:vi.
24. Ibid., "The Great War," 1:180–183; "The Rise of Christianity," 1:224–229; "Pauline Schism," 1:229–234.
25. Ibid., 307–377.
26. The preceding eight chapter titles are: "Jewish Society and Religion," "The Origins of Israel," "Kings and Prophets," "The Crucial Test," "The Expansion of Judaism," "The Great Schism," "The World of the Talmud," and "The Infidel."
27. Ibid., 2:3–8.
28. Ibid., 2:20.
29. Ibid., 2:27.
30. Ibid., 2:31.

31. Ibid.
32. Baron is technically correct in identifying the beginnings of historical writing organized around the lachrymose in early modern Europe. However, he significantly understates the rootedness of the lachrymose conception in traditional Jewish thinking. The lachrymose conception was grounded in a reading of the Hebrew Bible that projected horrific punishments for Jewish sinfulness. Jews from early on—long before the Jewish Middle Ages—projected Jewish exile and its attendant suffering as the results of just such sinfulness.
33. Baron, *Social and Religious History,* 2:31. The portrait of Jews with bundles on their backs is eerily reminiscent of the imagery used by Graetz in his statement on post-70 Jewish suffering noted earlier. Graetz created graphic imagery of the two aspects of post-70 Jewish experience—the painful suffering and the intense intellectuality. The former "represents subjugated Judah with the pilgrim staff in hand, the pilgrim pack upon the back, with a mournful eye addressed toward heaven"; Heinrich Graetz, *The Structure of Jewish History and Other Essays,* 125. Baron, deeply steeped in the work of his predecessor Graetz, absorbed much, even as he sought to distance himself from Graetz's views.
34. Here Baron even more significantly understates the traditional roots of the lachrymose conception of Jewish history, in this case the Christian version. For the Church Fathers, Jewish exile and suffering is the key motif of post-crucifixion Jewish history, serving as obvious evidence of Jewish sinfulness and divine abandonment.

4 Governmental Expulsions

1. Following the Babylonians, the Jews were ruled by Persians, Greeks, and pagan Roman authorities, none of whom exiled their Jewish subjects. There was no exile at the hands of the Romans at the end of the unsuccessful 66–70 rebellion, as we shall see.
2. Benjamin Z. Kedar, "Expulsion as an Issue of World History," *Journal of World History* 7 (1996): 166.
3. This is reminiscent of the Sherlock Holmes story about the dog that didn't bark.
4. There has been a widely shared sense that the Arch of Titus shows such Jewish captives bearing the looted sacred objects of the Jerusalem Temple. This view has been rejected convincingly by Steven Fine, "Who Is Carrying the Temple Menorah? A Jewish Counter-Narrative to the Arch of Titus Spolia Panel," *Images: A Journal of Jewish Art and Visual Culture* 9 (2016): 1–60.
5. For recent views of the Bar Kokhba rebellion, see Peter Schafer, *The Bar Kokhba War Reconsidered: New Perspectives on the Second Jewish Revolt Against Rome* (Tubingen: Mohr Siebeck, 2003).
6. For judicious consideration of the difficulties in reconstructing Jewish leadership and an emphasis on the support of the Roman authorities, see Seth Schwartz,

Imperialism and Jewish Society, 200 B.C.E. to 640 C.E. (Princeton: Princeton University Press, 2001).

7. See David Kraemer, "The Mishnah," in *The Cambridge History of Judaism*, vol. 4, ed. Steven T. Katz (Cambridge: Cambridge University Press, 2006), 299–315.
8. On Augustine and the Jews, see Jeremy Cohen, *Living Letters of the Law: Ideas of the Jew in Medieval Christianity* (Berkeley: University of California Press, 1999), chapter 1, and Paula Fredriksen, *Augustine and the Jew: A Christian Defense of Jews and Judaism* (New York: Doubleday, 2008).
9. Recall Kedar's placement of the onset of expulsion as a governmental technique at precisely this point in time.
10. The vitalization of western Christendom has been depicted by numerous scholars. Two of the most important are R. W. Southern, *The Making of the Middle Ages* (New Haven: Yale University Press, 1953), and Johannes Fried, *The Middle Ages* (Cambridge: Harvard University Press, 2015).
11. Recall the findings of S. D. Goitein on the diversified Jewish economy of the Mediterranean basin.
12. Deuteronomy 23:20–21.
13. See the valuable study of Rowan William Dorin, *Banishing Usury: The Expulsion of Foreign Moneylenders in Medieval Europe, 1200–1450* (unpublished doctoral dissertation, Harvard University, 2015). The Italian Christian moneylenders were in one sense more problematic than the Jewish moneylenders, since they were overtly contravening biblical and Church law; at the same time, they did not arouse the same level of popular animosity as the Jewish lenders did.
14. Recall again the Goitein findings cited above. The dramatic Gospel account of Jesus driving the money-changers out of the temple has often been cited as evidence of Jewish involvement in finance back in antiquity. That account—drama notwithstanding—of course proves nothing. All major shrines in antiquity—and in subsequent ages as well—have attracted large numbers of visitors and have thus required the services of money-changers.
15. For salient examples, see Robert Chazan, *Church, State, and Jew in the Middle Ages* (New York: Behrman House, 1980), 205–220.
16. For a fascinating example, see Robert Chazan, "Anti-Usury Efforts in Thirteenth-Century Narbonne and the Jewish Response," *Proceedings of the American Academy for Jewish Research* 41–42 (1973–1974): 45–67.
17. For fuller detail on the expulsion of 1182, see Robert Chazan, "The Onset of Medieval European Expulsions of Jews" (forthcoming).
18. William Chester Jordan, *The French Monarchy and the Jews: From Philip Augustus to the Last of the Capetians* (Philadelphia: University of Pennsylvania Press, 1989), 128.
19. Recall once again the parallel treatment of Italian moneylenders, as reconstructed by Rowan Dorin.

20. Chazan, *Church, State, and Jew in the Middle Ages*, 314–317.
21. Ibid., 80–83.
22. Alfred Haverkamp, ed., *Geschichte der Juden im Mittelalter von der Nordsee bis zur en Sudalpen* (Hannover: Verlag Hahnsche, 2002), vol. 2, *Ortskatalog*, provides a listing of Jewish settlements, with available documentation. Many of these sites show expulsions, often followed by return to the sites. My appreciation to my colleague David Engel for bringing this source to my attention.
23. For a comprehensive overview of the expulsion of 1492, see Haim Beinart, *The Expulsion of the Jews from Spain*, trans. Jeffrey M. Green (Oxford: The Littman Library, 2002).
24. See, for example, Ben Zion Netanyahu, *The Marranos of Spain from the Late 14th to the Early 16th Century* (New York: American Academy for Jewish Research, 1966), and Norman Roth, *Conversos, Inquisition, and the Expulsion of the Jews from Spain* (Madison: University of Wisconsin Press, 2002).
25. Jane Gerber, *The Jews of Spain: A History of the Sephardic Experience* (New York: The Free Press, 1992), 286.
26. Nicholas Terpstra, *Religious Refugees in the Early Modern World: An Alternative History of the Reformation* (Cambridge: Cambridge University Press, 2015), 1–2.
27. See the rich materials and valuable observations in Jeremy Cohen, *A Historian in Exile: Solomon ibn Verga's* Shevet Yehudah *and the Jewish-Christian Encounter* (Philadelphia: University of Pennsylvania Press, 2017).
28. Recall Baron's emphasis on expulsion as an innovation of medieval European society.

5 Flight from Governmental Repression or Popular Violence

1. For this analysis, see Bernard Bachrach, *Early Medieval Jewish Policy in Western Europe* (Minneapolis: University of Minnesota Press, 1977), chapter 1.
2. Chazan, *Church, State, and Jew in the Middle Ages*, 294.
3. The entire narrative can be found in A. M. Habermann, *Sefer Gezerot Ashkenaz ve-Zarfat* (Jerusalem: Tarshish, 1946), 19–21.
4. Abraham ibn Daud, *Sefer ha-Qabbalah*, ed. Gerson D. Cohen (Philadelphia: Jewish Publication Society, 1967), 88.
5. See David Corcos, "The Nature of the Almohad Rulers' Treatment of the Jews," *Journal of Medieval Iberian Studies* 2 (2010): 259–285.
6. Robert Chazan, *European Jewry and the First Crusade* (Berkeley: University of California Press, 1987).
7. Ibid.
8. Ibid., 225–226.
9. Ibid., 226.
10. Ibid., 227.
11. Ibid., 228–242.

12. Ibid., 273–287.
13. On the persecution of 1391, see Benjamin Gampel, *Anti-Jewish Riots in the Crown of Aragon and the Royal Response, 1391–1392* (New York: Cambridge University Press, 2016).
14. Shaul Stampfer, "What Actually Happened to the Jews of Ukraine in 1648?," *Jewish History* 17 (2003): 207–227.

6 Late Antiquity

1. Recall that I have defined "pre-modern" for this study as extending into the late eighteenth century, in accord with the periodization suggested for the onset of modernity by the Annales School.
2. The dates given for these periods are all round numbers. This reflects the general tendency among contemporary historians to diminish the significance of specific events in favor of broad tendencies.
3. With regard to this period, recall the limitation of source materials and see Collins, *Introduction to the Hebrew Bible*, chapter 21.
4. On this period, see Shaye J. D. Cohen, *From the Maccabees to the Mishnah* (Philadelphia: Westminster, 1987); Lawrence H. Schiffman, *From Text to Tradition: A History of Second Temple and Rabbinic Judaism* (Hoboken: Ktav, 1991); Peter Schafer, *The History of the Jews in the Greco-Roman World*, rev. ed. (London: Routledge, 2003).
5. Solomon ibn Verga's *Shevet Yehudah*, which is a sixteenth-century mélange of genuine historical materials, historical materials embellished by the author, and pure fabrications, tells a delightful tale of the first arrival of Jews in Iberia. According to ibn Verga, the sixth-pre-Christian-century Babylonian king, engaged in difficult combat with the Judeans, called in the king of Spain for assistance. When the war had been won, the Babylonian king offered his Spanish ally a choice of the spoils. The clever Spanish king asked for the Jews of the finest neighborhood of Jerusalem. Through this tale, the sixteenth-century author establishes two important realities—the very early arrival of Jews on the Iberian peninsula and the overall superiority of the Iberian Jews in the Jewish world.
6. Isaiah Gafni has edited a very useful set of Hebrew essays devoted to the relationships between the Jewish center in Palestine and the diaspora Jewish communities in late antiquity—*Merkaz u-Tefuzah: Erez Yisrael ve-ha-Tefuzot be-yemei Bayit Sheni, ha-Mishnah, ve-ha-Talmud* (Jerusalem: Merkaz Shazar, 2004). English summaries are available in the volume. While Gafni and most of the contributors note the shift in strength from Palestine to the eastern diaspora, no overarching position on timing and causation emerges.
7. On this process, see W. H. C. Frend, *The Rise of Christianity* (Philadelphia: Fortress, 1984); Robin Lane Fox, *Pagans and Christians* (New York: Knopf, 1987);

and Timothy David Barnes, *Constantine and Eusebius* (Cambridge: Harvard University Press, 1981).

8. Recently, Reza Aslan, *Zealot: The Life and Times of Jesus of Nazareth* (New York: Random House, 2013), has achieved enormous attention for suggesting that Jesus was an anti-Roman revolutionary. This view, however, has been recurrently voiced by a number of prior authors.
9. Muslim legalists and thinkers struggled with assessment of Zoroastrianism. Since Islam accorded special status to Jews and Christians as monotheists who received genuine revelation, it was important to decide whether Zoroastrians deserved to be included in this category, and the decision proved difficult.
10. Isaiah Gafni, "The Political, Social, and Economic History of Babylonian Jewry, 224–638 CE," in *The Cambridge History of Judaism*, vol. 4, 792–820.
11. For this analysis, see again Bachrach, *Early Medieval Jewish Policy in Western Europe*.

7 The Islamic World

1. On the early evolution of Islam, see the new and superb G. W. Bowersock, *The Crucible of Islam* (Cambridge: Harvard University Press, 2017).
2. For broad overviews of the Jewish experience in the realm of Islam, see S. D. Goitein, *Jews and Arabs: Their Contacts Through the Ages* (New York: Schocken, 1955); Bernard Lewis, *The Jews of Islam* (Princeton: Princeton University Press, 1984); Abelwahab Meddeb and Benjamin Stora, *A History of Jewish-Muslim Relations: From the Origins to the Present Day* (Princeton: Princeton University Press, 2013). Norman Stillman, *The Jews of Arab Lands: A History and Source Book* (Philadelphia: Jewish Publication Society, 1979), provides a brief overview as the introduction to his valuable collection of sources.
3. Recall the Christian acknowledgment of Judaism and its superiority over polytheism, discussed above.
4. Goitein's five-volume masterpiece, *A Mediterranean Society*, is grounded in his assiduous collection, transcription, translation, and interpretation of Cairo Genizah materials. For a recent and charming depiction of these materials, see Adina Hoffman and Peter Cole, *Sacred Trash: The Lost and Found World of the Cairo Genizah* (New York: Schocken, 2011).
5. Goitein, *A Mediterranean Society*, vol. 1.
6. Goitein published a collection of letters written by Jewish traders that indicates in rich detail the reality of this trade and travel; S. D. Goitein, *Letters of Medieval Jewish Traders* (Princeton: Princeton University Press, 1974).
7. The record composed by Benjamin of Tudela of his trip was published in a critical edition in 1840 and translated into English by Marcus Nathan Adler in 1907. The Adler translation has recently been reproduced, accompanied by a useful

introduction by Michael A. Signer as *The Itinerary of Benjamin of Tudela* (Malibu: Joseph Simon, 1983).

8. Note the remarkable portrait Benjamin provides of the city of Baghdad in general and of its Jewish community and leadership in particular; *The Itinerary of Benjamin of Tudela*, 95–102.
9. For full treatment of the Jews in crusader Palestine during the twelfth and thirteenth centuries, see Joshua Prawer, *The History of the Jews in the Latin Kingdom of Jerusalem* (Oxford: Clarendon Press, 1988), chapters 4–8.
10. Maimonides in his introduction to the *Mishneh Torah* clearly seeks to diminish the authority of the Mesopotamian *geonim*. The same is true for Abraham ibn Daud and his *Sefer ha-Kabbalah*, which we shall examine immediately.
11. The modern editor was Gerson D. Cohen, whose outstanding edition was titled *A Critical Edition with a Translation and Notes of The Book of Tradition by Abraham ibn Daud* (Philadelphia: Jewish Publication Society, 1967). Cohen's edition has served as a model for subsequent editions of medieval Hebrew texts and their analysis.
12. This famous story can be found in *The Book of Tradition*, 63–66.
13. Ibid., 88.
14. *The Book of Tradition*, 71–76.

8 Medieval Northern Europe

1. For a brief but incisive overview of this process, see Southern, *The Making of the Middle Ages*. For a recent and yet more expansive treatment of the growing strength and creativity of medieval Latin Christendom, see Fried, *The Middle Ages*.
2. There is an alternative view of the rise and development of northern European Jewry, which projects this rise and development as the result of the conversion of the Khazars, a central Asian people. For the characteristics shared by northwestern, north-central, and northeastern Jewish communities, see Chazan, *The Jews of Medieval Western Christendom*. The purported conversion of the Khazars has been closely examined and seriously questioned by Shaul Stampfer, "Did the Khazars Convert to Judaism?," *Jewish Social Studies* 19 (2013): 1–72.
3. On the Christian re-conquest of Iberia, see Joseph F. O'Callaghan, *Reconquest and Crusade in Medieval Spain* (Philadelphia: University of Pennsylvania Press, 2003).
4. Chazan, *Church, State, and Jew in the Middle Ages*, 69–70. For more such charters, see ibid., 70–75.
5. These two sources can be found in ibid., 58–59.
6. Habermann, *Sefer Gezerot Ashkenaz ve-Zarfat*, 21.
7. On very expensive items pawned with Jews, see Joseph Shatzmiller, *Cultural Exchange: Jews, Christians, and Art in the Medieval Marketplace* (Princeton: Princeton University Press, 2013).

8. Chazan, *Church, State, and Jew in the Middle Ages*, 84–88. For another important northeastern European charter modeled on that of Duke Frederick, see ibid., 88–93.
9. In the charter of 1244, Jewish physical security is addressed in clauses 9, 10, 11, 21, 24, 26, and 28, and the security of Jewish communal property is addressed in clauses 14 and 15.
10. These judicial issues are addressed in clauses 8, 16, 17, 18, 19, 20, 22, and 29.
11. Clause 1.
12. Clause 25.
13. Clauses 2, 3, 4, 5, 6, 7, 23, 27, and 28.
14. Clause 30.
15. Chazan, *Church, State, and Jew*, 59.
16. Chazan, *European Jewry and the First Crusade*, 225.
17. Note that the assaults, which were in any case quite restricted, took place only in limited areas of northern Europe.
18. R. I. Moore, *The Formation of a Persecuting Society* (Oxford: Blackwell, 2007).
19. See Robert Chazan, *Medieval Stereotypes and Modern Antisemitism* (Berkeley: University of California Press, 1997).
20. Recall the Graetz view of the role of the Church in pre-modern Jewish suffering.
21. Habermann, *Sefer Gezerot Ashkenaz ve-Zarfat*, 20–21.
22. Chazan, *Church, State, and Jew*, 31. This is the version enunciated by Pope Clement III, which was included in the official *Decretales*.
23. Ibid., 100–104, for Bernard's letter and 106–108 for Bernard's visit to the Rhineland.
24. Grayzel, *The Church and the Jews*, 1:268–271, #116.
25. Ibid., 274–275, #118.
26. Ibid., 308–309.
27. Ibid., 306–307.
28. See John Friedman, Jean Connell Hoff, and Robert Chazan, *The Trial of the Talmud: Paris, 1240* (Toronto: Pontifical Institute of Mediaeval Studies, 2012).
29. See Chazan, *European Jewry and the First Crusade* for an overview.
30. See the classic study by Gavin I. Langmuir, " 'Judei Nostri' and the Beginning of Capetian Legislation," *Traditio* 16 (1960): 203–269, reprinted in Langmuir, *Toward a Definition of Antisemitism* (Berkeley: University of California Press, 1990), 137–166.
31. Robert C. Stacey, *Politics, Policy, and Finance Under Henry III, 1216–1245* (Oxford: Oxford University Press, 1987), chapter 4.
32. Grayzel, *The Church and the Jews*, provides numerous examples of both kinds of papal communications.

9 Movement Eastward

1. Recall that there was no exile of Jews from Palestine in the year 70, as discussed above in chapter 4.

2. The fascinating reconstruction of Iberian Jewish history is offered in Solomon ibn Verga's *Shevet Yehudah.*
3. For some of the Church demands and governmental responses, see Chazan, *Church, State, and Jew in the Middle Ages,* 197–220.
4. Ibid., 318. Stacey, *Politics, Policy, and Finance Under Henry III,* argued that the extraordinary taxes imposed by Henry III in effect broke the financial backbone of English Jewry. Thus, Edward I could afford to be as pious as he sounds in this edict.
5. For full details of the royal profit, see Jordan, *The French Monarchy and the Jews,* chapter 12.
6. For the edict spelling out the complex details of the return in 1315, see Chazan, *Church, State, and Jew,* 79–83.
7. For full details on these events, see again Friedman et al., *The Trial of the Talmud.*
8. For this document, see Chazan, *Church, State, and Jew,* 89–93.
9. This massive migration has often been projected as involuntary, the result of the violence of the pogroms that began in 1881. The wellsprings of the massive migration have been carefully examined by the Nobel laureate Simon Kuznets in "Immigration of Russian Jews to the United States: Background and Structure," *Perspectives in American History* 9 (1975): 35–124. Kuznets's analysis concludes that this migration was overwhelmingly voluntary, sparked by the conviction that a better life could be found in America.
10. In a sense, the New Christians evoked the same anti-newcomer sentiment that the Jews making their way into vitalized northern Europe had encountered many centuries earlier.
11. See again Terpstra, *Religious Refugees in the Early Modern World.*
12. On the refugees from the Spanish expulsion, see the valuable study of Jonathan Ray, *After Expulsion: 1492 and the Making of Sephardic Jewry* (New York: New York University Press, 2013).
13. On the expulsion from Portugal, see François Soyer, *The Persecution of the Jews and Muslims of Portugal: King Manuel I and the End of Religious Tolerance, 1496–1497* (Leiden: Brill, 2007).
14. Mark Meyerson, *A Jewish Renaissance in Fifteenth-Century Spain* (Princeton: Princeton University Press, 2004).
15. See again Yerushalmi, *Zakhor,* chapter 3.

10 Return Westward

1. We shall deal in detail only with the first of these two stages, since this study concludes with the end of the eighteenth century.
2. This movement during the sixteenth through eighteenth centuries is featured in two major works on early modern Jewry: Jonathan I. Israel, *European Jewry in the Age of Mercantilism, 1550–1750* (Oxford: Oxford University Press, 1985), and

David B. Ruderman, *Early Modern Jewry: A New Cultural History* (Princeton: Princeton University Press, 2010).

3. Again, these developments lie beyond the limits of this study. Recall the ongoing discussion of the massive movement to America and the valuable Kuznets study that concludes that this movement was overwhelmingly voluntary.
4. Note the illuminating study of Peter H. Wilson, *The Thirty Years War: Europe's Tragedy* (Cambridge: Harvard University Press, 2009).
5. Again see Soyer, *The Persecution of the Jews and Muslims of Portugal.*
6. On the growth and development of the Jewish community of the Netherlands, see Miriam Bodian, *Hebrews of the Portuguese Nation: Conversos and Community in Early Modern Amsterdam* (Bloomington: Indiana University Press, 1997), and Steven Nadler, *Spinoza: A Life* (Cambridge: Cambridge University Press, 1999), chapter 1.
7. Nadler, *Spinoza: A Life* offers a fine overview of Spinoza's life.
8. To be sure, rulers often diverged from the idealized norm, pursuing their own interests and neglecting or opposing the demands of the Church.
9. John Locke, *A Letter Concerning Toleration* (Amherst, N.Y.: Prometheus, 1990), 18.
10. Ibid., 70.
11. For the extent to which the American colonies had absorbed Enlightenment ideals, see Bernard Bailyn, "Political Experience and Enlightenment Ideas in Eighteenth-Century America," *American Historical Review* 67 (1961–1962): 339–351. To be sure, adoption of Enlightenment principles with respect to Jews was by no means uniform across the diverse spectrum of the colonies. For a nuanced portrait of differences in this regard, see William Pencak, *Jews and Gentiles in Early America* (Ann Arbor: University of Michigan Press, 2005).
12. Mendes-Flohr and Reinharz, *The Jew in the Modern World,* 126.
13. Ibid., 127–128.
14. Kuznets, "Immigration of Russian Jews to the United States."

Epilogue

1. On the earliest human migrations, see for example Clive Gamble, *Timewalkers: The Prehistory of Global Colonization* (Cambridge: Harvard University Press, 1994), and Chris Stringer and Robin McKie, *African Exodus: The Origins of Modern Humanity* (London: Jonathan Cape, 1996). In 2015, PBS aired an impressive series entitled *First Peoples,* which traces effectively the spread of humanity through these earliest migrations.
2. See Collins, *Introduction to the Hebrew Bible,* 331–352.
3. Jeremiah 29:10–14.
4. Jeremiah 29:5–6.
5. Jeremiah 29:7.
6. See Collins, *Introduction to the Hebrew Bible,* 536–543.

INDEX

www.ingramcontent.com/pod-product-compliance
Lightning Source LLC
LaVergne TN
LVHW091214060825
817692LV00003B/26/J
9780813133805